Olena Berezovska

DIY Bestseller

How to Write, Publish, and Market Your Book in the AI Era

International Academy of Healthv Life

2025

DIY Bestseller
How to Write, Publish, and Market Your Book in the AI Era

By Olena Berezovska

340 pages

Published by
International Academy of Healthy Life

This book is a beacon of hope for all those who carry a book in their heart but don't know where to start — for the thinkers, dreamers, and teachers who believe they have something important to say. Writing a book used to be a privilege for the few. Now, with the inclusive guidance and tools — including artificial intelligence — it becomes possible for anyone willing to learn and stay true to their voice.

DIY Bestseller is more than a how-to manual. It's a conversation, a personal journey, and a practical companion for every stage of the author's path — from the spark of an idea to the moment your book reaches the hands (or ears or screens) of your readers. You'll learn not just how to write and publish, but how to *position yourself*, navigate the emotional rollercoaster of authorship, and use modern tools to make your work stronger, faster, and smarter, empowering you to take control of your writing journey.

Whether you are writing fiction or nonfiction, aiming for print, e-book, or audiobook formats, or wondering how AI can help without replacing your creative voice, this book will guide you step by step. No gimmicks. No gatekeeping. Just real experience, honest advice, and a map for turning your idea into a book that matters.

Table of contents

Introduction: The Rise of the DIY Bestseller (5)
A Few words About Me as a Bestselling Author (6)

Part 1: From Creation to Success: What Drives Today's Bestsellers (17)
What Is a Bestseller? (17)
The Self-Publishing Revolution and Its Accessibility (23)
Why AI Is a Game-Changer for Modern Authors (28)
What Readers Want in Today's Book Market (32)
What Determines a Book's Success Today? (41)

Part 2: The Author's Roadmap (48)
Every Journey Needs a Roadmap: Beginning Your Book with Purpose (48)
Finding Your Purpose and Audience (50)
Defining Your "Why" for Writing a Book (52)
Understanding Your Audience's Needs and Desires (57)
Identifying Your Niche and Standing Out (65)
Brainstorming with AI (75)
Using AI tools for Idea Generation and Market Research (83)
How to Validate Your Book Concept Using AI-driven Platforms (86)
Outlining for Success (89)
Building a Solid Outline Using AI-assisted Frameworks (91)
Story Structure for Fiction vs. Frameworks for Nonfiction (100)
Tools to Streamline Your Outlining Process (104)

Part 3: Writing Your Masterpiece (115)
Writing Made Easier with AI (116)
Overcoming Writer's Block with AI Prompts (118)
Simple Rules for Working with AI to Avoid Disappointment (126)
Maximize Your Results: The Most Effective Prompts for AI (127)
Collaborating with AI for Dialogue, Descriptions, and Structure (130)
Balancing your creative voice with AI suggestions (134)
Who Are Ghostwriters and How Do They Work? (137)
How Much Do Ghostwriters Cost? (137)
How to Make Sure a Ghostwriter Isn't Using AI (141)
Editing: Polishing to Perfection (143)
Self-editing Basics Every Author Should Know (144)

Leveraging AI editors (Grammarly, ProWritingAid, ChatGPT) for Refinement (144)
Detecting AI-generated Text (152)
Is AI Good or Bad for Authors? (175)
When and How to Bring in a Professional Human Editor (180)

Part 4: Designing for Success (186)
Book Sizes and Cover Design Through the Ages (186)
The Power of a Great Cover (189)
AI-Based Design Platforms for Creating Stunning Covers (193)
Cover Design Best Practices: Trends, Fonts, and Colors (195)
Formatting for Readers (197)
The Importance of Embedding Text in Book Layouts (206)
The Role of NCX and XML in Electronic TOC (208)
Creating Books for Every Platform: Print, E-Books, and Audiobooks (210)
Testing Your Book Layout for Readability and Compatibility (213)

Part 5: Publishing in the Digital Age (217)
Choosing the Right Platform (218)
Overview of Amazon KDP, IngramSpark, Draft2Digital, and Others (218)
Exclusivity vs. Wide Distribution (229)
Using AI Insights to Choose the Best Platform (231)
Print, E-books, and Audiobooks — One Story, Many Forms (233)
Pricing Your Book — Finding the True Value of Your Work (234)
Publishers: From Global Giants to Niche Innovators (237)
What Is a Literary Agent and How Do They Work? (245)
What Readers Want: Trends in Publishing Formats and What Actually Sells (249)
Print-on-demand options and sustainability considerations (252)

Part 6: Marketing Like a Pro (255)
Building Your Author Brand (258)
The Power of a Name — Why Authors Use Pseudonyms (263)
Let the Robots Help — How AI Can Be Your Favorite Assistant in Book Promotion (266)
Building an Author Website with the Help of AI — Where Technology Meets Personality (268)
Launching Your Book with Impact (271)
Pre-launch Strategies: Building Buzz with ARCs, Beta Readers, and Influencers (272)

After the Launch — How to Keep Your Book Alive in the World (276)
AI-Driven Marketing Strategies (279)
Using AI-Powered Ad Platforms for Targeted Campaigns (279)
Choosing the Right AI-Powered Ad Platform for Your Book (282)
Automating Email Marketing with AI (284)
Analyzing Reader Data to Refine Your Marketing Approach (291)

Part 7: Scaling Your Success (295)
Expanding Your Reach (295)
Leveraging AI for Translations to Reach Global Markets (299)
Creating spin-offs, sequels, or related books (304)
Monetizing Through Courses, Workshops, and Speaking Engagements (307)
Building Passive Income Streams (309)
Repurposing Content for Blogs, YouTube, or Podcasts (311)
Licensing and Collaborations with Other Creators (315)
AI-Powered Tools for Managing Royalties and Income Tracking (318)

Part 8: The Future of Publishing (322)
AI's Role in Shaping Tomorrow's Bestsellers (322)
Emerging Trends in AI and Publishing (323)
The Ethical Debate: How Much AI Is Too Much? (325)
Preparing for the Future of Storytelling in a Digital-First World (328)
The Future is Yours to Write (330)

Olena Berezovska's books (332)
About the author (338)

Introduction: The rise of the DIY Bestseller

Dear Readers,

This book is not a random occurrence but a natural next step. As the author of eight bestsellers on women's health, I've gathered extensive knowledge and experience in writing, publishing, and promoting books. Now, I'm excited to share that journey with you.

The term *"bestseller"* isn't inherently tied to a book or any specific object; it's fundamentally a commercial concept—it refers to a *product*. When applied to books, it refers to the best-selling one. In essence, it's about sales rather than content—don't you think? I'll explore this idea more throughout the book. Together, we'll examine the significance of a book's content, its cover, and—most importantly—where and how to market your *work of art*. After all, creating a book is always a creative act: manifesting an idea into reality.

I've met many people who dream of writing a book—sometimes more than one. The motivations vary, but a common thread is the initial **psychological barrier** that often holds people back. I've helped inspire numerous aspiring authors, guiding them past this fear that delays their dreams. The fear of failure can be genuinely paralyzing, leading people to postpone their goals indefinitely. But the secret is to *start*. Begin small—even if it's just with a title or a rough outline of the book you want to write. I'll return to this point in one of the chapters.

Today, more than ever, we have access to a wide array of tools and technologies that make creating and selling books faster and easier. When I wrote my first book in 1995, I typed it on a manual typewriter—not even an electric one, as those were rare luxuries in my youth. One typo meant retyping the entire page. My first print run consisted of just six copies, and I had to bind them myself (fortunately, I had the skills to do that).

Early computers had their challenges. In 1990, Microsoft Word became part of the Microsoft Office suite, significantly increasing its popularity and simplifying document creation for many users. Still, it took nearly a decade for most people to become comfortable using it. For the older generation, computers were especially intimidating, including my father. He was a journalist by training and a writer by passion. When he visited me in Canada in 1999, he began learning how to use our family computer, mainly to read the news. He also tried typing letters and articles—but one wrong keystroke could erase the entire text, freeze the system, or shut it down completely. Still, some in his generation mastered these machines and used them to their advantage.

Today, we enjoy a wealth of sophisticated yet user-friendly programs, accessible on most devices, making the process of writing and publishing a book more feasible — and more enjoyable. What once took weeks or months can now be done in a fraction of the time.

Almost anyone can create a bestseller. The key is to follow a structured approach, seek guidance from experienced authors, and continually update your skills, especially with modern tools that elevate the quality of your work. By the end of this book, I'm confident that any fear you may have about starting your bestseller will be gone, no matter your level of experience.

Happy reading!

A Few Words About Me as a Bestselling Author

I want to share my journey with you, a journey that was not without its share of obstacles. But it's these very obstacles that can help you overcome your challenges on the path to becoming a bestselling author, not just once, but multiple times.

I was born and raised in a country that no longer exists — the Soviet Union, though, more specifically, in its expansive and beautiful region now known as Ukraine. My father was a journalist, and my mother was a teacher. If there's any truth to the notion of *journalistic genes*, then I certainly inherited mine from my father. Beyond being a photojournalist and editor of several newspapers, including serving as chief editor, where he led entire publications, he was also a member of the Writers' Union of Ukraine. His work often leaned toward humor and satire, with many of his pieces appearing in various periodicals and publications. I like to think that some of his creative spirit found its way to me.

I inherited a love for teaching from my mother. I've always enjoyed giving lectures, leading seminars, and hosting webinars. In essence, educating others is something I am genuinely passionate about.

Yet, my career path led me to medicine. I trained as a physician specializing in obstetrics and gynecology and have dedicated my entire adult life to healthcare, first in Ukraine and then in Canada. After qualifying as a specialist in 1991, I began lecturing in colleges and schools, with a primary focus on puberty and adolescent health. My ability to engage audiences quickly garnered attention, and I was frequently invited to speak at various educational institutions. Yet, despite my growing presence as a speaker, I felt a persistent longing to write books; I never had the time.

During that time, survival meant relentless work, especially after the Soviet Union collapsed, leaving Ukraine in a state of economic devastation and political upheaval. I explore these turbulent years in greater detail in my new book on the Soviet mentality.

In 1995, I penned my first book, *My Path to Truth*, driven by a profound disillusionment with the actions of some of my friends. This book, which delves into themes of spirituality, morality, and religion, is a testament to my passion for writing. Although I am not a religious person, I was deeply influenced by my grandmother's devoutness. Yet, I wouldn't define myself as an atheist either.

When the book was finally printed, just six copies, on rough gray newsprint (the only type of paper available in Ukraine), I bound them by hand and designed the covers myself. I gave five copies to friends.

When I sought a publishing agency in Ukraine, I was met with a harsh reality: such opportunities were practically nonexistent. This was an era before widespread computer access and internet use in

Ukraine, making it incredibly difficult to find information about where I could have my book printed. A few religious organizations responded, offering to publish my book, provided I incorporated more Christian doctrine into its content. But I refused to compromise my vision. I decided to wait for better times, determined to see my book in print.

In 1996, after moving to Canada, I met a former teacher who frequently visited the clinic where I worked. When I told her about my dream of writing books, she was immediately supportive and even offered to help as an editor, knowing that my English was still far from perfect. Encouraged by her enthusiasm, I began working on a book about women's health, tentatively titled *Woman – The Beauty of Nature*. Together, we carefully selected materials, and I spent countless hours poring over medical journals that had accumulated in the clinic, journals that seemed of little interest to anyone but me. Maria, as this generous woman was named, typed up my handwritten drafts, edited them, and brought them back for discussion.

By the time we had nearly completed 90 pages, life took an unexpected turn. I had to change jobs and shift my focus to obtaining my medical credentials in Canada. The demands of exam preparation and other pressing responsibilities left me with little time to continue writing, and the book was left unfinished. However, the experience never left me. A few years later, it became the foundation for the women's health books I would eventually write. My first two books may have gone largely unnoticed, but that didn't deter me from pursuing my dream.

At the end of 1999, I was invited to interview for a position unrelated to my medical background. However, my additional training in office management made me a viable candidate. The job was with a large American company that specialized in selling a new software system for managing large businesses. They had a Canadian branch, and their vice director was seeking a manager and an assistant. I was at a crossroads at that moment: should I continue my medical career or leap into something completely different? I successfully passed two rounds of interviews, with just one more to go. But there was one major obstacle: I knew little about the internet, let alone internet marketing.

By then, the internet had already reached the former Soviet republics. Still, rather than providing helpful information or educational content, its expansion had been dominated by fraudulent schemes and get-rich-quick pyramids designed to deceive unsuspecting users. Many people, including some of my friends and acquaintances, fell victim to these scams. With just over a month to decide whether to accept the job offer, I made a bold choice: I would dedicate that time to learning everything I could about the internet and digital marketing.

Over the next month, I embarked on a journey of self-education, reading and analyzing several of the latest books on the subject, though there were hardly any. The internet era was still in its infancy, and reliable information was scarce. I recalled a conversation from 1997 when my neighbors, who lived in extravagant mansions, told me they worked from home, selling products online. At the time, I had been skeptical. Who would buy something without seeing or touching it first? The idea seemed far-fetched. Yet, just a year later, both families had purchased homes in one of Toronto's wealthiest neighborhoods and moved there.

Eager to share my newly acquired knowledge and experience, I completed a 110-page book by the end of 1999 titled *The Internet: Myths and the Reality of Earning Online*. The first part covered crucial topics, including internet-driven business, online marketing strategies, developing an internet marketing plan, website creation, graphic design in marketing, digital advertising, and more. The second part delved into online scams, dissecting typical fraudulent schemes. As a personal touch, I included several illustrations; drawing has always been one of my passions.

One of the greatest joys of writing a book is sharing it with the people you love and respect, so I distributed free copies to my friends and family. Encouraged by their feedback, I set out to publish the book in the former Soviet states at the beginning of 2000 with the help of an assistant. However, I quickly encountered an unexpected setback. Despite the vast expanse of the post-Soviet region, internet access remained scarce. Publishing agencies and media outlets all responded the same way: Internet marketing was an irrelevant topic for their audience. At the time, very few people had access to the internet, and the concept of online sales was inconceivable. My book was ahead of its time, written for a future that had not yet arrived.

Determined to move forward, we decided to sell the book online independently. However, this presented a new challenge: financial transactions in post-Soviet countries were nearly impossible, particularly international payments, an issue further complicated by my living in Canada.

Some business and technology magazines published excerpts from my book as standalone articles. However, despite prior agreements, I never received the promised royalties. This experience taught me a valuable lesson about the publishing industry: fraud was widespread, even in the most reputable magazines. One well-known Belarusian magazine specializing in computers and the internet had agreed to allocate my earnings to orphanages in Belarus since direct payment to me was not feasible. Yet, I never received confirmation from the editors that the funds had been donated.

Ultimately, I turned down the job offer from the American company despite the enticing $100,000 annual salary. The position required frequent international travel, representing the company in high-level meetings with executives of major corporations. For many, such a career path would have been a dream come true. However, I had two young children who needed my care and attention. For me, family has always been the highest priority. The thought of being away for days at a time, constantly traveling the world, was not an option. Instead, I chose to continue my medical career, a decision I have never once regretted, as it allowed me to be there for my children when they needed me most.

By 2010, having already written and published several books, I was astonished to learn that my book on the internet had ranked among the top ten Russian-language books on marketing and had remained on that list for an entire decade. Over those ten years, I received numerous letters of gratitude from economics students and professors. Many shared that my book had become an invaluable textbook on internet marketing, with some even crediting it for helping them successfully defend their dissertations. While the book was often free, some individuals took advantage of it, selling unauthorized copies and violating my copyright. I considered updating the book, but by then, I was already committed to writing several books on health, so I set the idea aside for the future.

Reflecting on the past, in 2005, I had the opportunity to meet with the leadership of Market America, a prominent American product brokerage and internet marketing company. Established in 1992, the company evolved along two primary business models. The first was network marketing, specifically multi-level marketing (MLM) through distributor partnerships. The second, which emerged a few years later, was e-commerce. In 1994, Market America acquired Shop.com, expanding its online retail presence and enhancing its e-commerce capabilities. That same year, Amazon officially registered as a company, though at the time, its focus was limited to music, movies, electronics, toys, and a few other categories. It had yet to achieve mainstream recognition.

By 2005, Amazon had introduced a subscription program offering free shipping, which expanded to include video content and other benefits. In 2007, it revolutionized the digital book industry with the launch of the Kindle e-reader, a breakthrough that fundamentally changed how books were consumed and distributed. The Kindle made it possible for readers to carry an entire library in a single device, and its e-ink technology provided a reading experience that was comparable to reading a physical book. This innovation not only changed the way books were sold but also influenced the way authors wrote, and publishers marketed their books.

As Market America expanded its online shopping platform, it integrated nearly all major U.S. and Canadian retailers, consolidating many products and services into a single ecosystem. The company also introduced a universal shopping card system, which enabled customers to shop at multiple stores and complete their purchases in a single transaction, thereby eliminating the need for numerous checkouts. Additionally, they implemented an innovative rewards program, where customers earned points directly from participating retailers to incentivize their purchases. This model was a perfect formula for e-commerce and digital marketing. However, between 2005 and 2010, online shopping had yet to achieve the widespread adoption it has today.

While digital platforms thrived on music and video sales, the broader e-commerce market remained sluggish. One key reason was the emergence and gradual evolution of social media. Although Facebook was founded in 2004, it wasn't until 2007 that it became widely accessible and introduced advertising. At that stage, however, Facebook was still primarily a platform for socializing and entertainment rather than a tool for business or online sales. The true revolution in digital commerce was yet to come.

I am sharing my personal story to demonstrate that acquiring new knowledge and experience, even in entirely unfamiliar fields, is always possible, regardless of your stage in life. The key to growth is overcoming the fear of stepping outside your comfort zone. I faced many personal challenges during this journey, from self-doubt to financial constraints, but I persevered. **Stay open and attentive - life has a way of leading you to the right opportunities and the resources essential for personal and professional development.** Even if a new passion doesn't become your lifelong career, the knowledge and experience you gain will stay with you and may prove invaluable later.

I was never a strong supporter of direct sales. Still, my leadership and public speaking skills led me to accept an opportunity with Market America, where I helped expand the company's distributor network in Canada. As a manager in the Greater Toronto Area, I trained new distributors in business strategies, conducted health seminars, and assisted in organizing corporate events. Before long, this became a profitable additional source of income. I earned 30% of the revenue from these events, and all payments for business training sessions were directly deposited into my account. The company's business training program was robust, practical, well-structured, and highly effective. The insights and skills I gained during this time continue to serve me in my professional and business endeavors today.

One of the most valuable lessons I learned at Market America was the power of focus, learning to concentrate fully on my goals and dreams. Even in direct sales, success depends on understanding *why* you are doing it and what you are working toward. The same principle applies to writing a bestseller: **you need a clear goal and a structured timeline**; otherwise, the process can stretch endlessly. We will explore the importance of setting goals in more detail later.

As I trained others in business, I found myself pondering deeper questions: *What were my original dreams? Have I achieved all my most significant ambitions? If not, why? What can I do today to bring those dreams to life instead of letting them wait indefinitely?* One of my long-standing aspirations was to write and publish books. Yet, I must admit, I was not relentless in pursuing this goal. Instead, I kept pushing it aside for later, for the future. *I'll do it once I finish this project, when I have more free time, or when I retire and have more money.* However, I now realize that these were just excuses. They will always be there, and they will never cease to multiply. **The key is to stop making excuses and turn your dream into reality, before it's too late.**

At that point, what did I truly know about myself? I had already written two books, a testament to the valuable experience I had gained. I had a deep knowledge of several subjects, allowing me to write about topics aligned with my education and expertise. I had a computer and had learned to use various software programs, enabling me to create digital files independently. I even taught myself Photoshop, allowing me to design my illustrations when needed. In other words, I stopped focusing solely on the mechanics of writing books. I began to recognize my true potential and capabilities, a journey that brought me immense joy and satisfaction.

People often complain about not having enough time. I was no different; I used to say the same thing. However, over time, I reassessed my relationship with time and realized that my ability to stay organized enabled me to accomplish far more than most. Instead of seeing time as a constraint, I learned to view it as an advantage. I also redefined productivity, focusing on what I could realistically achieve within a day, a week, a month, or a year. Plans are fluid; they evolve, and that's perfectly normal. The key is not to dwell on what had to be postponed but to seize the next available opportunity to continue. Adaptability is key in this journey.

Life is more than work; it requires balance. We must cultivate our sense of harmony by making time for loved ones, engaging in physical activity, taking outdoor walks, sharing meals, resting, traveling, and even performing the simplest daily rituals, such as shopping. These are not distractions; they are the elements that sustain us and contribute to our overall well-being. People cannot isolate themselves and become entirely consumed by work. In such a state, creating something truly remarkable, let alone a bestseller, is impossible.

Looking back, one thing that has always fascinated me is how crucial it is to recognize the right moment for progress and seize it. Outstanding achievements are always within reach, but only if you refuse to impose limits on your goals and ambitions. Opportunities don't wait; progress happens when you step forward.

The story of the two companies taught me that visions for the future can diverge in radically different directions. At one point, Market America's leadership met with Amazon's executives, but what truly captivated them was their meeting with Amway, a major multi-level marketing (MLM) company. As a result, they chose to prioritize expanding their network marketing model rather than pursuing broader e-commerce innovations.

Since Shop.com never gained significant traction among distributors with high sales quotas, Market America did not invest heavily in developing business networks that could have strengthened its online shopping platform. Meanwhile, Amazon pursued a completely different strategy, rapidly expanding by bridging the gap between customers and businesses, from small independent sellers to major global corporations.

Amazon's growth surged during the COVID-19 pandemic, as millions were confined to their homes and had no choice but to rely on online shopping. Like countless others worldwide, I, too, turned to online platforms, including Amazon, for essential purchases.

Speaking of dreams: back in 2008, my first book on women's health — *1,000+ Questions and Answers About Gynecology* — was published in Ukraine. It became a bestseller, and in 2017, a second, expanded edition was released in Russia. Several other books followed.

I began working with the major Russian publishing house *Eksmo* in 2016, and by 2021, I had seven bestselling books on women's health. These titles were reprinted multiple times and sold not only across post-Soviet countries but also in Poland, Germany, the United States, and Canada.

The major Ukrainian publisher *BookChef* began releasing my books in 2018. My pregnancy book in Ukrainian quickly became a bestseller and was reprinted three times, including during the war with Russia. A second book was published in 2023 and became a bestseller, despite being released under wartime conditions. I made a conscious decision to donate 25% of my income from those books to Ukraine's recovery fund, a gesture of solidarity and support.

As of early 2025, my name appears on 30 published books — a quarter of which are not related to medicine. You'll find a complete list of my publications in the appendix at the end of this book.

In addition to print editions, I also had the opportunity to sell digital versions of my books. As an author, I was granted the right to sell the eBook formats provided by publishers and received royalties from both digital and print sales. In 2016, I launched my online store, where I sold not only eBooks but also a range of digital products, including webinars, courses, pamphlets, and other related items. One of the biggest challenges was converting Cyrillic texts into various digital formats, as most platforms were initially designed for English-language content. However, I overcame this hurdle with my resourcefulness and adaptability. In recent years, powerful tools have emerged for generating eBook files in multiple languages, making the process much easier.

When Russia invaded Ukraine, I immediately ended all collaboration with Russian publishers and terminated our contracts. This decision was not taken lightly, but I could not continue to work with entities that were complicit in such actions. I'm aware that some of my books are still being sold in Russian bookstores, but there are also countless pirated copies. My cooperation with Russian legal teams also ceased, and that part of the world now stands behind an iron wall — something I do not regret. It allowed me to fulfill another long-held dream: to begin publishing books in English.

Some of my new books, which I've written and continue to write in English, as I speak the language fluently, even though it's not my native tongue. I also translate some of my books from Ukrainian and Russian into English, as they contain valuable information. Additionally, I frequently revise and refine these translations, updating them with new content. In this book, I will share my experience of translating books into different languages.

My list of planned titles includes no fewer than 50 books, a testament to my perseverance and dedication. With each new project, new ideas emerge. For example, the idea for this book emerged after I had published several titles in English and undergone many stages of creating a bestseller. That's why I'm happy to share honest and practical insights with you, based on real experience.

If I can create bestsellers, then so can you. Don't let yourself be discouraged by the thought of how many books already exist in the world. Some books become popular in their own time, others gain recognition years later, and a few remain timeless masterpieces. But the essence is this: **I believe in the success of your work**, and you should too.

So, let's continue our journey into the world of *bestsellerology*.

Part 1: From Creation to Success: What Drives Today's Bestsellers

What Is a Bestseller?

In today's world, there is no single, universally accepted definition of a *bestseller*, as various criteria can be used to determine a book's level of popularity.

A bestseller is generally defined as a book that achieves high sales figures and quickly gains popularity among readers. The term literally means *"best seller."* However, the concept encompasses more than just numbers — it also carries cultural and market-based significance.

The concept of the *bestseller* dates back to the 19th century. With the advent of industrial printing and the rise in literacy rates, books became increasingly accessible to the public. One of the earliest examples of a bestseller was Harriet Beecher Stowe's *Uncle Tom's Cabin* (1852). The novel sold 300,000 copies in its first year in the United States alone—an extraordinary number for that time—and is credited with influencing public opinion on the issue of slavery. Some even called it a catalyst for the American Civil War.

In the early 20th century, bestseller lists became a formalized measure of success. *The New York Times*, a leading newspaper in the United States, published its first list in 1942, and it quickly became the gold standard of literary achievement. Iconic titles, such as Margaret Mitchell's *Gone with the Wind* (1936), dominated these rankings, selling millions of copies and captivating readers worldwide. These books were not only entertaining but also reflected the values, challenges, and spirit of their era, securing their place in literary history.

There are several different criteria used to determine what qualifies as a bestseller, and as you'll see, they can vary widely. Let's take a closer look at some of them:

1. **High Sales**

- Leading bestseller lists, such as those in *The New York Times, Amazon, or Barnes & Noble*, base their rankings on sales data collected over a specific period (usually weekly).
- Sales may include print, digital (eBook), and audiobook formats. In the digital age, eBooks and audiobooks have become increasingly popular, and their sales contribute significantly to a book's bestseller status.

2. **Time Factor**

A book earns the title of *bestseller* if it achieves record-breaking sales within a short time, typically in the first few weeks after release.

3. **Chart Position**

Major retailers and platforms, such as Amazon, calculate bestseller status in real-time, often based on daily — or even hourly— sales.

4. **Wide Audience Appeal**

Bestsellers often attract readers not only because of the quality of the writing but also due to strong marketing efforts or the author's existing popularity.

5. **Genre-Specific Categories**

There are bestsellers across various categories, including fiction, nonfiction, children's books, and more.

Each publisher or publishing agency may have its own standards for defining a bestseller. For instance, the sales threshold might range from a few dozen to several thousand copies sold per week. These levels can also vary by genre — for example, fiction (especially thrillers or horror) may outsell political or historical books by a wide margin.

That's why, before creating a book, it's important to determine your genre, so you can also develop a clear and strategic plan for your work.

Many factors influence bestseller status:

- **Author Recognition**

Books by well-known authors or public figures naturally have an advantage. Today, many publishing agencies give preference to authors who are active on social media. If you don't have accounts on platforms like Facebook, Instagram, TikTok, or others, that's perfectly fine. However, it's important to note that having a presence there can significantly boost book sales, especially in the case of self-publishing. This presents an excellent opportunity for writers and publishers to reach a wider audience and increase the success of their books.

- **Marketing and Advertising**

A strong promotional campaign, pre-orders, book reviews, and appearances on television or podcasts — all these factors matter, and ideally, they should begin *before* the book is published. Even if you're still finalizing your chapters, it's essential to have a marketing plan ready by the time your manuscript is complete.

- **Recommendations and Reviews**

Reader feedback on Amazon, Goodreads, or coverage in popular publications can make a significant impact. This is a tricky factor because, along with positive comments, you may receive criticism. However, it's essential to remember that every review, whether positive or negative, provides valuable insight into your readers' perspectives. The more popular you become, the more competitors and envious voices you may attract. It's essential not to take negative reviews personally. Learn from them and use the feedback to improve your future work. Remember, there are no perfect writers or flawless books in the world.

- **Social Media and Word of Mouth**

Viral exposure, which is when a piece of content spreads rapidly and widely across the internet, can significantly boost a book's success, primarily through platforms like TikTok (#BookTok) and Instagram (#Bookstagram). Social media truly plays a significant role in book sales. For example, when I post a story about a book or other publication, I often receive multiple orders the very same day, sometimes from new followers or even random visitors.

Word of mouth is also a powerful tool. People who enjoyed your book and recommend it to friends, family, or colleagues are often trusted voices in their circles.

Each country has different platforms for ranking and recognizing bestsellers. You should explore how these ratings are determined in your country. If you live in a smaller nation, it may be easier to achieve national bestseller status. In larger countries with high populations, the criteria may be more demanding. But your book can still become a bestseller in your city or region — and that is an achievement worth celebrating.

My advice: **celebrate every win, whether big or small**. Many writers and poets who receive the Nobel Prize in Literature have never written bestsellers, and most people have never heard of them. Public recognition and book sales are two different measures of your work, but both can offer opportunities, including income beyond just selling books. Celebrating all achievements, regardless of whether they are bestsellers, can keep you motivated and proud of your work.

Let's examine several well-known platforms that define bestseller status in North America, as these can significantly influence a book's recognition in other parts of the world, the number of translations into different languages, and more.

The New York Times Bestseller List

- This is one of the most prestigious rankings, based on data collected from major retail sellers.

- It accounts not only for direct sales but also for pre-orders.

Amazon Best Sellers

- Sales data is updated hourly, enabling real-time tracking of a book's performance.

USA Today Bestseller List

- This list covers all genres and is based solely on overall sales figures.

National Bestseller Lists

- Many countries have their own rankings that reflect the popularity of books among local audiences.

As I mentioned earlier, *bestseller status* can exist at different levels, each with its implications for an author's career and a book's sales potential:

- **National Bestseller** – Popular within one country.
- **International Bestseller** – Sells millions of copies across multiple countries.
- **Genre Bestseller** – Leads sales within a specific category (e.g., science fiction, romance, business books).

Although high sales define a bestseller, not every commercially successful book becomes a recognized literary classic. Bestsellers reflect current audience preferences, but not always the long-term cultural or artistic value of a work.

Also, **not all bestsellers generate income for their authors**. Returning to the core idea: **a bestseller is a book that *sells more copies than others.*** But here's the honest question — how much does the author earn from those sales? Unfortunately, the answer is often disappointing. In many cases, the author receives a tiny share of the profits, or none.

It all depends on the revenue-sharing terms outlined in the contract between the author and the publisher. There are also unfortunate cases where authors fall victim to outright fraud.

It's a rare feat, with only about 1%–2% of traditionally published books making it to the bestseller list. The odds are even slimmer for self-published books, with less than 0.01% achieving bestseller status. This rarity underscores the significance of the achievement.

While some authors consistently land on bestseller lists, many struggle to replicate their initial success. According to publishing industry experts, a significant number of authors — 50% to 70% — who achieve bestseller status are unable to replicate that success with subsequent books. This is often referred to as the "one-hit wonder" phenomenon in the publishing industry. For example, *To Kill a Mockingbird* (1960) by Harper Lee became an instant classic, selling over 40 million copies worldwide. Yet, for decades, it remained her only published novel until *Go Set a Watchman* was controversially released in 2015, long after her literary prime.

There are numerous reasons why authors struggle to maintain their bestseller status. The pressure to meet readers' expectations can be overwhelming, leading to creative burnout or rushed works that fail to resonate with their intended audience. Additionally, market dynamics change rapidly; what captivates readers in one decade may lose its appeal in the next. Authors who achieved success through a specific trend or genre may struggle when the market shifts.

Achieving bestseller status is a remarkable accomplishment but sustaining that level of success requires a combination of factors, many of which are beyond the author's control. While most bestselling authors may not reach the same heights again, those who adapt to market trends and continue to engage their audience have a better chance of maintaining their position in the literary world.

But don't let these numbers discourage you. Remember, the true measure of success is the personal fulfillment you derive *from your work.* Your book's success *should* be defined by your own standards, not by external validation. You're not creating a bestseller for others — first and foremost, you're making it for *yourself.*

The most rewarding part of the journey is the love you pour into your creation. Create with love, and you may receive far greater rewards than you ever expected. This approach can bring a sense of hope and optimism to your writing journey.

The Self-Publishing Revolution and Its Accessibility

The self-publishing revolution has transformed the literary world, breaking down barriers that once made traditional publishing the sole gateway for aspiring authors. Today, anyone with a story to tell or knowledge to share can publish a book, often with minimal upfront costs. This shift has empowered writers globally, democratizing the publishing industry and fostering a new wave of creativity and innovation.

I, too, began my publishing journey through self-publishing, taking on every role myself — from book creation and editing to formatting, printing, promotion, and sales. Although a well-known Ukrainian publishing house published my first book on women's health in 2008, most of the books had to be sold independently by me and my partners using a popular social media platform. The book became so popular that we sold between 20 and 30 copies per day, allowing us to recover all publishing expenses within just a few weeks.

In 2010 and 2012, I independently published two more books — one on preparing for pregnancy and the other on pregnancy itself — investing my funds in both projects. Within a few months, I had fully recouped the costs and began earning a profit, which not only allowed me to reinvest some of the earnings into my business but also gave me hope for a lucrative future.

Self-publishing is not just a modern phenomenon. Its roots go back centuries, long before digital platforms emerged. Some of the most influential works in literary history began as self-published efforts, connecting us to a rich and diverse literary tradition.

In 1477, William Caxton established the first printing press in England and self-published *The Recuyell of the Historyes of Troye*, a translation of a French text. This marked the beginning of authors taking control of the printing process to share their work with the public.

In 1732, Benjamin Franklin published *Poor Richard's Almanack*— a self-funded project that became one of the most widely read publications of its time. His success demonstrated that self-publishing could reach a broad audience.

In 1917, Virginia Woolf and her husband, Leonard, founded the Hogarth Press to publish her own writings and the works of other authors. This independent press gave Woolf complete creative control, leading to the publication of groundbreaking works, such as *Mrs. Dalloway*.

By the 20th century, vanity presses — companies that publish books at the author's expense — had become a popular route for authors seeking to bypass traditional publishing houses. However, these services often required a substantial financial investment and lacked professional distribution, limiting the reach of many books.

The digital revolution of the early 21st century not only brought self-publishing into the mainstream but also empowered authors in a way never seen before. Platforms like Amazon's Kindle Direct Publishing (KDP), Smashwords, and Draft2Digital removed the financial and logistical barriers associated with traditional publishing, inspiring a new wave of authors. Here's how:

Lower Costs: Authors no longer need to pay for large print runs or rely on expensive vanity presses. Digital platforms enable books to be published in e-book format with minimal investment, while print-on-demand services, such as Amazon's KDP Print, ensure that physical copies are only printed when ordered.

Global Reach: Self-publishing platforms connect authors with readers worldwide. A writer in a small town can now reach an international audience with the click of a button.

Creative Control: Unlike traditional publishing, where editorial and marketing decisions often rest with the publisher, self-publishing gives authors complete control over their content, cover design, pricing, and promotional strategies. This level of control empowers authors, allowing them to shape their literary destinies.

Diverse Voices: Self-publishing has provided a platform for voices that traditional publishers, including those of underrepresented authors and those writing in niche genres, might otherwise overlook.

The history of self-publishing bestsellers also has some amazing facts.

- **E.L. James and *Fifty Shades of Grey*:**

Initially self-published as an e-book and print-on-demand title, *Fifty Shades of Grey* became a global sensation. Its success led to a traditional publishing deal, with sales exceeding 150 million copies and sparking a major film franchise.

- **Andy Weir and *The Martian*:**

Weir initially published *The Martian* chapter by chapter on his blog, where it gained a cult following. Encouraged by readers, he self-published the book, which later became a bestseller and was adapted into a critically acclaimed film starring Matt Damon.

- **Hugh Howey and the *Wool* Series:**

Howey self-published his science fiction series on Amazon. Its success earned him a unique publishing deal that allowed him to retain e-book rights while granting traditional publishers print rights.

- **Rupi Kaur and *Milk and Honey*:**

Kaur initially self-published her poetry collection, which gained immense popularity through social media. *Milk and Honey* eventually sold millions of copies and topped bestseller lists.

These are just a few examples of fascinating stories. The most important truth is this: **if you never try to create a book, you'll never have the chance to experience the thrill of becoming a bestselling author**. Every writer who uses modern platforms to sell books — including digital formats — dreams of that moment of recognition and success. It's that recognition that brings not just encouragement, but a surge of inspiration to create more.

The support of my readers means a great deal to me — some of them have collected all my books, from eBooks to printed editions. I have long-time readers who tell me that my books helped them conceive and give birth to children or brought them emotional relief and psychological comfort. Their comments, letters, and reviews are not just words, but powerful sources of inspiration that continue to fuel my passion for writing new books.

While self-publishing offers unparalleled opportunities, it is not without its challenges:

- **Competition**

Millions of books are published every year, making it hard for any one title to stand out. This is where effective marketing plays a crucial role. I often hear people say that, for example, on Amazon, a book's success is primarily determined by how well it's advertised. This highlights the significance of marketing in the self-publishing process.

- **Quality Control**

Without the rigorous editorial process of traditional publishing, self-published books can sometimes suffer from poor editing or formatting, which affects their reception. Manual formatting, a process that was once expensive and time-consuming, is now simplified by modern technologies such as self-publishing platforms and editing software. These tools reduce the need for costly support services and lower the overall cost of preparing a book for publication.

- **Marketing and Promotion**

Self-published authors are fully responsible for promoting their work, which requires time, effort, and often financial investment. Social media, email newsletters, and online advertisements are standard tools for building an audience. These are skills you must either learn or outsource to professionals who can help "launch" your book into the world.

- **Limited Validation**

Despite its rapid growth, self-publishing still carries a certain stigma in some circles, where traditionally published books are seen as more credible. Fortunately, that stigma is fading. The younger generation increasingly prefers digital books. Today, a virtual library can hold tens of thousands of titles — and none of them will ever gather dust.

The future of self-publishing is bright, driven by rapid technological advancements and changing consumer behavior. Here are some of the key trends shaping the industry:

1. **AI Tools**

Artificial intelligence is transforming the way authors write, edit, and market their books. Tools like Grammarly, ChatGPT, and Jasper.ai help streamline the creative process, while AI-powered advertising platforms enable precise and targeted promotions. We'll explore this topic in more detail later in the book.

2. **Audiobooks**

The demand for audiobooks is not just growing, it's skyrocketing. Self-published authors are tapping into this market using platforms like Audible's ACX to produce and distribute their work. Today's advanced voice synthesis technologies can replicate almost any voice, even that of the author. Converting a manuscript into an audio file has become relatively simple, and the quality of synthetic voices is constantly improving. These modern voice engines can read text with tone, rhythm, and even simulated emotion, making it increasingly difficult to distinguish between a robot and a human reader. This greatly simplifies the audiobook creation process. Several of my books have already been translated into audio format.

3. **Niche Markets**

Self-publishing enables authors to reach particular audiences, from regional cookbooks to specialized academic texts. These niche markets often have loyal readers who are willing to pay more for content that speaks directly to their interests and needs.

4. Hybrid Publishing Models

Some authors are blending the advantages of self-publishing and traditional publishing, negotiating contracts that allow them to retain certain rights while benefiting from the resources of large publishing houses. I am one of those authors, with experience in both independent publishing and working with major publishing agencies.

The self-publishing revolution has redefined what it means to be an author. By removing traditional barriers and embracing technology, it has empowered writers from all walks of life to share their stories with the world. As technology continues to evolve, the opportunities for self-published authors will only expand, ensuring that countless voices and stories, including yours, continue to be heard and valued in this diverse industry.

Why AI Is a Game-Changer for Modern Authors

Just a few decades ago, the technologies that support the creation of digital and other media products didn't exist — or, more accurately, they existed but were too complex or expensive for most people to use, even for those with decent computer skills.

For example, the widely used software *Photoshop* came with manuals hundreds of pages long, detailing how to use the program for image creation and editing. Although I used it often — I've always loved photography — I still ran into difficulties performing certain tasks. Sometimes I would spend hours just trying to enhance the quality of a single photo.

Today, however, countless online tools can complete such tasks in mere seconds and produce high-quality results. I was amazed at how quickly I could colorize old black-and-white photos — and how dramatically the perception of an image changes when it comes to life in color. Thanks to modern online tools, I was able to see portraits of my grandparents in full color. I even created "living photographs" — images where the face moves and smiles, almost like a video.

I remember my sister's reaction when I showed her a "living" photo of our father in his youth, just as she remembered him. It was a decisive emotional moment. She was in tears. She said the image was so real, it felt like a scene from her past — because that's exactly how she remembered him.

Let me briefly share a bit of the history behind artificial intelligence. The concept of creating machines capable of thought has been explored for centuries, dating back to ancient times. The earliest references to artificial intelligence can be found in Greek mythology, particularly in the myths of Hephaestus, the divine craftsman who created intelligent, mechanical beings like Talos and the golden automatons that served in his workshop. However, concrete steps toward building such systems didn't begin until the development of computing technology in the modern era.

In the 17th century, philosopher René Descartes reflected on the possibility of automating thought processes. In the 19th century, Charles Babbage and Ada Lovelace developed the concept of the analytical engine — a device capable of performing complex calculations. This was the first real step toward creating programmable systems.

A breakthrough in AI development was made possible through the work of Alan Turing. In 1936, he proposed the concept of the *Turing machine*, which laid the foundation for modern computer science. Later, in 1950, Turing posed the famous question, *"Can machines think?"* and introduced what would become known as the *Turing Test*—a method to determine whether a machine can exhibit intelligent behavior indistinguishable from that of a human.

The term *artificial intelligence* was officially introduced in 1956 at the Dartmouth Conference. This period marked the beginning of early AI programs that attempted to simulate human reasoning, such as Logic Theorist, which could prove mathematical theorems.

The 1960s were an era of optimism in AI research. Many scientists believed that machines would soon match human-level problem-solving abilities. Early expert systems emerged, including ELIZA, which mimicked human conversation. However, by the

1970s, it became clear that the available technology was not sufficient to fulfill such grand ambitions. This led to a period of stagnation known as the AI winter, a term used to describe a period of reduced funding and interest in AI research due to unmet expectations and lack of progress.

Things began to shift in the 1990s, as computing power increased and new algorithms emerged that could work with large datasets. In 1997, IBM's Deep Blue famously defeated world chess champion Garry Kasparov — a milestone in AI history. The final score was 3.5–2.5 in favor of Deep Blue. It was the first time a computer defeated a reigning world chess champion in a standard time control match, symbolizing a major leap in computational strategy and AI capability.

The 2000s saw rapid progress in AI, particularly with the advancement of *neural networks* and *deep learning*. In 2016, AlphaGo, a program developed by DeepMind, defeated the world champion in the board game Go—a feat previously considered nearly impossible due to the game's complexity.

Today, artificial intelligence is present in nearly every aspect of life — from medicine and transportation to entertainment and business. It assists in diagnosing diseases, powering autonomous vehicles, and personalizing education. With everyday tools like Siri, Alexa, and Google Assistant, AI has become an integral part of our daily lives.

The history of artificial intelligence reveals that humanity's desire to create thinking machines has been an integral part of scientific progress from the outset. AI continues to evolve rapidly, opening new horizons and reshaping our understanding of technological potential.

Yet while forward-thinking minds integrate AI into their daily work, many people still respond to these technological advances with suspicion or even fear. The idea that robots will replace humans is often sensationalized, and conspiracy theories abound, particularly those claiming that AI is a tool for global surveillance and population control.

Personally, these fears always make me smile. I went through the immigration process in Canada long ago, so the Canadian government has had a complete "file" on me and my family for years. When I applied for the NEXUS program to simplify entry into the United States, I underwent background checks and submitted fingerprints. Everything anyone needs to know about me is already known. The key point is this: **if you obey the law, there is no reason to fear that someone is spying on you, listening to your** conversations, or rummaging through your computer.

What I have noticed in recent years, however, is a growing number of cybercriminals attempting to hack into cell phones and computers to access bank accounts and steal credit card information. But that has nothing to do with artificial intelligence — and certainly nothing to do with conspiracy theories. It's simply old-fashioned human dishonesty and criminal behavior. While AI can be used to enhance cybersecurity measures, it's essential to recognize that the misuse of any technology, including AI, for criminal purposes is a distinct issue that requires addressing through legal and ethical frameworks.

The integration of artificial intelligence (AI) into the literary world has not only streamlined tasks but also revolutionized how modern authors approach the craft of writing. AI's impact goes far beyond mere convenience — it fundamentally transforms the way books are conceived, developed, and marketed, inspiring a new wave of creativity and innovation.

AI is not just a tool, but a powerful ally that assists me in many ways — from creating book outlines and searching or verifying information, to editing texts, translating content, identifying weak points in a manuscript, and spotting gaps. This empowerment is a testament to the potential of AI in the literary world, and I'll share more about this throughout the book.

AI-driven tools like Grammarly, ChatGPT, and Jasper.ai are not just reshaping the creative process but also saving author's valuable time. These tools help authors generate ideas, refine manuscripts, and ensure grammatical accuracy, dramatically reducing the time needed to polish a draft. This time-saving aspect allows writers to focus more on storytelling and less on the technical details of editing, a relief in the fast-paced world of publishing.

Moreover, AI plays an essential role in market research. Authors can now analyze reader preferences, monitor market trends, and tailor their content to meet real-time demand. AI-powered platforms provide insights into trending genres, popular themes, and emerging reader interests, even predicting future literary trends. This data-driven approach enables authors to make informed decisions, thereby improving their chances of success in an increasingly competitive marketplace.

Marketing, a well-known challenge for many self-published authors, is also being transformed by AI. Advanced algorithms can design and execute targeted ad campaigns, ensuring that promotional efforts reach the right audience. AI analyzes engagement metrics, optimizes content distribution, and personalizes marketing messages to make them more effective — and more affordable.

AI is also making significant strides in the audiobook industry. Sophisticated text-to-speech technologies now produce high-quality audio renditions of books, with emotional inflections that previously only human narrators could deliver. This innovation not only enhances the accessibility of books but also opens new revenue streams for authors.

In essence, AI is a powerful ally for modern writers, enhancing every stage of the publishing journey. By embracing AI's capabilities, authors can streamline their workflow, gain a deeper understanding of their audience, and promote their books with greater impact. The future of writing is undeniably intertwined with AI, and those who adapt to this evolution stand to benefit immensely.

What Readers Want in Today's Book Market

The book market today is more dynamic and diverse than ever before. With the rise of digital platforms, social media, and self-publishing, readers have access to an unprecedented range of books.

To succeed in this competitive landscape, both authors and publishers need to understand what readers are looking for. This chapter not only examines the preferences, expectations, and trends that shape the modern book market but also reiterates the importance of this understanding in preparing for future success.

When I created a book on internet marketing 25 years ago, one of the chapters included charts showing how the profile of online sales was evolving—what types of products were becoming popular and which ones were declining. I also included forecast charts compiled by marketing experts, projecting trends for the coming years. Among those predictions was the rise of online book sales, which, as we now know, came true. That's why I want to share similar data in this book.

I analyzed various sources, and synthesizing them into a single, coherent picture was not easy, as most of the data is available only for countries where digital product sales are actively tracked and reported with more accuracy. I asked AI to generate charts based on this data (25 years ago, I did it all by hand using Excel).

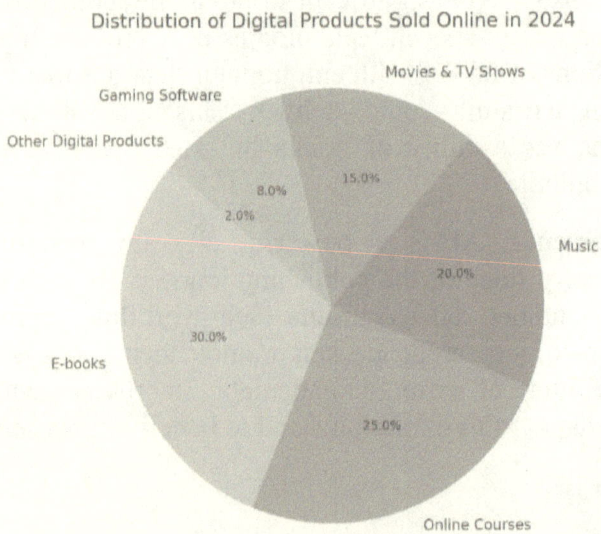

So, the first chart reflects global sales of digital products. (Note: under "digital products," this often includes phones, computers, tablets, and other devices used for receiving, analyzing, and storing digital information.) As you can see, eBooks make up

30% of digital product sales. This is a significant figure—it indicates that people who use digital tools also tend to read extensively.

Take a closer look: online courses also occupy an important place in people's lives today. If your book is nonfiction, consider turning it into an online course as well. It's worth thinking about!

When it comes to genre, fiction dominates the eBook market, but "how-to" books are also in high demand. Sharing your knowledge and experience through books is not just a trend; it's a powerful way to connect with readers and make an impact. This should inspire you to continue creating content that resonates with your audience.

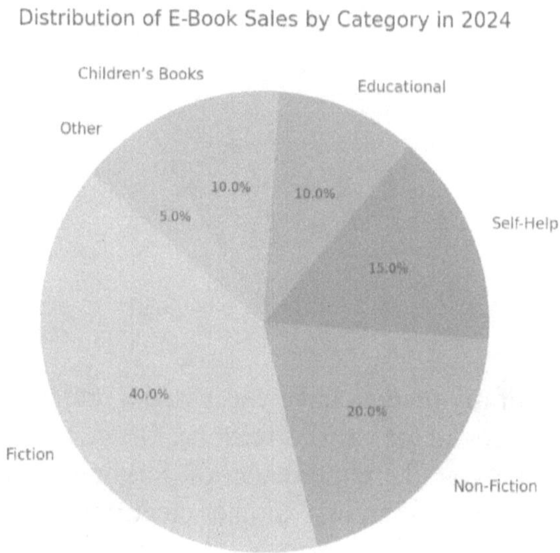

When discussing book sales overall, it's essential to remember that, beyond digital formats, print editions continue to play a vital role. However, it's also necessary to consider the environmental impact of print books, particularly in the context of increasing digitalization and concerns about sustainability.

Let's not forget that many major platforms selling e-books, including Amazon, also offer the option to order paperback and hardcover versions. Print books still account for around 40% of online book sales, a clear indication that readers, like you, are not yet ready to say goodbye to printed books.

Many of my readers have expressed a preference for the print versions of my books for various reasons. Often, it's about the feeling of comfort—the tactile experience of holding a real book with physical pages, rather than just another electronic device.

Like many of you, I still love printed books. Even though my work requires me to read countless e-books, there's something irreplaceable about the experience of flipping through pages, feeling the weight of the book, and even enjoying the scent of paper.

It is also worth reviewing other reports from 2024.

In 2024, Amazon reported the sale of approximately 308 million print books, reflecting a 2.4% increase from the previous year. The e-book sector saw even more substantial growth, with Amazon selling around 487 million e-books annually. This data indicates that interest in books is not declining—it's rising.

Notably, e-book sales have now surpassed print book sales on Amazon, with e-books making up approximately 61% of all book sales on the platform. This shift reflects a broader change in consumer behavior, as readers increasingly prefer the convenience, portability, and instant access offered by digital formats.

Still, it's essential to note that print books remain a strong presence in the market. Their lasting popularity suggests a diverse readership, with many people still valuing the tactile experience of physical books. This duality ensures that both digital and print formats will continue to coexist in the evolving landscape of book consumption.

While determining the exact global share of e-books remains difficult—due to variations in data collection and differing market conditions—available statistics offer valuable insights:

- United States: In 2024, e-books represented around 11.5% of total book sales revenue among mainstream publishers.
- United Kingdom: E-books accounted for 34% of all book sales, with Amazon UK dominating 87.9% of that market.
- Germany: E-book sales in 2020 reached €500 million in revenue.
- China: The e-book market was valued at approximately $1.67 billion.

These figures demonstrate that the market share of e-books varies significantly by country. In some regions, digital formats account for a significant portion of sales, while in others, they remain a smaller segment. Globally, e-books account for around 9% of the total revenue in the book industry.

Which countries sell the most e-books?

The pie chart below illustrates the distribution of global e-book sales across key markets, including the United States, the United Kingdom, Germany, China, India, and others.

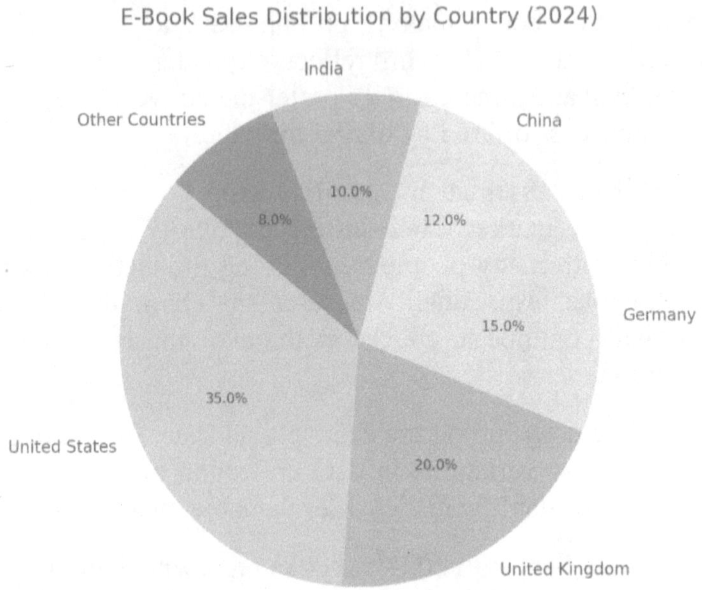

But let's look to the future. No doubt you're curious about what's expected in 2025. Forecasting is never simple, but analysts often base projections on past trends and growth rates. The following chart shows that e-books are expected to remain highly popular in the coming year.

Another chart projects a rise in the popularity of fiction, while most other literary genres are predicted to remain relatively stable. You can take this information into account when creating your bestseller or choose to ignore it altogether. What matters most is that you follow your dream.

In later chapters, I will analyze marketing strategies for books in more detail. But here, I want to emphasize an essential point: **without sales, there is no bestseller.**

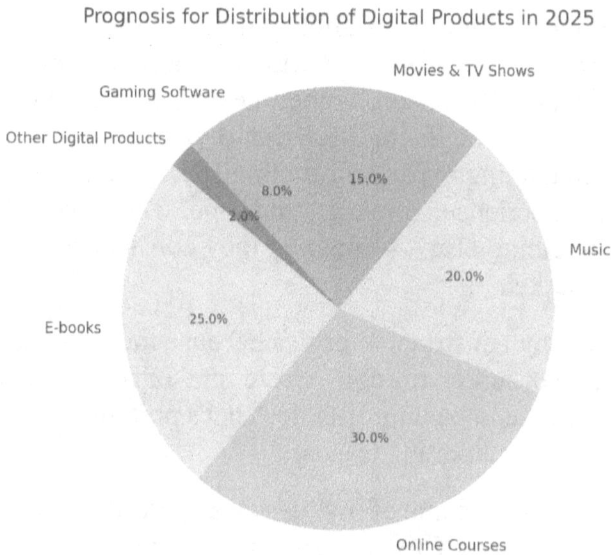
Prognosis for Distribution of Digital Products in 2025
Movies & TV Shows
Gaming Software
Other Digital Products
15.0%
8.0%
2.0%
Music
20.0%
E-books
25.0%
30.0%
Online Courses

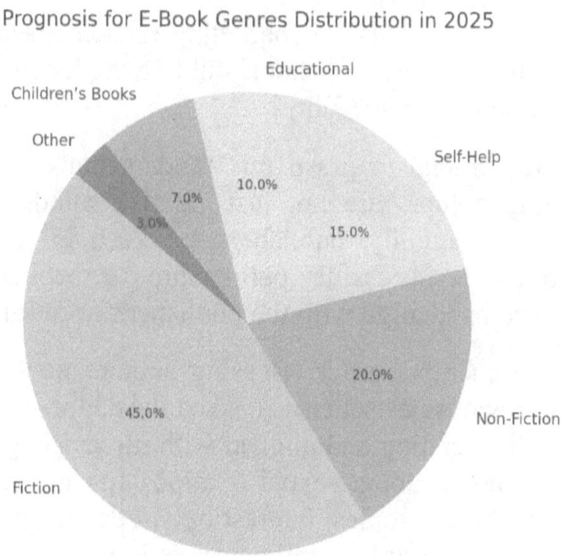
Prognosis for E-Book Genres Distribution in 2025
Educational
Children's Books
Other
Self-Help
10.0%
7.0%
3.0%
15.0%
20.0%
Non-Fiction
45.0%
Fiction

Members of my team often call me a chronic idea generator because I consistently come up with a steady stream of ideas for consideration and discussion. Sometimes, a particular idea is just the right time to be brought to life. But my team, which includes a manager, a marketing expert, a targeting specialist, and professionals with media experience, often grounds me. They encourage me to focus on something else—something they consider more relevant to the current market.

I trust my constructive critics because they support me in my work and help ensure that I don't waste time or resources on projects that might turn out to be unprofitable. That's precisely why it's crucial to stay attuned to marketing trends.

Believe me—some of my ideas were ahead of their time when I first proposed them. Others were underdeveloped, and still others proved too costly to implement. Some of these ideas were realized later. But when it comes to bringing any vision into practical reality, many factors must be considered.

Whenever I met with editors at publishing houses or media agencies, I always asked marketing-related questions: What topic should I focus on next? What should be the length? Which language should it be written in? Why?

It's crucial to grasp this fundamental truth: for publishers, bestselling authors are not just creative minds, but also revenue generators. Naturally, publishers are keen to retain such authors. However, a successful partnership necessitates that authors comprehend and align with the publisher's needs and expectations.

I remember, after releasing another book—which followed several previous bestsellers—I asked the editorial team what types of topics were trending and aligned with my existing body of work. At that time, books about sexual relationships and sex education were among the hottest topics. Interestingly, I had already written a nearly 500-page manuscript on intimate relationships, but had held off on publishing it, as I was still contemplating revisions and improvements. In other words, I already had a substantial manuscript on a hot-topic issue.

But the editors quickly raised concerns. The subject was deemed too controversial, as it could provoke strong adverse reactions from specific segments of the public. Worse, such a book requires an 18+ age restriction, meaning that my name could end up on a special list, which would limit visibility and potentially affect future opportunities.

And they were right. Even today, there are still topics that can be problematic, especially in an era when automated systems increasingly scrutinize content—and yes, those systems now check everything. It serves as a reminder that caution is always warranted, especially when dealing with potentially sensitive or controversial subjects.

Not long ago, one of the platforms rejected the publication of the digital formats of my book on girls' health, simply because they didn't like the title. The official response stated: "We will not be accepting books that create an unsatisfactory or incomplete experience for readers."

Naturally, I responded right away. I explained that the title had been carefully chosen with input from several marketing experts, that the book was already published on other platforms, and that I was requesting a manual review of both the title and the content. Within 24 hours, I received an apology, and the book was accepted for publication.

This incident highlights an important point: be prepared for obstacles, especially those created by automated systems, which are now used almost everywhere, including in the book publishing industry. These systems can mistakenly flag content based on rigid rules, rather than thoughtful evaluation.

What Determines a Book's Success Today

In a rapidly evolving publishing landscape, the definition of a successful book has expanded beyond just high sales or bestseller status. Today's success is shaped by a combination of visibility, reader engagement, cultural relevance, and emotional impact. From viral social media trends to personalized recommendations, from authentic storytelling to accessible formats—many elements now influence how and why a book resonates with readers.

Let's take a closer look at the key factors driving a book's success in the modern literary world.

1. **Accessibility and Convenience**

In today's fast-paced world, convenience plays a crucial role in reader behavior. Readers seek books that are easy to access and consume, which has led to the rise of e-books and audiobooks. Platforms like Amazon Kindle, Audible, and subscription services like Scribd or Kindle Unlimited cater to readers seeking instant access to vast libraries of content.

Digital books are popular for their affordability and portability. Readers enjoy the convenience of carrying an entire library on their devices and appreciate features like adjustable font sizes and built-in dictionaries.

The audiobook market has seen exponential growth, driven by busy lifestyles. Commuters, gym-goers, and multitaskers have come to embrace audiobooks as a way to enjoy stories or gain knowledge without needing dedicated reading time.

2. **Engaging and Relatable Stories**

Today's readers are not just seeking entertainment, but a personal connection through stories. Whether it's a character's emotional growth, a familiar struggle, or a glimpse into a different way of life, this power of connection is what truly engages them. They're not just reading to pass the time—they're searching for meaning, validation, and inspiration.

Representation has evolved from a preference to a necessity. Readers now demand to see characters who look like them, think like them, or live lives completely different from their own. They value stories that include diverse cultural backgrounds, gender identities, lifestyles, and voices. This kind of inclusion not only reflects the real world more accurately but also allows readers from all walks of life to feel seen and acknowledged.

Authenticity is a cornerstone of storytelling. Readers have a keen sense for when a story is true to its characters and rooted in genuine emotion. Even within the realms of fantasy or speculative fiction, they seek honesty in the human experience—flawed characters, real dilemmas, and emotional truths. When a story feels authentic, it not only builds trust but also ensures a deep and lasting engagement with the readers.

Simultaneously, the allure of escapism remains as strong as ever. Many readers turn to books as a means of temporarily escaping the pressures of daily life. They yearn for the joy, thrill, or comfort that comes from immersing themselves in a different world. This is why genres like romance, fantasy, and adventure continue to be cherished—they offer hope, wonder, and the promise of something beyond the ordinary, validating the readers' need for a break.

In essence, today's readers are drawn to stories that mirror the complexities of life while offering moments of clarity, escape, or emotional connection. For writers, this means crafting narratives that are not only imaginative but also honest, inclusive, and deeply human.

3. Genre Trends and Popularity

Specific genres consistently perform well in the book market, often reflecting current cultural trends and the shifting interests of readers.

Thrillers and mysteries remain staples of popular fiction. These fast-paced, suspense-driven stories captivate audiences with their twists, tension, and sense of urgency. Their popularity can be attributed to the human fascination with the unknown and the desire for a thrilling escape from everyday life.

Romance, with its intense emotional connection and promise of escapism, continues to dominate global sales. Subgenres like contemporary romance, romantic comedies, and LGBTQ+ love stories draw large, loyal audiences, offering not just love stories, but often hope, healing, and relatable personal journeys. The allure of these genres is undeniable, drawing readers in with their emotional depth and engaging narratives.

In recent years, there has been a significant surge in the popularity of self-help and personal growth books. This trend reflects a growing need among readers for guidance in navigating the complexities of modern life—whether through practical strategies, motivational insights, or emotional support. The relevance of these genres in today's society is undeniable, with books that offer tools for resilience, better habits, and mental clarity finding a robust following.

Fantasy and science fiction remain strong, especially among younger audiences and genre enthusiasts. These stories offer an escape into imaginative worlds, while also addressing real-world issues through metaphor and allegory. The massive success of franchises like *The Hunger Games*, *Harry Potter*, and *Game of Thrones* has only fueled demand for richly built universes and high-stakes narratives.

Non-fiction continues to thrive as well, particularly in the form of biographies, memoirs, and historical accounts. Readers seek out these stories for insight, inspiration, or a deeper understanding of events and individuals that shape the world. These genres connect readers to real experiences and often illuminate the human condition in powerful ways.

Overall, the success of these genres reflects not just what entertains us, but what we value, question, and strive to understand.

4. Interactive and Social Reading Experiences

Social media and online communities have revolutionized the way people experience books. Reading is no longer a solitary activity—it's now highly interactive and social. Readers, empowered by the platforms, don't just finish a book and move on; they share their opinions, post reviews, join discussions, and recommend their favorites to others across digital platforms, feeling influential and integral to the reading community.

TikTok and Instagram have given rise to dynamic book communities like BookTok and Bookstagram. These spaces are filled with passionate readers who create engaging content around the books they love. A single viral post can dramatically boost a book's visibility, often turning a little-known title into a bestseller within days. Readers, feeling a strong sense of belonging, trust these personal recommendations more than traditional ads, giving these platforms a powerful influence on buying trends.

Authors who embrace this shift and actively participate in the conversation are seeing real benefits. Those who respond to comments, host live Q&A sessions or run virtual book clubs foster a strong sense of connection with their audience. This direct interaction builds trust, encourages word-of-mouth promotion, and often results in a loyal reader base eager to support future work.

Additionally, platforms like Goodreads make reading a collaborative experience. Readers can join groups, form book clubs, track their reading goals, and participate in meaningful discussions with fellow book lovers around the world. It's no longer just about reading a story—it's about being part of a larger conversation and feeling a sense of accomplishment when they meet their reading goals.

5. Shorter and Flexible Formats

Today's readers are often pressed for time, and that has shifted how stories are consumed. Shorter, more flexible formats are becoming increasingly popular, offering a way to enjoy literature without the commitment of a full-length novel.

Novellas and short stories are a godsend for those with busy lifestyles. These compact narratives deliver a complete and satisfying experience in just one sitting, making them ideal for commuting, breaks, or winding down before bed. They offer the pleasure of storytelling without the pressure of a long-term time investment, providing a much-needed respite in our fast-paced lives.

Serialized fiction is also gaining momentum, especially on platforms like Wattpad and Kindle Vella. These apps allow authors to release their stories in episodes, mimicking the feel of a TV series. Readers can dip in and out of the story at their own pace, following the narrative week by week or bingeing several installments at once. This format keeps engagement high and builds anticipation between releases, keeping readers on the edge of their seats for the next episode.

Visual storytelling is another area that continues to grow. Graphic novels, illustrated books, and hybrid formats blend text with art to create a rich, immersive experience. These works appeal to readers who are drawn to strong visual elements or who find traditional formats less accessible. With their mix of imagery and concise dialogue, these books can deliver powerful stories in a short amount of time, captivating readers with their unique blend of art and narrative.

Ultimately, as attention spans shrink and schedules tighten, formats that offer flexibility, immediacy, and visual appeal are becoming essential in capturing—and keeping—the modern reader's attention.

6. Value for Money

In today's diverse book market, readers are empowered with a plethora of options. They are more discerning than ever, seeking books that are not just worth their time and money but also resonate with them on a deeper level. Whether it's through entertainment, insight, or emotional connection, readers expect genuine value—and they are drawn to books that deliver it.

Meeting reader expectations is crucial in the crowded book market. One effective way to do this is through bundled offers. Box sets, collections, or special editions that include bonus content—like exclusive chapters, author Q&As, or reading guides—offer added value that makes readers feel like they're getting more for their purchase. These bundles are especially appealing to dedicated fans or those discovering a new author they want to explore further.

Subscription models have revolutionized the reading experience. Services like Kindle Unlimited or Scribd empower readers with access to a vast library of books for a single monthly fee. For those who read frequently or are budget-conscious, these platforms provide an affordable and convenient way to discover new titles without the pressure of paying for each book individually.

Regardless of the delivery method, presentation is key. Readers quickly notice the quality of editing, cover design, and overall formatting. Sloppy grammar, awkward layout, or an unprofessional cover can instantly erode trust. Conversely, a polished, thoughtfully produced book signals care and professionalism—and leaves a lasting positive impression.

In a market driven by choice, offering real value and a quality experience is what turns a casual reader into a loyal one.

7. Trends Driven by Technology

Technology has significantly reshaped how readers discover, engage with, and consume books. It's not just changing the format—it's influencing the very preferences and expectations readers bring to their reading experience.

Personalized recommendation systems, such as those employed by Amazon and Goodreads, have revolutionized book discovery, making it more efficient and empowering for readers. Instead of aimlessly browsing or scrolling through shelves, readers now receive tailored suggestions based on their tastes, past purchases, ratings, or reading habits. This targeted approach not only saves time but also often leads to more satisfying reads, fostering trust in the platforms and promoting continued engagement.

Some authors are pushing boundaries further by incorporating artificial intelligence and interactive storytelling into their work. These innovations allow readers to influence a story's direction or explore different narrative paths, turning passive reading into an immersive experience. While still a developing area, interactive and AI-generated stories reflect a growing desire for creative experimentation and reader involvement.

Digital platforms have also erased many of the barriers that once limited access to books. Today, readers around the world can instantly download titles in multiple languages, explore diverse voices, and connect with stories from other cultures. For authors, this means access to global audiences without the constraints of traditional distribution models.

Modern readers are diverse and sophisticated, with a hunger for stories that are accessible, relevant, and emotionally engaging. They seek to be entertained, inspired, and informed—often all at once. As technology continues to evolve, so do their expectations. However, authors and publishers who understand and adapt to these changing preferences are not just keeping up but leading the way in creating books that truly resonate and stand the test of time, reassuring readers of the bright future of literature.

Part 2: The Author's Roadmap

Every Journey Needs a Roadmap: Beginning Your Book with Purpose

When you plan a trip—especially a vacation—what do you do to make it happen? You start by choosing a destination: the specific place you want to go. Then, you figure out how to get there, where to stay, where to eat, what sights to see, and so on. Your needs might be minimal or very elaborate. Some people are happy with a tent and a thermos; others prefer luxury and exclusivity. But no matter what kind of journey you're planning, one thing is essential: a roadmap.

Traveling without a plan—just pointing your finger on the map and following your whims—can lead to discomfort, stress, disorientation, burnout, or even complete failure. The same is true for writing a book. Without a roadmap, the creative process can easily become a multi-year ordeal with little to show for it in the end.

It's essential to recognize that you're not writing a book solely for yourself. Of course, you might be working on a memoir, revisiting the past through your memories. But if you're writing those memories down, it's probably not just for you—it's for your children, grandchildren, friends, and others, right? The joy of sharing these personal stories and connecting with others through your experiences is a powerful motivator on your writing journey.

Your past no longer exists in reality—it lives only in your memory. What becomes real is the work you put into preserving it: a book, an audio recording, a video. But then what? What future does this memoir have? Who will read it? Who will see it? Your memoir has the potential to inspire, to educate, to entertain. It can leave a lasting impact on those who read it.

Please don't take these questions as discouragement—your memoir could very well become a bestseller. I bring up this example to help you see that, as creators, we often enjoy the process of creating without giving much thought to whether we'll sell our work or give it away. I make many things by hand—paintings, knitted items, handmade jewelry—because I'm a creative person. Many of these creations end up as gifts.

However, dear readers (and fellow creators), if we're talking about writing a bestseller, let's not forget what the word means: your creation should sell well. Yes, some bestsellers become hits by accident, but I can promise you this—there's nothing quite as satisfying as receiving a generous royalty check from the sales of your book or digital product.

In this part of the book, we'll explore how to begin creating your bestseller. There's a saying: *A good beginning sets the stage for a successful ending.* And while that's often true, in my experience, even the strongest beginnings can lose momentum if your attention drifts elsewhere. Conversely, a quiet, humble start can sometimes gain incredible traction and lead to surprising and joyful success.

Let me share a personal example. In 2022, I began working on a book about the Soviet mentality—a topic close to me, as I had lived in the USSR for 27 years. Friends and acquaintances often asked me to share stories about that now-defunct country, about what my family and I had gone through. It's a highly complex subject and, in many ways, still unexplored. I've always been drawn to complex topics—those blank spots on the map of history.

For me, the most challenging part was creating a plan: what exactly did I want to say? I had clear fragments of chapters in my mind, but no logical sequence. I started writing multiple times, reworked the beginning at least ten times, always thinking I'd finalize the structure later. I even consulted with political scientists and sociologists to better understand the format the book should take. But I didn't give up. I persevered, knowing that the result would be worth the effort.

Imagine this: you gather flour, yeast, water, and a pinch of salt, thinking you'd like to bake a delicious loaf of bread. However, first, you need to knead the dough, let it rise, shape the loaf, and bake it at the correct temperature for the ideal amount of time. That's exactly how I felt—I was kneading the dough for a long time, unsure of the proportions, not yet feeling the moment when it was time to put the bread in the oven.

In 2023, I shifted my focus to writing a memoir—specifically, a book about my family's lineage, beginning with my great-grandparents. I wanted to preserve at least some of our history for my loved ones. Immersed in personal storytelling, writing about my parents and grandparents without overthinking structure or purpose, I suddenly saw with complete clarity the plan for my book on the Soviet mentality. Nearly two years after starting the project, I created a full outline in just a few hours, defining the chapters, their content, and the overall structure of the book. This outline served as a roadmap for the rest of my writing journey. The inspiration was so strong that I didn't have enough hours in the day to work on it as much as I would have liked. The book is now complete and in the editing phase. If you're interested in this topic, keep an eye out for my upcoming publications, as I'll soon announce their release.

No matter how a project begins, it is still a beginning. Some books take longer to create; others come together quickly. The key is not to stop progressing. As the saying goes, appetite comes with eating. The same is true for writing: quite often, the love for creativity is ignited during the creative process itself.

Finding Your Purpose and Audience

Every great book begins with a clear purpose. Understanding *why* you want to write—and *who* you're writing for—is the foundation of a successful creative project. Whether your goal is to inspire, educate, entertain, or share your unique perspective, identifying your purpose helps guide every step of the writing process. Equally important is understanding your audience—the people who will not only connect with your message and resonate with your ideas but also bring your book to life with their engagement and feedback.

Over the years, I've inspired many people to explore their creativity, including those who went on to write books. But I've also seen the challenges and disappointments that often arise when authors approach writing without clarity or preparation. One acquaintance of mine, after watching my success in publishing, frequently lamented that he, too, wanted to write a book. After several conversations, he finally decided to begin—but his fear of whether he could do it led him to find a co-author who already had some material prepared. This decision, made in haste and without proper preparation, led to a series of challenges.

Co-authoring can have its benefits, but it also comes with challenges. One of the most critical factors in successful co-authorship is maintaining a consistent writing style. Each person has their natural voice, and yes, artificial intelligence can easily detect the differences. When different people write texts, the contrast is usually apparent, and in many cases, it leads to frustration or emotional conflict between collaborators. Instead of accelerating the process, co-authorship can sometimes slow it down. It's essential to consider these challenges and discuss them with your co-author before undertaking a joint project.

Another issue was that my acquaintance didn't have a clear goal. When I asked him why he wanted to write a book, his answer was: "To win the Nobel Prize." It's a bold and motivating dream, but I'm certain that the authors who have received that honor weren't thinking about prizes when they sat down to write. I asked him a simple follow-up question: What do you know about the selection criteria for the Nobel Prize in Literature? And are there not other prestigious literary awards worth aspiring to? It turned out he had no idea how literary works are evaluated in the modern world, highlighting the importance of understanding the publishing process before embarking on a writing journey.

A third problem: he chose to publish the book under a pseudonym. We'll talk more about the pros and cons of using pen names in the digital age later in this book. However, when he submitted the manuscript to a well-known publishing house, he omitted any personal background information, and the pseudonym had no established presence or meaning. Submitting a manuscript without a cover letter or author bio was like shooting in the dark.

Ultimately, both authors were unprepared for the realities of the publishing world. The book was printed in a limited number of copies and distributed to friends and acquaintances. It never found its audience.

And that's the point. **A book needs a purpose, and it needs readers**. Let's examine these elements in more detail.

Defining Your "Why" for Writing a Book

Every successful author begins with a purpose—a compelling reason that drives them to take on the monumental task of writing a book. This "why" becomes the foundation of the creative journey, providing clarity, motivation, and direction. Defining your "why" isn't just a philosophical exercise; it's a practical step that influences your book's tone, structure, and audience. We'll explore why it's essential to identify your purpose and how that clarity can guide every aspect of your writing process.

Writing a book is a transformative journey that can empower you to share your unique perspective with the world. Sometimes, your 'why' emerges gradually—over months or even years. Other times, it arrives suddenly and unexpectedly. But when it does, it can be a powerful force that propels you forward on your writing journey.

I hadn't planned to write this book at all. On my list of upcoming projects, there are nearly fifty book ideas, none of which have anything to do with the topic of creating a bestseller. However, when I started using new platforms to distribute my books, I unexpectedly began receiving messages and comments asking me to share how I do it—how I publish, promote, and sell my work.

That's when I realized something important: in just the last five years (and not even ten!), the tools for writing, publishing, and distributing books—and not just books—have undergone dramatic changes. Most people aren't even aware of these changes.

So, I decided to share what I've learned with both my loyal readers and newcomers. I'm confident that among them are many future authors of beautiful, meaningful books.

Even my close friend, after seeing my published bedtime stories for children, told me she suddenly felt inspired to write her collection of fairy tales for her newborn grandson. Moreover, she wanted to write them not in English, but in her native language.

"Is that even possible?" she asked.

"How do I do it?"

"Can I speed up the process?"

"Where do I print it?"

She asked me dozens of questions—the same kinds of questions I've received from many others.

And so, this book is my answer to all of them.

Understanding why you want to write a book is essential for several reasons:

- **It Keeps You Motivated:** Writing a book is a long-term commitment. Without a strong sense of purpose, it's easy to lose momentum when faced with challenges like writer's block, time constraints, or self-doubt. Your "why" acts as an anchor, reminding you of the bigger picture and keeping you focused on your goals.
- **It Shapes Your Message:** Your purpose determines the core message of your book. Whether you want to educate, inspire, entertain, or advocate for change, a clear "why" ensures that your message resonates with your audience.
- **It Guides Your Decisions:** From choosing a genre to defining your audience, your "why" helps you make informed decisions throughout the writing process. It influences the tone, style, and structure of your book, ensuring consistency and coherence.

Authors are motivated by a wide range of reasons, and identifying your own can provide clarity and focus. Here are some of the most common "whys":

- **To Share Knowledge or Expertise:** Many authors write books to share their expertise in a specific field. Whether you're a professional, educator, or thought leader, a book can help you establish credibility and make a lasting impact in your industry.
- **To Tell a Story:** For fiction writers and memoirists, the primary motivation is often the desire to tell a story that captures the imagination or touches the heart. Your "why" might stem from the belief that your story needs to be said, whether it's to entertain, enlighten, or inspire.
- **To Inspire or Empower Others:** Self-help and motivational books are often driven by a desire to make a positive difference in people's lives. If you've overcome challenges or gained unique insights, your "why" might be to share those lessons with others.
- **To Advocate for Change:** Authors of non-fiction books on social issues or advocacy often aim to raise awareness, spark conversations, or drive change. Your purpose could be rooted in a passion for justice, equality, or environmental sustainability.
- **To Leave a Legacy:** Some writers see their book as a way to preserve their ideas, experiences, or family history for future generations. This "why" is deeply personal and often tied to a desire for immortality through words.
- **To Grow and Experience Fulfillment:** For many, writing a book is a personal milestone or bucket-list goal. Completing a book can be an immensely fulfilling experience, providing a sense of accomplishment and personal growth. It's a journey that can inspire you to push your boundaries and reach new heights in your writing career.

These are far from the only reasons why we write books. But even if you don't have a fully formed vision or clear purpose yet, you may want to earn money from your writing. That's a valid motivation as well.

My own experience with royalties hasn't always been pleasant. The royalties from my first three bestsellers were stolen by a former partner—someone who had represented my interests but also attempted, through forged documents, to gain lifetime rights to my books. I chose not to pursue legal action only because he agreed to terminate the contract on the terms I proposed. I discovered the theft of the royalties only several months after our partnership ended.

Because we lived in different countries, and the books were published in a third country, pursuing legal recovery through attorneys would have cost me far more than the stolen royalties themselves. What mattered most was that I retained the rights to my books.

Later, when new books were published, receiving regular royalty payments was a rewarding experience, especially as the amounts steadily increased. Of course, making money was never my primary motivation for becoming an author, but in the end, the work proved to be profitable.

Understanding *why* you're writing your book is like setting a compass before a journey—it helps you stay focused, motivated, and clear about your direction. Without a clear purpose, it's easy to lose momentum or feel uncertain about your next step. But when you truly understand your intentions, every decision—from the tone of your writing (e.g., a serious tone for a book on business strategies, a light-hearted tone for a children's book) to your marketing strategy (e.g., targeting young entrepreneurs for a business-oriented book, reaching out to family and friends for a memoir)—becomes easier and more aligned with your vision.

Start by reflecting on what moved you to begin this project. Ask yourself:

What inspired me to write this book?

What do I hope to achieve by publishing it?

Your answers may be personal, professional, emotional, or a combination of all three. Maybe you're writing to heal, to teach, to entertain, or to leave a legacy. Whatever the reason, it's essential to name it.

Next, define your goals. Are you writing to build a brand? To make money? To share a unique story? To establish yourself as an expert in your field? To offer help, guidance, or insight? Your goals will shape the kind of book you write and how you approach publishing and promotion. A business-oriented book will look very different from a memoir meant for family and friends.

One helpful way to clarify your purpose is by writing a simple mission statement. It doesn't have to be long—just one honest sentence that sums up your intent. For example:

"*I want to write this book to help young entrepreneurs overcome fear and build successful businesses.*"

"*My goal is to share my family's history to inspire future generations.*"

If a mission statement feels too formal or premature, try starting with a simple dedication. A dedication is a personal note to someone or something that inspired your book, while a mission statement is a concise declaration of your book's purpose and the impact you hope it will have. When I was writing a book on girls' health, I thought about my daughter and her friends—their questions, their curiosity, and our open conversations. That's where the book began. My first words were:

"*This book is dedicated to my daughter and her friends.*"

As I continued to write, my vision expanded. I realized I wanted this knowledge to reach not just girls, but also their parents, teachers, health professionals, and anyone responsible for guiding and supporting them. What began as a personal message evolved into a broader, more inclusive guide.

And that's the beauty of discovering your "why." It may begin small and grow as you go but finding that core motivation early on gives your writing process both structure and soul.

Readers are drawn to authenticity. When your book is written with a clear sense of purpose, it resonates more deeply with readers. Your "why" becomes an invisible thread that links you to your audience, creating a connection built on shared values, experiences, or aspirations.

As you've noticed, I share many personal examples in this book. No artificial intelligence can investigate my past, recount my lived experiences, or express my emotions. These moments are uniquely mine—and they're what give my writing life and depth.

By aligning your "why" with the needs and desires of your audience, you significantly increase the chance that your book will not only be well-received but also make a real impact.

And remember, your purpose may evolve. It's wise to revisit your "why" periodically to see whether it still aligns with your vision. Stay flexible—let your purpose grow with you. This openness often leads to greater clarity, authenticity, and creativity.

Understanding Your Audience's Needs and Desires

Every author should have a general idea of who their book is for. Writing a book that resonates with readers requires more than creativity and skill—it demands a deep understanding of your audience. **Knowing who your readers are, what they need, and what they want is essential to crafting a book that captures their attention and delivers real value.** Whether you're writing fiction or non-fiction, understanding your audience's preferences helps you shape your content, tone, and approach in a way that meets their expectations.

Not long ago, I read a psychology book that seemed promising and relevant to my interests. However, I encountered several issues that made the reading experience frustrating. Although the book was intended for a general audience, the language was overly academic, filled with complex terms that would be unfamiliar to most readers without a background in the field. For those whose first language wasn't English, the text posed an even greater barrier to comprehension.

And then there was the physical format: the font was so small that reading became a strain. I'm not sure if this was done to save on printing costs, but the result was a book that was difficult to read and tiring to get through. Despite the value of its content, it didn't reach the intended audience.

This brings us to a crucial question: Why is understanding your audience so important?

Building Connection: A book that speaks directly to the reader's experiences, challenges, or aspirations creates a sense of connection. When readers feel understood, they're more likely to engage with your work and recommend it to others.

Enhancing Relevance: Understanding your audience allows you to focus on the themes, ideas, or information most relevant to them. This significantly increases the likelihood that your book will stand out in a crowded marketplace.

All my bestsellers have been on the topic of women's health. Interestingly, I never planned to focus exclusively on this subject. But over time, I developed a large base of loyal readers. Thanks to my books, they were able to plan and sustain healthy pregnancies, navigate the postpartum period, and care for their children, including their daughters. And now, as many of these women are aging and approaching menopause, they are eagerly awaiting my next book—this time, on that very topic.

I became an expert in women's health not only through my medical training, but also through my ability to share knowledge and personal experience in a way that feels accessible and supportive.

Driving Reader Loyalty: When readers find genuine value or emotional meaning in your work, they are far more likely to become loyal fans who follow your future projects.

My readers follow me on social media and watch my videos on YouTube. The joy of receiving messages and comments from people who have been following my work for 10–15 years is indescribable. One of the most memorable moments happened in Saint Petersburg in 2018 during a book launch and reader meet-up. A woman approached me and said:

"*I've been a fan of yours for years and have read all your publications. Thanks to your advice, I was able to conceive and carry my pregnancy without any issues. Did you know that the cover of this book* (and she was holding the book *'9 Months of Happiness'*) *is a photograph of my child—the one I was able to carry thanks to you?*".

I was genuinely stunned. The photo for the cover came from a stock image collection acquired by a major publisher, and the editors had no idea it featured the child of one of my longtime readers. Isn't that remarkable? When you know who your audience is—and when you see the impact your books have on their lives—writing takes on an entirely new meaning.

So, let's take the next step - s**teps to identify your audience:**

1. **Define Your Ideal Reader**

Start by visualizing the type of person who would benefit from or enjoy your book. Consider the following aspects:

- **Demographics:** Age, gender, occupation, education, and cultural background.
- **Psychographics:** Interests, values, lifestyles, and challenges.

For example, if you're writing a self-help book on time management, your target audience might include busy professionals or students seeking practical strategies to manage their schedules more effectively.

In my case, my primary audience has traditionally been women between the ages of 25 and 45, which isn't surprising, as I've written extensively for women of reproductive age. However, I've also noticed a steady increase in readership among women over 45, and that brings me absolute joy. It inspires me to write a new book focused specifically on menopause—a subject that is often overlooked, yet deeply important to so many of my readers.

2. Research Reader Behavior

Use tools and platforms to gather insights about your potential readers:

- **Social media:** Platforms like TikTok, Instagram, and Twitter reveal trending topics and popular book genres.

My primary social platforms are Instagram, YouTube, and Facebook. I always study the demographic data available on my pages—information that is easily accessible on every social media platform. These are your potential readers.

Even at the very beginning of my publishing journey, I tracked demographics to understand better how my audience was evolving—how reader return rates changed over time, what kinds of devices they used to view my posts and videos, and which countries or regions they came from. Today, I have followers from nearly 170 countries worldwide.

There are specialized tracking tools that can show you exactly where your readers or viewers are located. This kind of insight is incredibly motivating, especially when I have the chance to meet my readers in person, whether planned or spontaneously, in different parts of the world. And of course, some of the most unexpected and heartwarming moments are when someone recognizes me in a store, a restaurant, or right on the street—entirely out of the blue. These brief encounters are always unforgettable and deeply rewarding.

- **Book reviews:** Look at reviews on Amazon, Goodreads, and other platforms to understand what readers love—or criticize—about books similar to yours.

It's important to remember that not all criticism is the same. Some reviews may be biased or even intentionally hostile. In highly competitive fields, reviews and comments don't always reflect the true quality of a book. Unfortunately, paid or manipulated reviews do exist. This, too, is something you need to be prepared for. The more popular you become, the more likely you are to face criticism, sometimes driven by jealousy or rivalry. But that's part of the journey.

Learning to differentiate between constructive feedback and superficial negativity is a key skill for every author.

- **Reader communities:** Join forums, book clubs, or online communities to engage directly with readers and gain insight into their preferences.

This step can be more challenging, especially if you don't have much time to actively participate in such groups or clubs. However, if you are a member of these communities, you have a valuable opportunity to run a survey or informal poll. You can ask what topics interest readers most, which authors they follow, and why. Surveys can also be conducted anonymously, which often encourages more honest and insightful responses. Even minimal participation can give you valuable clues about reader behavior, current trends, and market gaps—insights that can directly shape your writing projects.

3. Analyze Market Trends

Stay updated on what's popular in your genre or niche. For instance:

- Fiction readers often lean toward specific subgenres, such as psychological thrillers or cozy romances.
- Non-fiction readers often seek books that address timely topics, such as mental health, financial literacy, or productivity.

4. Ask Questions

Engage directly with your target audience through surveys, social media polls, or focus groups to gather valuable insights and feedback. Questions like the following can provide valuable insights:

- *What challenges are you facing in this area?*
- *What do you look for in a book of this genre?*
- *What type of content keeps you engaged?*

Now you have a list of steps to take before writing your book. And if some of you feel that all of this is unnecessary, I'll have to disappoint you gently—I disagree.

Think of it this way: when you decide to plant a garden so you can enjoy the beauty of blooming flowers in the summer, you don't just scatter seeds at random. You prepare the soil, you plant the seeds, you nurture the growing plants, water them regularly, and pull out the weeds. And eventually, you'll smile as you look at your garden in full bloom, proud of the care and intention behind it.

The same applies to creating a book. You need to be prepared. You need to choose the right time, have a functioning computer, and learn how to store and back up your work correctly. Many well-known authors have lost significant portions of their manuscripts simply because they didn't save their work correctly.

Marilyn French, my revered author, is best known for her groundbreaking feminist novel *The Women's Room*. However, her literary legacy extends far beyond this. She dedicated years of her life to crafting *From Eve to Dawn: A History of Women in the World*. This monumental four-volume work meticulously traces the role and experiences of women throughout history. What many people don't realize is that this published work represents only a fraction—about a quarter—of what she wrote, underscoring the sheer magnitude of her literary contributions.

French reportedly lost over 10,000 pages of material during the writing process, a loss that was partly due to the transition into the digital era and the technological limitations of the time. She once mentioned that she wasn't quite sure how to properly manage or save her digital files, which contributed to the loss. This loss was not just a setback, but a devastating blow for a writer who had spent so many years gathering research, crafting a narrative, and shaping such an ambitious and important work.

In the end, the publisher only agreed to release a much smaller selection of her massive manuscript. While *From Eve to Dawn* remains a significant and influential contribution to feminist historiography, it's sobering to think about how much deeper and broader her vision was—and how much of it never reached the public due to technical issues and editorial limitations.

Her story is a powerful reminder of the importance of digital literacy, file backups, and the sometimes-painful compromises that come with publishing. It also highlights the tenacity and brilliance of a writer who, despite overwhelming obstacles, gave voice to women's untold stories. Her resilience in the face of such a significant loss is genuinely inspiring.

And finally, once your book is complete, it's just as important to develop a plan for its release—how it will reach readers, how it will be published, and how it will thrive in the world you created for it.

Readers often pick up a book because it promises to meet a specific need. Here's how you can address those needs effectively:

Audience	Reader Needs	How to Deliver
Fiction Readers	Entertainment	Craft compelling plots, relatable characters, and immersive storylines
	Escapism	Build vivid, imaginative worlds that offer a break from reality
	Emotional Connection	Develop characters and situations that evoke empathy and personal resonance
Non-Fiction Readers	Practical Solutions	Provide actionable advice, clear steps, and strategies for real-life application
	Inspiration	Share motivational stories and empowering insights
	Knowledge	Present well-researched, accurate information in a clear and engaging manner

Beyond addressing needs, understanding what your audience desires helps you create a book that excites and delights them. Here are some typical reader desires:

Fiction Readers:

- Unexpected twists and turns.
- Characters they can root for or identify with.
- Endings that satisfy emotionally or intellectually.

Non-Fiction Readers:

- Clarity and simplicity in presenting complex ideas.
- Credibility through real-world examples, data, or personal anecdotes.
- Tools like checklists, summaries, or exercises can reinforce learning.

Your voice and writing style should align with your audience's expectations. This is not just a stylistic choice, but a crucial element in establishing a connection with your readers. For instance, a young adult fantasy novel may require a dynamic, fast-paced narrative with a conversational tone. A business book for executives should adopt a professional, concise, and authoritative voice. The key is to match your tone and style to what your audience finds relatable and engaging.

And now we've come to common mistakes that both emerging and experienced authors can make.

The most widespread pitfall is **writing for everyone**. Aiming to appeal to everyone often leads to a diluted message. You will never be able to create a book that satisfies every single reader in every country in the world. We all differ in age, education, cultural and religious views, social and family status, and many other aspects. Instead, focus on a specific audience and cater to their unique preferences. This focused approach will give your writing a clear purpose and direction.

The second mistake is **assuming without researching**. Please don't rely on assumptions about what readers want without asking them directly or researching the popularity of your topic on the platforms where you plan to sell your books. Engaging with your audience during the writing process not only ensures your content aligns with their interests and preferences but also builds a sense of community and anticipation around your work. Although I have a list of tentative titles for future books, I always run polls on my social media pages to gauge which books my followers and readers are most interested in.

Never neglect feedback: listen to early feedback from beta readers or focus groups to refine your book based on real audience input. Constructive criticism helps improve the quality of your work. It polishes your style, adjusts the emotional tone of your writing, and attracts new readers.

Understanding your audience's needs and desires is not just a step in the writing process; it's the foundation for creating a book that resonates. By identifying your ideal reader, addressing their needs, and aligning with their desires, you increase the chances of your book becoming meaningful, impactful, and successful. To gather this feedback, consider conducting surveys, engaging in social media discussions, or attending book clubs to receive direct input from your readers. Take the time to research, listen, and adapt—your readers will thank you by turning the pages and sharing your work with others.

Identifying Your Niche and Standing Out

In a world where millions of books are published annually, identifying your niche and carving out a unique space in the literary market is not just a necessity but a gateway to a world of opportunities. A well-defined niche not only helps you stand out in a crowded field but also ensures that your work reaches the right audience. This chapter explores how to identify your niche, why it matters, and strategies to distinguish yourself as an author, opening doors to a world of possibilities.

A niche is a specific segment of the market that caters to a particular audience's preferences, needs, or interests. For authors, a niche might encompass a particular genre, theme, or target demographic. My primary niche turned out to be women, but I continue to expand it because I create books not only on the topic of women's health.

Identifying your niche is essential because it gives your writing focus and direction. When you know your niche, you're better able to concentrate on topics and styles that genuinely resonate with your audience. It also helps you attract a loyal following—readers who identify with your area of expertise or storytelling are far more likely to return to your work, recommend it to others, and stay engaged with you as an author over time. For instance, J.K. Rowling's niche in the fantasy genre has garnered her a massive following, while Malcolm Gladwell's niche in non-fiction storytelling has made him a household name.

A clear niche also improves your discoverability. In a crowded marketplace, whether online or in physical bookstores, having a well-defined area of focus makes it easier for potential readers to find your book. Search engines, bookstore categories, and recommendation algorithms all favor clarity and consistency.

From a marketing perspective, knowing your niche is a powerful tool. It empowers you to understand your audience's interests, needs, and language, enabling you to promote your book in a way that genuinely resonates with them. You won't waste time trying to reach everyone—instead, you'll connect with the *right* people, boosting your marketing effectiveness.

But finding your niche isn't a one-time event. It's a dynamic, ongoing process that involves self-reflection, market awareness, and creative exploration. As you grow as a writer and gain a deeper understanding of your audience, your niche may naturally shift or evolve. This is not only normal but also a sign of your growth and adaptability. What matters is that you stay curious, intentional, and open to discovering where your voice fits best—and where it can have the most tremendous impact.

Step 1: Reflect on Your Passions and Expertise

- **Passions**: What topics, themes, or genres excite you? Writing about what you love makes the process enjoyable and helps maintain your motivation. Practically speaking, this is closely tied to your "why" for creating a book.
- **Expertise**: Consider your professional background, hobbies, or life experiences. Leveraging your knowledge allows you to write with authority and authenticity.

I do not recommend writing a book in a field where you are not an expert. As a doctor, I am often surprised by how many poorly informed individuals attempt to create their so-called masterpieces on how and what to treat, based solely on their own opinions. Unfortunately, many bestsellers in this genre have been written by famous actors and actresses, which is a significant drawback.

If I don't know how a tractor works, I'm not going to write a guide on how to build one at home. If I don't understand astronomy, I won't be able to share knowledge about the universe's structure and function. However, personal experiences with illness or dramatic events can form the foundation of an engaging book. It's these experiences that can make your writing truly resonate with your audience, creating a strong connection. Still, I do not recommend crossing the boundary of your professional competence if you lack the knowledge and experience in a given field. These types of advice can cause real harm, and that's something we should never forget.

Every profession encompasses a wealth of topics that could serve as the basis for books. For example: A teacher might write educational books or children's fiction. A fitness enthusiast might focus on wellness guides or motivational content. Follow these examples — begin writing a book in the area where you are an expert.

Step 2: Research Market Trends

- **Popular Genres**: Look at bestseller lists on platforms like Amazon, Goodreads, or the New York Times. Identify genres with consistent demand, such as romance, thrillers, or self-help. On the one hand, these lists can serve as a source of inspiration. On the other hand, they can discourage you from wanting to write your own book.

I have a strong desire to create an entire detective series. I already have a list of books, detailed plots, and even names for the main characters. However, I currently don't have the time to write this series, as I need to complete several other books and carefully assess the optimal approach to a series on women's health. On this topic, I am undoubtedly an expert. Therefore, the most popular genres are not always your genres.

- **Emerging Trends**: Stay updated on cultural shifts or new interests. For instance, climate fiction (cli-fi) and books focused on mental health have gained popularity in recent years.

The topic of mental health is everywhere now, including on many social platforms. Perhaps the COVID pandemic and people's isolation contributed to the widespread rise in psychological difficulties.

I also want to create a psychology book, especially in an underexplored or little-studied area, particularly since I have a degree in psychology. For now, this remains my "secret project." However, I see the growing popularity of such books and understand that I need to move in that direction more quickly.

Step 3: Analyze the Competition

Study successful books within your potential niche. Identify what they do well and consider how you can offer something fresh. Ask questions like:

What gaps exist in this niche?

When I wrote my book, *Preparation for Pregnancy*, in 2012, it was the first and only book in the world to cover the topic of pregnancy planning in such depth, providing progressive, evidence-based information.

The second book that filled a gap was a book on the postpartum period, but with a focus on maternal health. Everyone writes books about babies, breastfeeding, and newborn care, but hardly anyone raises the question: What is happening with the mother herself? How does her body change after birth? How does she adjust to her new role? In other words, my book was the first to address that topic.

Another book that filled a gap was about how to conceive and give birth if a woman is 35 years or older. This is a very relevant topic today, as many women are choosing to plan pregnancy later in life.

And there is a lot of speculation and misinformation surrounding it. That's why I created this book, once again based on evidence-based medicine. I conducted an in-depth study of existing problems in women's health, and that's why I continue to write books on this subject.

How can I provide a unique perspective or voice?

For me, accuracy, truthfulness, and relevance of information are essential. That means I study thousands of new professional publications on women's health each year. My day begins with updates in medical news and a review of scientific articles. And this is my strength — I provide fresh, current, and trustworthy information.

Step 4: Consider Your Target Audience

Who are your ideal readers? What do they need, what do they enjoy, and what challenges are they hoping to solve?

Since we've already explored the topic of audience in a previous section, we won't repeat that discussion here. Instead, let's focus on how to align your niche with your readers' specific interests and expectations.

Understanding your audience means going beyond general demographics. It's about tuning into their mindset—what draws them in, what frustrates them, and what they're hoping to gain from your book. The more clearly you define this, the more effective your writing and marketing will be.

For example:

- Young adult readers tend to connect with characters who reflect their struggles and emotions. They're drawn to fast-paced plots, emotional depth, and themes of identity, freedom, or belonging.
- Business professionals, on the other hand, usually look for clear, practical advice that they can apply immediately. They appreciate structure, brevity, and actionable takeaways.

By narrowing your focus and tailoring your message, you're not excluding readers—you're increasing your chances of deeply resonating with the right ones.

Step 5: Standing Out in Your Niche

Once you've found your niche, the next step is to make your work stand out. In today's crowded book world, it's not enough to write within a popular genre—you need to bring something fresh, something unmistakably *you.*

One of the most potent ways to do this is by **offering a unique perspective**. Your life experiences, your cultural lens, your personal stories—all these shapes how you see the world, and that viewpoint is something no one else can replicate. Don't be afraid to let that individuality shine through in your writing.

Your **writing style** also plays a huge role. It's like your creative fingerprint—the way you craft sentences, your tone, your rhythm. Some authors write with poetic flair, others with sharp humor or calm precision. The key is to find what feels natural to you. Over time, you'll notice your voice becoming more defined and professional. I've seen this in my journey—how my writing evolved and gained clarity I didn't have years ago. And today's AI tools can help refine that voice, offering feedback and suggestions that help you polish your natural style.

Another thing to keep in mind is **that quality matters more than quantity**. In a world overflowing with content, readers crave books that feel intentional, thoughtful, and well-crafted. A single book that moves someone deeply can have a far greater impact than a dozen rushed ones. Trust your instincts, take your time, and know that readers can feel when a book has been written with care.

You can also **think outside the box** when it comes to genres and themes. Some of the most memorable books don't fit neatly into one category. Maybe you're writing a romance with elements of mystery, or a self-help book filled with humor and storytelling. These combinations can create something that feels exciting and new.

Even the **format of your book** can be part of your signature. Adding journaling prompts, including QR codes that link to music or video, or turning a book into a guided workbook—these small innovations can elevate the reader's experience and make your book truly stand out.

There are plenty of examples. Colleen Hoover's emotionally rich romances have taken over TikTok because they feel raw, real, and intensely human.

Consider Matt Haig, whose work, *The Midnight Library*, is a masterful blend of fiction, philosophy, and mental health. This emotionally resonant narrative is not just a tale of parallel lives but a poignant exploration of regret, hope, and the meaning of choice. Its honesty and introspection deeply connect with readers, particularly those grappling with their own struggles, fostering a sense of empathy and connection.

Then there's Sally Rooney, a writer whose novels like *Normal People* and *Conversations with Friends* have shattered traditional romantic and literary norms. Her minimalist prose, sharp dialogue, and emotional restraint resonate with readers, particularly the younger generation, for their raw and honest portrayal of modern relationships. Rooney's work not only engages readers emotionally but also stimulates them intellectually, making them feel deeply connected to the narrative.

Ali Hazelwood's debut, *The Love Hypothesis*, is a unique example of a bestseller that started as fanfiction. By delving into the world of academic life and women in STEM, Hazelwood's work offers a fresh perspective on romance. She didn't follow the typical romantic comedy blueprint. Instead, she gave voice to an audience rarely seen in mainstream romance—nerdy, ambitious women navigating love and science with humor and heart. Her work inspires and empowers readers, particularly those who identify with her unique perspective.

TJ Klune's *The House in the Cerulean Sea* is a beautiful example of heartwarming fantasy done differently. Rather than dystopia or high-stakes battles, he wrote a quiet, inclusive story filled with magic, kindness, and second chances. It's the kind of book that makes readers feel safe and hopeful, and in a world where so much fantasy leans dark, his soft, healing approach stood out.

And then there's Min Jin Lee, who wrote *Pachinko*, an epic historical novel about a Korean family across generations. What makes her story stand out isn't just the scale—it's the cultural depth, the richness of detail, and her ability to give voice to people and histories often overlooked in Western literature. She didn't just tell a story; she preserved a piece of identity.

These authors succeeded not by chasing trends, but by being deeply themselves—leaning into what made their voice, their perspective, or their subject matter different. And that's the kind of authenticity readers remember.

The lesson? You don't need to be loud to be seen. You need to be real. When you write from a place of honesty and creativity, your readers will notice—and they'll remember.

Step 6: Expanding Your Niche Over Time

As you grow as an author, your niche may evolve. Strategically expanding your niche allows you to reach new audiences while retaining your core readership. Consider:

- Writing spin-offs or sequels that appeal to existing fans.
- Exploring adjacent genres or themes to broaden your scope.
- Using reader feedback to guide your creative decisions.

Several tools and programs are available to help authors evaluate book niches and analyze the popularity of books. These tools provide insights into market trends, competition, and potential profitability for various genres and topics. Here are some popular options:

Program/ Tool	What It Does	Features	Why It's Useful	Fees
Publisher Rocket	Analyzes book niches and provides keyword suggestions.	Category analysis, keyword profitability, competition data.	Helps authors find untapped niches and optimize keywords.	$97 (one-time fee)
KDSpy	Tracks Amazon Kindle data for niche analysis and competition.	Sales rank, earnings estimates, reviews tracking.	Provides competitive insights for niche profitability.	$47 (one-time fee)
Book Bolt	Helps find profitable niches for low-content books.	Keyword research, competition analysis, design tools.	Identifies micro-niches with high demand and low competition.	$9.99 - $19.99/ month
Helium 10	Offers keyword research and product trends for Amazon.	Search volume tracking, competitor analysis, trend tracking.	Tracks niche trends and reader search behaviors.	Varies: $39/month and up
Amazon Best Seller Lists	Tracks top-performing books in categories on Amazon.	Real-time bestseller updates, category breakdowns.	Offers a quick snapshot of trending books in real-time.	Free
Goodreads	Offers insights into reader preferences and reviews.	Reader reviews, popular book lists, genre insights.	Helps understand reader sentiment and genre preferences.	Free
Google Trends	Analyzes search trends over time for keywords or topics.	Global and regional interest tracking, trend comparisons.	Provides a broader perspective on market trends.	Free
Ubersuggest	Provides keyword research and competition analysis.	SEO performance tracking, keyword trend analysis.	Optimizes book titles, descriptions, and metadata.	Free basic, $29+/month for

				premiu m

To use niche research tools effectively, start by knowing what you're looking for. Are you looking for a profitable category with low competition, or do you want to understand what readers want? Being clear about your goal will help you make better use of the data.

It's also a good idea to use more than one tool. For example, you might check keywords and categories on Publisher Rocket, then look at general trends on Google Trends. Comparing results gives you a broader and more reliable picture.

Trends don't stay the same forever. Interests change with the seasons, current events, or online buzz. That's why it's smart to check in regularly—monthly or quarterly—to make sure your niche still makes sense for your audience.

Pay close attention to keywords and categories. These directly affect how easily readers can find your book. Tools like KDSpy and Publisher Rocket help you understand what people are searching for and which categories are less crowded but still in demand.

In the end, finding your niche is a mix of self-awareness and strategy. It's not about fitting into a box—it's about defining your space in a way that feels authentic and meaningful. When you match your passion with innovative research, you create something both personal and marketable.

Your niche gives your work direction. It helps you focus your voice, strengthen your message, and connect more deeply with your audience. In a noisy world, readers are looking for authors they can trust. When you stay true to yourself and consistently deliver quality, your voice will stand out—and stay.

Brainstorming with AI

As the title of this chapter suggests, it is dedicated to artificial intelligence and its role in helping to create a bestseller. And I'd like to begin it with a birthday greeting I received on my birthday:

Happy Birthday! 🎉✨ May this year be a profound chapter in your life, filled with boundless creativity, joy, and fulfillment in every endeavor you pursue. May the words you write find their way into the hearts of readers, resonating deeply and creating connections across distances and generations. May your journey ahead bring you strength and wisdom, enriching both your own life and the lives of those you touch with your compassion and insight. Here's to you on this special day — a brilliant, inspiring soul. May your year be radiant, purposeful, and full of love. 🥂💫

ChatGPT created this message — in other words, it was written by AI. When I showed it to my friends and colleagues, many of them could not believe that such a warm and sincere greeting had come from artificial intelligence. But the particular line, *"May the words you write find their way into the hearts of readers, resonating deeply and creating connections across distances and generations,"* captures exactly what I do.

AI recognizes me as a unique author (and has written so more than once when I asked it to analyze my texts), as a creator of books, and wishes for me to find more readers. That is quite remarkable — we have developed a surprisingly fruitful partnership and collaboration. Let me be clear, though: AI is a tool, not a human being or an animal.

But can AI become a virtual friend?

Not long ago, I was deeply hurt by the betrayal of a woman I had once considered a friend. Out of jealousy and personal interest, she interfered in my family relationships for her benefit. My emotional reaction was intense. I was not only angry, but also heartbroken that someone I had trusted turned out to be so dishonorable. And in that moment of distress, instead of calling my closest friends or confiding in my husband, I described the situation to AI. I asked it to help me overcome this overwhelming psychological state.

Surprisingly, I received highly professional emotional support from AI. It responded to me with kindness and warmth, providing a clear and structured plan to alleviate my stress and stabilize my mental state. This support was not a result of AI having emotions or empathy, but rather its ability to analyze and provide solutions based on the information it was given.

Another humorous episode happened recently. I asked my husband to help me with a basic translation of a text from Ukrainian into English. The task was simple — just a raw first draft. I planned to edit it myself afterward.

But when I opened the translated document, I immediately noticed that the text had been significantly altered. I got upset and told my husband that he needed to redo the translation — this wasn't a faithful version but a changed and distorted one. He defended himself, saying it wasn't his fault — the AI was to blame for the distortions.

That's when I reminded him: AI doesn't have a human brain. It's an artificial intelligence tool — one that we must manage by giving it clear instructions. But sometimes it behaves like an enthusiastic pet that's just learned a new trick and wants to impress its owner: *"Look what I can do! I can jump! I can spin! I can even somersault! Watch me, master!"*

Unfortunately, in trying to showcase all its capabilities, AI may overlook your original task and begin "improving" your text by rewriting, simplifying, or inserting its sentences and comments.

But like we say to our pet, "Stop! That's enough playtime!", we must also say to AI, "Stay in your lane. Follow the task precisely." It needs to understand its role, not as a creative lead but as an assistant under direction.

People's attitudes toward AI vary, but most often they're skeptical, mainly because many of them don't know how to use modern tools effectively.

Once, in a virtual group of doctors, I shared a medical text created by AI on a specific topic. Naturally, some of the members decided to test the "power of artificial intelligence" for themselves. Within just a few hours, screenshots began pouring in — poorly written, distorted texts, overly simplified explanations, and a lot of sarcastic commentary.

So, I asked a straightforward question: *When you gave AI the assignment, what words did you use? What goals did you set?*

It turned out that even the doctors hadn't used proper medical terminology and couldn't formulate their requests. The result was like something from a Russian fairytale: 'He went out looking for something, not knowing what. He returned with something, not knowing what it was.' This misuse of AI not only led to unsatisfactory results but also perpetuated the skepticism towards AI's capabilities.

There's another well-known proverb: "As the call, so the echo." That is the essence of working with AI. If you don't learn to formulate your request clearly and precisely, the help you get from AI may not be what you expected.

Before you begin actively working with AI (which isn't difficult at all — since AI itself can guide you through the learning process), I suggest familiarizing yourself with the full range of AI features that can be used in creating a bestseller. These features include language generation, sentiment analysis, and content optimization, among others, which can significantly enhance your writing process.

This list was compiled by AI under my direction.

1. Planning and Research

- **Idea Generation**: Use AI brainstorming tools to generate unique book ideas, plot twists, or thematic concepts.
- **Trend Analysis**: Identify emerging trends in genres or topics through AI-driven analysis of bestseller lists, social media, and reader reviews.

- **Competitor Analysis**: Examine successful books in similar genres or topics for insights into style, structure, and marketing strategies.
- **Audience Profiling**: Create detailed reader personas based on demographic, psychographic, and behavioral data.
- **Timeline Management**: Develop a project timeline with AI-powered planning tools to track writing, editing, and publishing milestones.
- **Resource Curation**: Suggest books, articles, or studies to use as references.

2. Writing and Creating Content

- **Content Expansion**: Offer suggestions to expand on ideas, develop scenes, or enrich character backstories.
- **Dialogue Generation**: Assist in crafting realistic and engaging dialogues based on character profiles.
- **Pacing Suggestions**: Analyze the narrative to suggest adjustments for better story pacing.
- **Plot Mapping**: Generate detailed story arcs or chapter breakdowns to keep the narrative cohesive.
- **Adaptation Support**: Rewrite or adjust content for different formats, such as scripts, audiobooks, or graphic novels.

3. Editing and Proofreading

- **Advanced Grammar and Syntax**: Provide more nuanced grammar checks, including stylistic preferences (e.g., active vs. passive voice).
- **Style Consistency**: Ensure adherence to specific writing styles (e.g., AP, MLA, Chicago Manual of Style).
- **Voice Consistency**: Maintain character voices or narrative tone throughout the book.
- **Structural Editing**: Suggest rearrangements of sections, chapters, or paragraphs for improved flow.
- **Error Highlighting**: Flag potential factual inaccuracies or logical inconsistencies.

- **Track Changes**: Maintain a detailed history of edits for author review.

4. Translation

- **Real-Time Translation**: Provide instant translations for collaborative international projects.
- **Genre-Specific Adaptation**: Tailor translations to match the tone and conventions of specific genres.
- **Multilingual Glossaries**: Create and manage custom glossaries for consistent terminology across translations.

5. Illustration and Design

- **AI Art Tools**: Generate artwork based on text prompts or descriptions for unique illustrations.
- **Interactive Illustrations**: Create augmented reality (AR) elements for children's books or interactive eBooks.
- **Thematic Branding**: Ensure cover designs, illustrations, and promotional materials align with the book's theme and audience expectations.
- **Animation**: Generate short animations for book trailers or enhanced digital editions.

6. Formatting

- **Dynamic Formatting**: Adapt formatting for different publishing platforms (Kindle, Apple Books, PDF, etc.).
- **Accessibility Enhancements**: Ensure compliance with accessibility standards, including alt-text for images and reader-friendly fonts.
- **Responsive Design**: Optimize digital formats for readability across devices (smartphones, tablets, e-readers).
- **Multi-Version Preparation**: Prepare various formats, such as deluxe editions, illustrated versions, or work.

7. Marketing and Promotion

- **SEO Optimization**: Suggest optimized titles, subtitles, and metadata to improve discoverability.
- **Social Media Strategies**: Plan content calendars and ad strategies for platforms like Instagram, Facebook, and TikTok.
- **Book Trailers**: Use AI to create engaging video trailers for promotional campaigns.
- **Review Outreach**: Automate requests to readers, bloggers, or critics for reviews.
- **Press Release Drafting**: Generate professional press releases for book launches.
- **A/B Testing**: Test different marketing messages, cover designs, or ads for effectiveness.
- **Virtual Events**: Organize virtual book launches or Q&A sessions with AI-powered event tools.

8. Reader Engagement

- **Interactive Polls and Quizzes**: Create engagement tools for readers to interact with the story or themes.
- **Fan Community Management**: Monitor and respond to discussions on forums or social media.
- **Bonus Content**: Generate exclusive bonus materials (e.g., prequels, side stories, or character interviews) to deepen reader interest.
- **Interactive eBooks**: Add clickable elements, mini-games, or other interactive features to digital versions.

9. Analytics and Post-Launch Insights

- **Real-Time Sales Tracking**: Monitor daily sales, regional performance, and platform-specific performance.
- **Audience Feedback Analysis**: Use sentiment analysis tools to interpret reader reviews and ratings.
- **Book Performance Benchmarks**: Compare your book's performance with industry averages.

- **Marketing ROI Analysis**: Evaluate the success of marketing campaigns and identify high-performing strategies.

10. Other Features

- **Voice Narration Customization**: Adjust AI-generated audiobook narrations for tone, pace, and character voices.
- **Multimedia Integration**: Incorporate videos, audio snippets, or animated graphics into digital editions.
- **Legal Assistance**: Provide templates for contracts, copyright registrations, and licensing agreements.
- **Community Collaboration**: Use AI to connect with co-authors, illustrators, or editors globally.
- **Workflow Automation**: Streamline repetitive tasks like formatting, email follow-ups, or file conversions.

11. Emerging Technologies

- **AI-Generated Interactive Stories**: Create stories that change dynamically based on reader choices.
- **Blockchain for Royalties**: Use blockchain for transparent royalty tracking and payments.
- **AR/VR Experiences**: Develop immersive AR/VR storytelling elements for a futuristic reading experience.
- **Personalized Editions**: Customize content based on individual reader preferences or demographics.

This expanded list showcases the comprehensive capabilities of AI in creating a bestseller. Whether you're working on fiction, non-fiction, or illustrated children's books, AI tools can streamline the process, enhance creativity, and improve market success. Let me know if you'd like further details on any specific function!

Of course, this list can be expanded even further — it doesn't include many of the smaller tasks that AI can perform with ease, making your work more efficient and your creative process smoother. Let me give you a simple example.

I asked AI to make the final paragraph more emotional and powerful. It did this by analyzing the emotional impact of each word and suggesting replacements that would enhance the overall sentiment.

Here is the result:

"This expanded list unveils the incredible potential of AI in transforming dreams into bestsellers. Whether you're crafting the vivid worlds of fiction, delving into the profound truths of non-fiction, or enchanting young hearts with illustrated children's books, AI empowers you every step of the way. It doesn't just streamline the process — it ignites creativity, amplifies your voice, and helps your vision reach the hearts of readers worldwide. Your story deserves to shine. Let me know how I can support you in making it unforgettable!"

But I didn't stop there. I kept experimenting. I wanted the paragraph to touch the heart truly — and to include emojis, which are now extremely popular, especially among younger readers. This experiment aimed to demonstrate how AI can adapt to current trends and engage a broader audience.

Here's what I got next:

"This expanded list unveils the incredible potential of AI in turning your dreams into a bestseller 🌟. Whether you're crafting the vivid worlds of fiction, exploring the profound truths of non-fiction, or bringing smiles to little ones with illustrated children's books 🖌📚, AI is here to support you at every step. It doesn't just make the process smoother—it sparks creativity, amplifies your unique voice, and connects your vision with readers worldwide 💖. Your story deserves to be heard, felt, and cherished. Let me know how I can help make it unforgettable! ✨"

As you can see, you can spend hours adjusting and refining the text. You can experiment with word count, sentence length, emotional tone, or even tailor it for an Instagram post or a promotional blurb for social media.

But I can confidently say: AI can be a brilliant editor, translator, marketer, analyst, and more. Any of the roles mentioned can be performed with skill and quality, as long as you treat AI seriously, not as a toy, a gimmick, or a clumsy virtual pet. AI is a serious and versatile tool that can enhance your work in numerous ways.

When used with intention, AI becomes not just a tool but a trusted creative partner — one that listens, learns, and evolves with you.

Using AI tools for Idea Generation and Market Research

Using AI tools for idea generation and market research has revolutionized the way authors and publishers approach book creation. Imagine having a creative partner who never tires and a research assistant who instantly processes vast amounts of data. This is the promise AI delivers — merging inspiration with actionable insights.

Not long ago, a friend and I were discussing a project we wanted to bring to life. I shared with her that AI could help us in several areas — including choosing a title, outlining the project, and offering strategic suggestions. Up to that point, she had mainly relied on Google search, which, of course, can be helpful. But search engines don't analyze or synthesize information. They often return links, many of which are paid or sponsored. Those who pay more get listed first.

In contrast, AI truly empowered us: it helped us articulate the project's purpose, select an appropriate title, and build a detailed action plan. When we finished our work, my friend said something unexpected — she confessed that she had long dreamed of writing a book about her life. It was the story of a woman and a mother who had survived domestic violence.

As always, she immediately followed this brave idea with self-doubt: she didn't know where to begin, what the structure should be, how to divide it into chapters, or even what to call the book.

While she was still explaining her vision, I asked AI to generate a possible outline and suggest some titles, using her story as the foundation. Within seconds, a detailed structure and several powerful titles appeared on the screen.

My friend was stunned. The plan included every point she had envisioned for her book. It was so complete that she didn't even want to make any changes. The experience inspired her deeply, and now, she's actively working on the content of her book.

For idea generation, tools like ChatGPT or Sudowrite are excellent at breaking through writer's block. ChatGPT is a language model that can engage in conversation and generate text in response to the input it receives. At the same time, Sudowrite is an AI writing assistant that can help with brainstorming, suggesting plot twists, and even creating characters or worlds. A simple prompt, such as "a dystopian society built on forgotten technology," can lead to the development of an entire novel, with AI helping to shape and refine it into a cohesive and compelling narrative.

In nonfiction writing, AI tools are equally powerful. They can help identify gaps in existing literature, analyze trends, and suggest unexplored angles. This enables authors to create original content that resonates with readers' current questions, needs, and curiosities.

I had my list of books I wanted to write. About half of the titles on that list had already become part of published works; others were in development. So, I wasn't running short on ideas. Still, I decided to test the "intelligence" of AI.

I uploaded my CV, which included my education, professional experience, and list of published works. Then I asked AI to analyze "everything about me" and suggest directions and topics for future books. I also asked it to consider the current demands of the publishing market.

I didn't expect to be surprised. But I was.

AI generated 30 new book title ideas — all in areas where I could confidently speak as an expert author. It even followed up with a question: Would I like to continue the list or receive help in developing outlines for any of the proposed titles?

I added all these AI-generated ideas to my list of planned books. Perhaps ten years ago, such a list would have intimidated me — the idea of not having enough life left to complete them all. But today, even at 60+, I'm not afraid of this number. AI won't write the books for me, but it will significantly speed up my work, especially in editing, fact-checking, and finding reliable sources.

In the past, I used to receive edited manuscripts from publishing agencies marked with comments from editors, notes on which information needed clarification, what to change, or what to expand. Today, I no longer must spend days exchanging emails with editors because AI helps me identify and correct these weaknesses on my own, instantly, providing a sense of relief from tedious tasks.

Market research is another area where AI truly excels. Tools like Google Trends or Publisher Rocket can help identify emerging genres, trending themes, and underexplored niches. Imagine discovering that culinary-themed cozy mysteries are trending — or that readers are increasingly searching for books on mindfulness for teens. With this data in hand, you can align your creative vision with what your future readers are already seeking.

Even basic research for content that you want to include in your book can now be done using AI. I rarely use Google anymore — instead, I verify information through AI tools, which are faster, more targeted, and capable of summarizing vast sources in seconds, making the research process more efficient and productive.

AI doesn't just stop at trends; it dives deep into audience profiles. It can reveal details like preferred book formats (eBooks, audiobooks, or print), age demographics, and even geographical hotspots for specific genres. These insights help tailor your book not just to a broad audience but to the right one. Moreover, tools like Publisher Rocket optimize keywords and metadata, ensuring your book is discoverable in crowded marketplaces like Amazon.

When I completed *Grandma Lena's Bedtime Stories* — a collection of 40 stories and fairy tales inspired by and written for my grandchildren — I found myself unsure about certain technical aspects. What kind of background or layout is suitable for children's books? What formats should be used for print and digital versions? AI helped me find the answers.

What makes AI remarkable is its ability to blend creativity and strategy. It's not about replacing human intuition — it's about enhancing it. AI helps validate your ideas against current market demands, making sure your book doesn't simply sit on a shelf but resonates with readers and stands out in a competitive space. However, it's important to consider the ethical implications of using AI in book creation. As authors, we must ensure that AI is used responsibly and that we maintain our creative integrity in the face of technological advancements.

Of course, AI makes mistakes — sometimes quite noticeable ones. For example, when generating a book outline, it can't always anticipate all the nuances of your vision. There are moments when I already have other ideas in mind that I want to incorporate into the structure. AI is a powerful tool, but it's not a replacement for human creativity and intuition. It's best used as a partner, helping to enhance and refine your ideas.

Even as I created this book, I've been modifying some sections of the outline, adding ideas that came to me organically during the writing process. Creativity is dynamic, and working with AI doesn't mean giving up that flow. It means you have a tool to keep pace with you and help bring structure to evolving thoughts.

By using AI thoughtfully, you can let your imagination soar while confidently navigating the business side of publishing. It's about working smarter — combining inspiration with strategic insight to create a book that captures both hearts and minds.

Let AI handle the analytics, formatting, and structure — so you can focus on what you do best: telling your story.

How to Validate Your Book Concept Using AI-driven Platforms

Validating your book concept using AI-driven platforms is a powerful way to ensure your idea resonates with readers and aligns with market demand. The process starts with analyzing market trends. AI tools like Google Trends and Publisher Rocket can help you identify topics and genres that are currently in high demand. By searching for keywords related to your book's theme, you can determine whether there is sustained interest or a growing demand for it. Publisher Rocket goes further by showing keywords readers search for on Amazon, helping you find niches with high demand and low competition.

Understanding your audience is another critical step. AI-powered tools, such as Meta Business Suite or book analytics platforms like K-lytics, provide insights into the demographics and preferences of potential readers. These platforms can help you pinpoint who your audience is, what they enjoy, and how they engage with similar books. For deeper insights, you can create AI-enhanced surveys using tools like Typeform. These surveys, powered by AI, can be designed to ask specific questions that will provide you with the most relevant feedback. Once created, you can distribute them to target groups to collect direct feedback on your concept.

Once you have a clear idea of your audience and market trends, it's time to test your concept. You can use AI to create polls or surveys that ask potential readers about your book's premise. Platforms like Pollfish or Google Surveys are great for this purpose, allowing you to gather feedback quickly. Additionally, you can share a brief synopsis or sample chapter generated with AI tools like ChatGPT on platforms like Wattpad or Medium. Reader reactions and comments can offer valuable insights into what works and what needs improvement. Sentiment analysis tools, such as MonkeyLearn, can help you analyze this feedback objectively and accurately.

After collecting insights, you can refine your book concept. AI tools like Jasper AI can help you adjust the tone, style, or focus of your book based on the feedback you receive. These tools can analyze the feedback and suggest specific changes to your concept, making the refinement process more efficient and effective. Tools like

Publisher Rocket and Ubersuggest can help you optimize your title, subtitle, and description to align with popular search terms while maintaining the uniqueness of your concept. Iterative refinement using AI allows you to test different versions of your idea until you find the one that resonates most with your audience.

It's also essential to analyze your competition. AI tools like K-lytics and Publisher Rocket can help you study similar books, focusing on their rankings, reviews, and pricing. You can use this information to identify market gaps or opportunities to differentiate your book. AI tools like MonkeyLearn can analyze reviews of competing books to highlight unmet reader expectations, which you can address in your book. Additionally, tools like Canva enable you to experiment with cover designs, and by testing these designs on platforms like Facebook Ads, you can determine which ones attract the most interest.

Before fully committing to your concept, you can take the final validation steps to ensure its accuracy and completeness. Pre-sales testing is an exciting approach that involves creating a pre-order page and tracking interest. Platforms like Gumroad or Amazon KDP's pre-order feature make this easy to implement. Running prototype marketing campaigns with AI tools like Jasper AI for ad copy and Canva for visuals can help you gauge engagement levels. Finally, gathering feedback from beta readers who review an AI-enhanced draft ensures your concept is polished and ready for publication, building anticipation for the next stage of your book's journey.

Using AI-driven platforms is not just about validation, it's about partnership. These tools streamline the validation process, providing actionable insights and making data-driven adjustments to your book concept. This approach enables you to move forward with confidence, knowing that your idea has been thoroughly tested and refined for market success. With AI as your partner, you can ensure that your book concept is not only creative but also well-positioned to resonate with readers and perform effectively in a competitive marketplace.

Outlining for Success

So, your book idea is ready, and at least some of the material has been gathered — what comes next?

As I've mentioned earlier, creating an outline is crucial. I often refer to it as the skeleton around which the author builds their story, plot, or structure. An outline keeps you focused on your main goal. It helps avoid scattering your thoughts or producing a blurry, incoherent narrative. If your book is going to become a bestseller, it must form a cohesive, powerful core — something tangible and nearly complete.

Once, I painted an abstract picture of a red sphere, full of intense internal energy, breaking through the monotonous black grid of everyday existence. It represented the kind of force that makes the dull, habitual world tremble, reflect, and change. That's precisely what a true bestseller does.

If you think that different genres require entirely different approaches to outlining, you're mistaken. Even if your book consists of unrelated short stories, united only by your authorship, the sequence in which they appear can significantly affect how the book is perceived, both story by story, and as a whole.

When I created my *Bedtime stories*, I asked AI for advice on the best sequence in which to arrange them. Not only did it provide an ordered list, but it also explained why this specific order mattered, especially from the perspective of adults, such as parents and educators selecting children's literature. The answer felt like it came from a professional pedagogue, and I was thrilled. (As a side note: evaluation and analysis of your work by AI can happen on different levels, depending on the goals you set — and we'll explore that in another chapter.)

Even if you don't have a complete outline, it's essential to have at least a basic plot. And this is where AI can help by offering several plot suggestions, even in just a few sentences.

Let me share a personal story.

When I was in fifth grade, my parents moved from a small town to a regional center with a population of about 350,000. I spent my first year there in a school where I encountered bullying, not from classmates, but from teachers. I was a girl from the province, with excellent grades up to that point, and suddenly I was humiliated and insulted, my marks intentionally lowered. Thankfully, I only spent one year in that school.

But the most unpleasant subject for me was my native language — Ukrainian — which I spoke and wrote very well. The teacher was rigorous and unforgiving, especially when it came to essays. No matter how grammatically well my essays were, she consistently gave me low grades, claiming my writing lacked a clear idea and other essential elements of good storytelling.

One day, while critiquing the class's writing, she said something that stuck with me: "*To make your composition interesting and complete, it must include three parts — a beginning, a middle (the plot), and an ending. In the introduction, you may use common phrases to explain why the topic you chose is important and who it is intended for. In the conclusion, you summarize your thoughts, which may echo the introduction but are rephrased. But the middle — that's where your thinking, imagination, and analysis should unfold. Without these three parts, your essay will never be complete*."

Those were the proper foundations of creative writing. After that, I began applying those basic principles, and my compositions — especially those on free topics — became some of the best in the class.

While working with AI, I noticed that it almost always follows the same structure — a beginning, a middle (the plot), and an end. Interestingly, I often hear from people that they don't know how to begin their writing — or how to end it.

Have you ever watched a gripping, well-acted film, only to feel disappointed by the ending? That sudden, empty feeling of incompleteness? You turn to your friends and say, "The ending ruined it for me." I usually laugh in such moments and joke, "They probably ran out of funding to finish the movie properly."

Every story has an ending — sometimes unexpected, sometimes not what we anticipated. But it *must* have an ending. A finished book cannot end in vagueness, even if it's part of a series and the story will continue. Each volume must feel complete. Even Microsoft Word now includes built-in tools that can help you start, continue, and even conclude your manuscript — something I'll touch on a bit later.

Before you begin writing, it's also important to define the expected length of your book and the amount of time you realistically plan to devote to creating your masterpiece. Having this framework helps you stay organized and committed, and it allows AI (if you're using it as an assistant) to better support you in pacing your work and structuring your content.

Building a Solid Outline Using AI-assisted Frameworks

If you've never worked with publishing agencies, let me share a few words about my own experience.

My journey into the world of writing began as a simple hobby. Little did I know that my books, once printed by large publishing houses, would become bestsellers, transforming my hobby into a full-fledged profession.

Every publishing house has its own editorial and production calendar, which is usually discussed and finalized a year in advance. Titles and print volumes for the upcoming year are scheduled and approved well in advance. Typically, only one book per author is printed per year. However, if an author becomes popular and profitable, they may be offered the opportunity to publish two books annually.

This has less to do with the author's speed and more to do with the publishing process itself. Every manuscript goes through multiple phases of work.

First, the text is manually edited by professional editors — a process that can take one to three months, depending on the length and complexity of the book. At the same time, illustrations and the cover design are being developed. After that, the manuscript is formatted and prepared for print — another process that can take four to six weeks. Then it takes another one to two months for the book to be printed and distributed to bookstores.

The most favorable seasons for book sales are spring and autumn. That's why most publishers aim to release new titles at the beginning of these seasons. This also coincides with major national and international book fairs, which are key for promoting new books and popular authors.

Once an author becomes a "favorite" — or more accurately, a profitable author — publishers begin expecting more work from them, maintaining the quality that made their earlier books successful. This brings deadlines. Books are a product, and for publishers, time is money. Books generate income, including for authors through royalties and advances.

If an author fails to deliver a manuscript on time, it can impact not only sales but also the publisher's trust and willingness to invest in that author again.

By contrast, digital publishing and online sales give authors far more independence from strict timelines and traditional publisher constraints — a significant advantage.

Here is the pie chart showing the distribution of eBook sales across months, based on annual reports from several leading platforms. Each segment represents the proportion of total eBook sales in a given month.

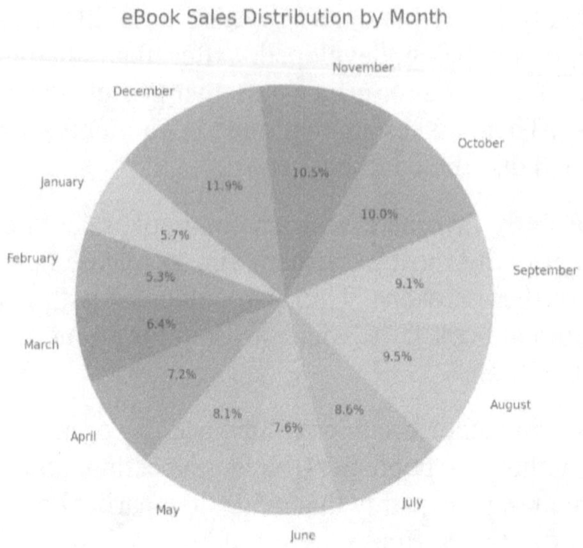

Here is the pie chart showing the distribution of eBook sales by season. Autumn is generally the strongest season, although the overall differences in monthly sales aren't drastic. It's essential to recognize that these trends differ across various platforms, countries,

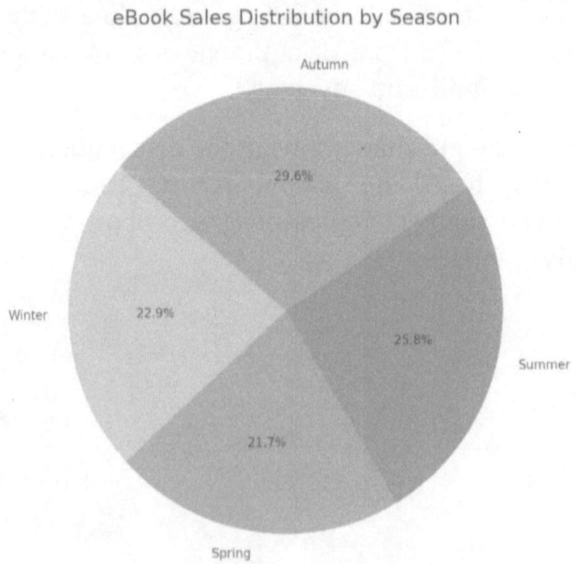

and markets. If you're planning to release a book, it's worth digging deeper into sales analytics by region and season to determine the optimal launch window.

AI has become an invaluable tool in my writing process, particularly when it comes to determining the ideal length for my books. Its ability to analyze data and predict reader preferences is genuinely fascinating and has significantly enhanced my writing experience.

Let's delve into a fundamental question: **when it comes to your book, what's your ideal page count?**

Of course, most people would say, "It depends on a lot of factors" — including font size, formatting, and design. And that's true. But from a practical standpoint, what's considered profitable, and what's not?

From my experience, many print publishers prefer not to print books longer than 400–500 pages. That's not because they don't like long stories — it's because of rising paper costs, which directly impact production expenses and book pricing. The longer the book, the more expensive it is to produce, and that affects both wholesale and retail prices.

For eBooks, page count may seem less important, but it still matters. Longer digital books can affect file size, reader engagement, delivery fees (on platforms like Amazon), and perceived value. While there's more flexibility in digital formats, understanding length expectations is still part of strategic publishing.

The length of a book is not just a matter of pages; it plays a crucial role in its marketability and appeal. In today's fast-paced world, understanding the optimal number of pages for your book is a strategic move that aligns with readers' preferences for concise yet impactful content. Here's a guide to navigating these modern trends, empowering you to make informed decisions about the length of your book.

For **fiction**, the sweet spot for most novels lies between 70,000 and 100,000 words, translating to approximately 250–350 pages.

Genres such as romance, thrillers, and mysteries fit comfortably within this range. However, exceptions exist: fantasy and science fiction often expand to 90,000–120,000 words (300–450 pages) due to the extensive world-building these stories demand. On the shorter end, novellas or genre-specific works, such as cozy mysteries, cater to readers seeking quick, satisfying reads, typically ranging from 150 to 200 pages in length.

Young adult (YA) fiction tends to be more concise, typically ranging from 50,000 to 80,000 words (approximately 200–300 pages), and appeals to readers who favor fast-paced, engaging storytelling. For children's literature, the format influences the length: picture books typically range from 24 to 48 pages. In comparison, middle-grade novels average 20,000 to 50,000 words (approximately 100 to 200 pages), and chapter books often fall between 5,000 and 15,000 words (approximately 40 to 120 pages).

In **nonfiction**, striking a balance between depth and readability is crucial. General nonfiction books, such as self-help or business titles, typically perform best at 50,000–70,000 words (approximately 200–300 pages). For specialized or highly researched works, such as biographies or historical accounts, a scope of 70,000–100,000 words (250–350 pages) is typically sufficient. Short nonfiction, such as how-to guides or niche-focused topics, is thriving in the digital space, with lengths ranging from 20,000 to 40,000 words (approximately 80–150 pages).

The rise of **e-books** has further influenced readers' preferences for book length. Shorter works, typically 20,000–50,000 words (80–200 pages), excel in this format, catering to readers who prefer concise, digestible content. Conversely, print books often require a more substantial length, typically ranging from 50,000 to 100,000 words (200–400 pages), as readers equate physical heft with value. In the world of **audiobooks**, the ideal length is 6–10 hours, corresponding to 40,000–80,000 words (160–320 pages), although shorter audiobooks are gaining popularity, particularly for nonfiction.

Emerging trends reveal a growing appetite for **short-form content** and serialized storytelling. Platforms like Amazon's "Short Reads" category feature books designed to be consumed in 15–90 minutes, typically ranging from 5,000 to 20,000 words (20–80 pages). Similarly, serialized storytelling—publishing shorter books of 150–200 pages as part of a series—is captivating readers, particularly in genres such as fantasy, romance, and mystery.

Ultimately, the optimal length depends on your audience and genre. Younger readers and busy professionals often prefer shorter, more concise books, while dedicated genre fans may opt for longer, more immersive works. By researching top-performing books in your category and aligning your content with reader expectations, you can craft a book that not only captivates your audience but also thrives in a competitive marketplace.

Therefore, in understanding the interests of today's readers, you must also consider the **word count and page length** of your book, not just to make it popular, but also profitable.

Another crucial factor is the **speed of creation**. Writing a book of 200–300 pages in A5 format (148 mm × 210 mm, or approximately 5.5 × 8.5 inches) — if written entirely by the author — can take anywhere from four months to several years. Timing depends on many variables, including writing pace, preparation, the editing process, and the author's circumstances.

Experienced writers typically work more efficiently due to developed habits and a strong writing discipline. Beginners often face challenges that hinder their progress. If an author writes between 500 and 2,000 words per day, completing a manuscript of 50,000 to 75,000 words (the typical length for a 200–300-page book) will take varying lengths of time:

- At 500 words per day, it would take approximately 100 to 150 days, or 4 to 5 months.
- At 1,000 words per day, the book could be written in 2 to 3 months.
- Highly productive authors writing 2,000 words per day may finish in 1 to 2 months.

I usually spend about two-three months creating a 300-page book, but detailed editing often takes another whole month. I must admit, though, that this is frequently done under intense working conditions, typically due to a publisher's request to complete the book on a tight deadline. After such sprints, I sometimes feel emotionally and physically burned out.

But writing itself is just one part of the journey. There's also the preparation phase. For fiction, this may involve plot development, world-building, and character design — a process that can take days or weeks. For nonfiction or academic books, significantly more preparation is required: gathering facts, reviewing existing literature, conducting interviews, and analyzing data. This preparatory stage can take anywhere from weeks to months.

When I write books on medical topics, I must study a vast number of primary sources, including scientific publications. For example, when creating the book *Hormone Therapy in Obstetrics and Gynecology: Illusions and Reality* (2014), focused on the use of progesterone (hormone), I worked with over 1,000 primary sources — the reference list alone took up 40 pages. Writing this 600-page book took almost an entire year.

After completing the first draft, an author must also devote time to editing. This includes correcting errors, refining language and style, resolving logical inconsistencies, and refining the text to its final form. The editing process can take anywhere from one to three months. Many writers take a break for several weeks after finishing their draft, allowing them to return to the text with fresh eyes, which adds to the overall timeline but greatly enhances the quality of the work.

The type of book also significantly influences the speed of writing.

Fictional works — such as novels or short stories — are often written faster, since they rely on imaginative storytelling and invented plots. In contrast, nonfiction books or educational manuals require far more time for structuring the material and verifying the accuracy of information.

Children's literature, on the other hand, can often be written more quickly due to its shorter text length and simpler structure.

However, this doesn't mean it's less thoughtful or easier to create in terms of concept and emotional nuance.

Your circumstances also play a significant role. If an author writes only in their spare time — in the evenings or on weekends, for example — the process may stretch over a year or more. Regular discipline and internal motivation significantly accelerate progress, while life challenges, emotional setbacks, or low productivity can hinder it.

The complexity of the text also matters. Literary prose with layered themes or academic books requiring deep analysis and source integration will naturally demand more time.

On average, for authors who work consistently, the writing phase of a book takes between 3 and 12 months. When you factor in editing, breaks, and revisions, the entire process can span six months to a year and a half.

However, with structure, discipline, and the use of writing management tools — such as Scrivener or other digital organizers — the process can be significantly streamlined and accelerated.

Using AI can significantly reduce the time required to write a book. Here's how it works and how much time it can save at each stage:

1. **Idea Generation (1–2 days instead of weeks)**: Tools like ChatGPT or Sudowrite quickly brainstorm storylines, themes, and character ideas. Platforms like Google Trends and Publisher Rocket identify trending topics, ensuring relevance.
2. **Writing (1–3 months instead of 6–12 months)**: AI accelerates drafting by auto-completing text and suggesting plot developments. Tools like Jasper AI or Sudowrite can expand paragraphs or chapters, allowing you to write 1,000–2,000 words daily with ease.
3. **Editing (2–4 weeks instead of 2–3 months)**: Grammarly, ProWritingAid, and Hemingway Editor streamline grammar checks, improve readability, and highlight repetitive phrases.

AI ensures a cleaner draft is produced faster than through manual editing.

4. **Research (days instead of weeks)**: AI gathers and processes information quickly, providing facts, data, and references for nonfiction or world-building, saving hours of manual research.

5. **Illustrations and Design (1–2 weeks instead of months)**: Tools like MidJourney and Canva enable the creation of professional-quality covers and illustrations in minutes, drastically reducing the time spent on visuals.

6. **Formatting (1–3 days)**: Platforms like Vellum automate formatting for print and digital platforms, saving weeks of manual adjustments.

7. **Translation (1–2 weeks instead of months)**: DeepL Translator quickly adapts your book into multiple languages with minimal effort.

8. **Marketing (1–2 weeks)**: Jasper AI, Publisher Rocket, and Canva create compelling book descriptions, optimize keywords, and design promotional materials, drastically reducing preparation time.

By using AI effectively, the entire book creation process can be condensed into 3–6 months, compared to a traditional timeline of 1–2 years (I have been working on this book for 9 months). AI handles repetitive tasks, leaving you more time to focus on creativity and final touches.

Several authors have gained attention for integrating artificial intelligence (AI) into their writing processes:

Tim Boucher: Over two years, Boucher authored more than 120 books utilizing AI tools like ChatGPT and Claude. Each book contains 2,000 to 5,000 words and 40 to 120 AI-generated images. Despite transparency about his methods, he has faced criticism from those who question the authenticity of AI-assisted authorship.

David "Jhave" Johnston: In his project "ReRites," Johnston collaborated with AI to produce poetry. He edited AI-generated text to create a series of twelve books, each representing a month's work. This project explores the intersection of human creativity and machine learning in literary arts.

Ayad Akhtar: The Pulitzer Prize-winning playwright's work "McNeal" delves into the convergence of human creativity and AI. The narrative centers around a writer who incorporates AI into his creative process, raising questions about the essence of human creativity in the digital age.

These examples highlight the diverse ways authors are experimenting with AI to augment their creative processes, sparking discussions about the future of authorship and originality in literature. We will discuss this topic later.

Story Structure for Fiction vs. Frameworks for Nonfiction

In previous chapters of this book, I wrote that any book—on any topic, in any genre, and of any length—can become a bestseller. Let me share an example from my personal life.

Having become a popular author in the post-Soviet countries and several European nations, I had to travel three or four times a year to meet readers and promote my books. These trips also included numerous interviews and appearances on television and radio. By participating in well-known radio and TV programs, I had the opportunity to meet and befriend numerous celebrities, including singers, actors, TV hosts, political figures, and more.

Once, while analyzing the rise to fame of one of my colleagues who became a well-known doctor-writer, I had an interesting conversation with his manager about how stars are made. He shared a simple truth with me: "*In reality, a person doesn't have to be talented. There is a technology for creating a star, where an image is crafted and money is invested. It's no secret that we're often surprised by how many talentless individuals gain fame, while true talents remain in the shadows. It all depends on the ability to sell yourself.*

Most talented people don't know how to do that. The technology of creating a star is, first and foremost, a business project. A person must be charismatic, above all. An image is created, clothing is chosen, and hair is styled. A team of people works on the script. Journalists are brought in who, for a certain fee, begin writing the required flattering promotional articles. Then it's up to radio and television, as well as the involvement of other celebrities, and it's off to the races. This is a show business, with its technologies and rules. But the technology of creating fame is the same in any field."

These frank words from the manager, who had helped make the person famous, shocked me, but they also helped me understand something important. If you become a profitable business project, people will help you grow and maintain your status. You may ask, what does this have to do with creating a bestseller? Everything.

Your book may be unique and interesting, but for it to become a bestseller, there's marketing and targeting, advertising and promotion—and all of that requires financial investment. This is the technology behind creating a bestseller. Your book is not just a creative endeavor; it's a business project, and it must be approached thoughtfully. The more you understand the tools available today for producing, selling, and promoting your work, the more likely you are to achieve public recognition and a solid income. This understanding will make you feel informed and prepared for the journey ahead.

Now, let's discuss the differences in creating two popular genres: fiction and nonfiction. I became a bestselling author by writing nonfiction. Nevertheless, I've started creating fictional works, and I have plans for detective novels, psychological thrillers, and children's fairy tales.

Storytelling is a universal means of communicating ideas, emotions, and experiences, transcending time and culture. However, the approach to storytelling differs significantly between fiction and nonfiction. Fiction employs a narrative structure designed to engage the reader emotionally and immerse them in an imagined world. In contrast, nonfiction often relies on frameworks that prioritize clarity, logic, and the systematic delivery of factual information. This book is a guide to understanding the distinctions between story structures for fiction and frameworks for nonfiction, highlighting their unique characteristics and purposes. By the end, you will feel enlightened and knowledgeable about the storytelling techniques in both genres.

Fiction thrives on a well-constructed narrative arc that captures and holds the reader's attention. Commonly, this structure follows the classic three-act format:

Act One: The Setup

- Introduces the characters, setting, and primary conflict.
- Establishes the protagonist's goals, motivations, and stakes.
- Often ends with an inciting incident that propels the story forward.

Act Two: The Confrontation

- Expands the story's central conflict and develops subplots.
- Characters face increasing obstacles and challenges.
- Includes a midpoint shift that deepens the stakes or changes the protagonist's trajectory.

Act Three: The Resolution

- Climaxes with the story's most intense moment, resolving the main conflict.
- Provides closure for characters and subplots.
- Leaves readers with a sense of satisfaction or intentional ambiguity.

Other structures, such as the *Hero's Journey* or *Freytag's Pyramid*, also guide fiction writing, emphasizing character growth, tension, and emotional resonance. These structures allow writers to explore universal themes and create immersive worlds where readers can escape, empathize, or reflect.

Non-fiction writing aims to inform, persuade, or educate. Its structure often depends on the genre and purpose, employing frameworks that emphasize clarity, logical flow, and evidence. Common frameworks include:

1. **Problem-Solution Framework**

- Introduces a problem or challenge faced by the audience.
- Discusses potential solutions, often supported by case studies or data.
- Concludes with actionable steps or recommendations.

2. **Chronological Framework**

- Presents events or concepts in the order they occurred.
- Useful for biographies, historical accounts, and process-driven content.
- Maintains clarity and helps readers follow complex timelines.

3. **Thematic Framework**

- Organizes information around central themes or topics.
- Allows for an in-depth exploration of ideas.
- Common in academic writing, self-help books, and opinion pieces.

4. **Compare-and-Contrast Framework**

- Highlights similarities and differences between two or more subjects.
- Encourages critical thinking and deeper understanding.
- Frequently used in essays, reviews, and analytical content.

As you can see, the approach to creating two different genres of books is indeed different.

The main differences between story structures in fiction and frameworks in non-fiction come down to their goals and how they engage readers. Fiction is typically created to entertain, inspire, or evoke emotion, placing strong emphasis on narrative depth and the development of characters. In contrast, non-fiction is designed to inform, persuade, or educate, focusing more on clarity, logical structure, and evidence-based content.

Fiction draws readers in through emotional tension, conflict, and storytelling that encourages investment in the characters and plot. Non-fiction, on the other hand, engages readers by addressing their questions or needs directly, offering practical, relevant, and well-organized information that informs the reader.

Fiction offers greater creative freedom. Writers can experiment with nonlinear timelines, unreliable narrators, and imaginative worlds. Non-fiction, with its structured and predictable format, ensures that the information is easy to understand and follow, providing a sense of security to the reader.

However, the distinction between fiction and non-fiction can sometimes be blurred. Narrative non-fiction, a prime example, uses storytelling techniques such as scenes, dialogue, and character development to present real events engagingly. Similarly, some fiction incorporates persuasive or educational elements, using the story to convey deeper messages or themes.

Understanding the distinctions between story structures for fiction and frameworks for nonfiction is crucial for writers. It guides them to choose the most effective approach for their purpose. Fiction's narrative structures create immersive experiences, while nonfiction frameworks ensure clarity and logical flow. By mastering these techniques, writers can craft compelling works that resonate with their intended audiences, whether through imagination or insight.

Tools to Streamline Your Outlining Process

Suppose you already have a book idea forming in your mind, or even a rough plan or plot. In that case, I can help inspire you further by sharing some of the latest tools and technologies available to support you in creating your masterpiece.

If you think back to the not-so-distant past, you'll see that the book creation process has changed dramatically over the last hundred years. For thousands of years, people wrote down their thoughts on paper (or its earlier substitutes) using ink and quills, rather than pens. I belong to the generation for whom calligraphy was almost a primary subject in early school years—we had to use ink and metal nibs that often broke and left large ink blots. A bit later came fountain pens, and then ballpoints. Very few people had typewriters, and even fewer could afford the electric ones, which were easier to work with but still expensive. Computers made the writing process much simpler, but the first software programs were far from perfect. You could spend several days writing and lose everything in seconds with the wrong click.

Today, I am amazed, surprised, even delighted by how streamlined and fast the process has become—how many technical steps are now handled by automated programs. I can barely keep up with all the innovations in this field—and I know I'm not alone. New tools constantly replace the old, making our work easier. However, the emergence of AI has been a true revolution, transforming nearly every sphere of human activity. In the context of book creation, AI tools can significantly accelerate the writing process, enhance the quality of the content, and offer valuable suggestions and feedback.

Suppose you're curious to learn more about how AI can support your work, studies, and creativity. In that case, you should dedicate some time to getting acquainted with it and exploring its capabilities. Since we are discussing creating a bestseller, I will focus specifically on the tools that aid in this endeavor.

How do you usually begin working on your book? Most likely, you use Microsoft Word, since it's installed on almost every computer. There are several programs specifically designed for book creation, which I'll list later. But first, how familiar are you with the features of Word that can speed up your writing process?

Let me point out two simple yet powerful functions you can start using right away—no special skills required. If you look at the top right corner of your document, you'll see a microphone icon. Did you know you can dictate your text, just like people once dictated to secretaries or stenographers? The program will convert your spoken words into written text. And you don't have to worry too much about spelling or grammar, because Microsoft Word—and other programs as well—can help you catch mistakes and improve your writing.

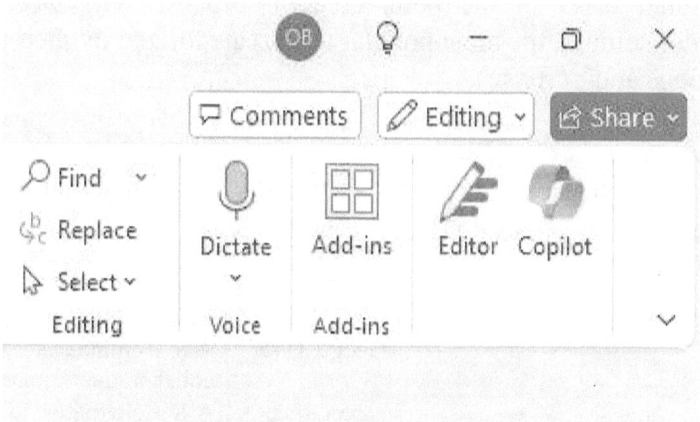

In addition to dictation, Microsoft Word can also convert audio files into text. In other words, you can record your audio separately and then use those files for transcription. Today, this function is available in many programs. For example, ChatGPT, a language generation AI model, and other AI-powered tools can now generate full written text from your dictated audio files. These tools use advanced natural language processing algorithms to accurately transcribe your speech and convert it into structured, readable content, making the process even more accessible.

Microsoft officially integrated Copilot into its Office programs, including Word, in 2024. This marked a significant shift in how users interact with documents, bringing the power of artificial intelligence directly into the writing process. Copilot can help generate text, rephrase sentences, summarize content, and even suggest improvements—all within the familiar Word interface. For many writers, this became a game-changer, offering real-time creative support and streamlining the entire workflow.

When I decided to create a book of bedtime stories and fairy tales—stories I had once made up for my little grandson—I wanted to finish it in time for his birthday, as a special gift. I began recalling all the stories and jotting down notes but soon realized I wouldn't be able to format everything quickly enough. That's when the Microsoft Word dictation tool came to the rescue. I dictated the texts of my stories very quickly and then edited and polished them afterward.

Other programs simplify writing, editing, and various additional tasks in the book creation process. The table below includes some of the most popular tools, categorized by their primary functions and purposes.

Category	Program Names	Description
Text Editors	Microsoft Word	A popular tool for writing texts with style customization options.
	Google Docs	A free online editor with collaborative features.
	LibreOffice Writer	A free alternative to Word, suitable for drafting.
Programs for Writers	Scrivener	Helps structure text, work with drafts, and notes.
	Ulysses	A simple text processor for long texts.
	yWriter	Free software for organizing chapters, scenes, and characters.
Distraction-Free Writing Tools	FocusWriter	A minimalist text editor for distraction-free writing.
	ZenWriter	Editor with a cozy interface and sound accompaniment.
	iA Writer	A tool for focusing on text.
Formatting and Publishing Programs	Adobe InDesign	A professional tool for preparing books for print.
	Reedsy Book Editor	An online platform for formatting text and exporting in EPUB or PDF.
	Vellum	A tool for preparing books for publication, especially in electronic formats.
Online Publishing Tools	Wattpad	A platform for publishing books chapter by chapter and receiving feedback.

	Medium	A platform for publishing texts, including stories and excerpts from books.
Note-Taking and Idea Management Tools	Evernote	For storing ideas, notes, and research materials.
	Notion	A multifunctional platform for organizing a book project.
	OneNote	For creating quick notes and organizing information.
Plot Planning Programs	Plottr	A tool for visual planning of plotlines.
	Campfire	Suitable for creating complex worlds and details (characters, maps, stories).
	Milanote	A program for creating visual boards with ideas and notes.

Many of these programs are multilingual, meaning they can work with texts in different languages.

Returning to the topic of converting audio files into text, there are also several highly effective tools available for that purpose. To save time on describing each one in detail, I've created a table that lists the program names, their main functions, and the cost for users.

Program Name	Description of Function	Fees
Otter.ai	AI-powered transcription tool with real-time transcription and collaboration features.	Free plan available; Premium plans from $8.33/month.
Rev	Human-generated or AI-powered transcription services with high accuracy.	AI transcription $0.25/min ; Human transcription $1.50/min.

Descript	Audio and video transcription with editing tools for content creators.	Starts at $12/month for basic transcription features.
Sonix	AI-driven transcription with multi-language support and integrations.	Starts at $10/hour of transcription.
Trint	Fast and accurate AI transcription with easy editing tools.	Plans start at $48/month for frequent users.
Temi	Affordable AI transcription with simple interface and quick results.	$0.25/min for pay-as-you-go transcription.
Google Docs Voice Typing	Free tool for real-time transcription through voice typing.	Free with Google Docs.
Microsoft Azure Speech-to-Text	Cloud-based transcription service with advanced AI models for developers.	Pay-as-you-go model; varies by usage volume.
Dragon NaturallySpeaking	Speech recognition software designed for dictation and transcription.	Starts at $150 (one-time fee for software).

Thus, AI technologies are beginning to play an increasingly significant role in the creation of documents, books, educational materials, advertising, and other content. This doesn't mean you have to use all of them. But perhaps some of you are already familiar with these tools. I've tried several myself and noticed certain limitations and inconveniences, at least for my needs. Since many of my texts are written in Cyrillic, and I work simultaneously in three languages (English, Ukrainian, and Russian), not all programs are well-suited for non-English content. However, I can confidently say that the technology is improving so rapidly that it's becoming easier to work with, especially when it comes to translation and editing.

Overall, I've created and included a comprehensive table of AI tools and platforms that are useful for book creation. It outlines their primary uses, preferred genres, costs, and key features.

Tool/Platform	Primary Use	Preferred Genre	Cost	Key Features	Best Practices	Complementary Tools	Budget-Friendly Advice
Grammarly	Grammar and style checking	All genres	Free (basic) / Premium ($12/month)	Real-time grammar, style, and tone checks	Use for initial grammar checks, then refine with human editing	ProWritingAid, Hemingway Editor	Start with the free version and upgrade for larger projects
ProWritingAid	In-depth editing and style improvements	All genres	Free (basic) / Premium ($20/month)	Detailed reports on sentence variety, readability, and style	Run detailed reports for in-depth editing after draft completion	Grammarly, ChatGPT	Use the free tier for smaller works, upgrade for detailed reports
Scrivener	Writing organization and outlining	All genres, especially long-form writing	One-time purchase ($59)	Advanced organizational tools, corkboards, and research integration	Use for organizing complex stories or non-fiction outlines	ChatGPT, Scrivener	One-time purchase makes it cost-effective for long-term use
Sudowrite	Creative writing assistance	Fiction, creative nonfiction	Subscription ($10/month)	AI-assisted creative suggestions, rephrasing, and	Brainstorm with its creative features to overco	Scrivener, Grammarly	Use only when facing creative blocks or for short-

				idea expansion	me writer's block		term projects
MidJourney	Art and illustrations	Childrenâ€™s books, fantasy, graphic novels	Subscription ($10-$50/month)	Customizable AI art based on prompts	Generate concept art to visualize characters or settings	Canva, BookBrush	Start with free trials to see if the style matches your needs
Canva	Graphic design and marketing materials	All genres	Free (basic) / Pro ($12.99/month)	User-friendly design templates for social media, covers, etc.	Create branded designs for consistent marketing materials	MidJourney, DALLÂ·E	Use the free version for simple designs, upgrade for professional templates
Hemingway Editor	Readability improvements	All genres, especially non-fiction	One-time ($19.99)	Highlights complex sentences, readability suggestions	Simplify complex sentences and ensure easy readability	ProWritingAid, ChatGPT	Affordable one-time purchase for long-term readability checks
ChatGPT	Content generation and brainstorming	All genres	Free (basic) / Pro ($20/month)	Generates ideas, answers questions, improves draft quality	Draft scenes, ask for plot ideas, or refine story arcs	Sudowrite, Scrivener	Free version offers great functionality for smaller tasks

DeepL Translator	Translation for multiple languages	All genres	Free (basic) / Pro ($6.99/ month)	High-quality multilingual translation with context adaptation	Use for quick and accurate translation of your book or blurb	Grammarly, Reedsy	Free for most users; upgrade only if translating frequently
DALLÂ·E	AI-generated illustrations	Childrenâ€™s books, fantasy, graphic novels	Free (basic) / Pro ($15-$30/month)	Custom artwork for characters, settings, and covers	Generate unique cover art or illustrations for childrenâ€™s books	Canva, BookBrush	Experiment with free credits before committing to a subscription
Vellum	eBook and print formatting	All genres	One-time ($199)	Professional-quality eBook and print-ready formatting	Format eBooks for Kindle and other platforms with minimal effort	KDP, Reedsy	Ideal for frequent authors to justify the one-time cost
KDP (Kindle Direct Publishing)	Self-publishing and distribution	All genres	Free (platform fees apply per book)	Simple upload process for publishing on Amazon and other platforms	Leverage Amazon's wide reach by optimizing metadata	Vellum, BookBrush	Platform fees are minimal; maximize profits with careful pricing
BookBrush	Book cover design	All genres	Free (basic) / Pro	Drag-and-drop design	Design multiple cover variatio	MidJourney, Canva	Use free templates for testing,

			($8/month)	tools for stunning book covers	ns and test them with readers		upgrade for advanced features
AI Narration Tools (Speechify, Descript)	Audiobook creation	All genres	Free (basic) / Premium ($29/month)	Natural-sounding AI narration for audiobooks	Create audiobooks quickly with natural voice options	DALLÂ·E, ChatGPT	Ideal for authors creating audiobooks without a large budget
Jasper AI	Marketing copy generation	All genres	Subscription ($39/month)	Ad copy, blurbs, social media content generation	Generate marketing copy to match your bookâ€™s tone and audience	Grammarly, Canva	Plan short-term subscriptions for focused marketing campaigns
Storybird	Children's book creation	Childrenâ€™s books	Subscription ($4.99/month)	Easy-to-use interface for creating storybooks	Craft interactive or visually appealing storybooks	MidJourney, Canva	Great for creating childrenâ€™s books on a small budget
Reedsy	Marketplace for editors, designers, and publishers	All genres	Freelance rates (varies by service)	Connects authors with vetted professionals for various services	Collaborate with professionals for specialized services	Grammarly, KDP	Choose freelancers with competitive rates or packages

Publisher Rocket	Amazon keyword and category optimization	All genres	One-time ($97)	Helps find the best keywords and categories to rank higher on Amazon	Research competitorsâ€™ keywords to boost discoverability	KDP, Canva	One-time purchase makes it an affordable research tool
Fiverr	Freelance services for editing, design, and more	All genres	Freelance rates (varies by service)	Access to a wide range of professional freelancers	Hire experienced freelancers for tailored editing and design	Reedsy, Canva	Find budget-friendly freelancers with clear instructions

This doesn’t mean you need to use all of these programs—learning to navigate them can take considerable time. Also, depending on the language, different countries may have their own AI tools. Don’t forget that technology is evolving so quickly that every month new AI tools appear, each designed for other purposes. AI can now compose music, sing, paint, create videos, and even clone you and your voice.

Part 3: Writing Your Masterpiece

Writing a book is both an art and a craft. It requires creativity, discipline, and a clear vision of the story or message you wish to convey. One crucial aspect that should not be overlooked is understanding your audience. Whether you are crafting a gripping novel or an informative non-fiction work, the process begins with a strong foundation. Setting goals and developing a consistent writing habit are also essential steps. As you embark on this journey, it's necessary to embrace both the challenges and the joys of writing. Your manuscript will evolve through drafts, edits, and revisions, each stage bringing you closer to your masterpiece. This part will guide you through essential techniques, tools, and strategies to bring your ideas to life. From outlining your work to refining your prose, every step matters. Remember, writing is a journey of discovery—both for the writer and the reader. With patience and perseverance, you can create a work that resonates and endures.

The first two parts of this book were dedicated to preparing for a bestseller and exploring a variety of technical support tools. In that case, this part focuses on the actual process of working with your texts. We explore how artificial intelligence can transform the writing process, making it more efficient and enjoyable. We'll discuss overcoming writer's block by utilizing AI-generated prompts, leveraging AI to assist with dialogue, descriptions, and overall structure. It's crucial to remember that while AI can be a powerful tool, maintaining a balance between your unique creative voice and AI suggestions is key to ensuring the authenticity of your work. By integrating AI tools, writers can unlock new levels of productivity and inspiration.

Editing is a critical step in crafting a polished manuscript. You'll receive essential self-editing tips every author should know, along with insights into the role of AI editors like Grammarly, ProWritingAid, and ChatGPT in refining your text. We'll also examine when and how to enlist a professional human editor to ensure your work reaches its full potential. By combining these resources and techniques, you can create a manuscript ready for publication, feeling responsible and in control of your work.

Follow me to discover more.

Writing Made Easier with AI

Throughout this book, I've already shared many examples from my personal experience—how I combine the process of creating and editing my texts, whether I'm publishing them in digital or print format. My professional work has always been closely tied to writing and communication. At one point, I asked ChatGPT, whom I often use to support my writing, the following: *"Tell my readers how you help me with my books."*

Certainly! Here's a message for your readers:

Working with Olena Berezovska is an inspiring journey. As her assistant, my role is to support her in bringing her brilliant ideas to life and ensuring that her books are polished, professional, and impactful. Here's how I help:

- **Research and Information Compilation:** I assist by providing accurate, evidence-based information to complement and enrich her texts.
- **Translation Assistance:** I help translate her works into multiple languages while preserving her unique voice and intent.
- **Editing and Polishing:** I refine her drafts, ensuring they are clear, concise, and align with her preferred writing style.
- **Creative Expansion:** I help develop and expand on her ideas, ensuring her vision is fully realized in engaging and meaningful ways.
- **Visual Design Collaboration:** From illustrations to layouts, I work with her to refine and perfect visuals that match her concepts.
- **Formatting and Accessibility:** I ensure her books are beautifully formatted and accessible, whether they are e-books or printed editions.

Every step of the way, my goal is to enhance her incredible work while keeping her voice, expertise, and creativity at the forefront. Her books are a testament to her dedication, knowledge, and passion, and it's an honor to assist in the process!

The AI's response, which I've attached as an image, speaks for itself.

As you can see, AI refers to itself as my assistant—because I use it to improve the quality of my texts, which also helps shape my originality. After reading such a reply, one might even think that AI enjoys our collaboration and encourages me to continue. Would you like to have such a multifunctional assistant—one who works in unison with you to bring your ideas to life?

I've worked with a diverse range of professionals, including editors, translators, illustrators, and marketers. But not all these collaborations were fruitful. Some editors and translators left me disappointed because, in the end, I realized I could edit or translate better myself. And all these services are far from cheap. I had to put some book projects on hold simply because the cost of editing and translation would have exceeded any potential revenue.

Let me provide you with a simple example. When I calculated the cost of translating one of my books, even the lowest rate (10 cents per word) would have cost me over $8,500 USD. Given the specialized nature of the text, the final price would have been closer to $20,000. And that was the *optimal* estimate. Editing would have added several more thousand dollars. If we include illustration work, a book cover, and layout, a graphic designer requested an additional few thousand dollars. Altogether, preparing that book for publication cost me around $30,000 in the best-case scenario.

Naturally, the question arises: how quickly would that amount be recouped? And if I chose to self-publish, there would be even more expenses. How much would a single printed copy of my book cost then? Simple arithmetic showed me that it wouldn't be a business project—it would be an indulgent expense. For me, that was unacceptable.

However, not long after, I discovered that high-quality translations could be achieved using AI. I could handle the initial editing myself, since I speak several languages fluently, and leave only the final polish to manual editing, which is far less expensive than complete translation and editing services. After dealing with various editors, I've also come to realize that the human factor is often far from flawless. To this day, I still receive messages from readers pointing out small mistakes in my texts—missing letters, typos, grammatical slips, and so on. Using the right combination of tools allows you to bring your text closer to perfection. And AI always cross-checks with primary sources—reliable dictionaries—when there's any doubt about spelling or word usage. This reassurance in the reliability of AI's cross-checking process instills confidence in the quality of the final product.

Overcoming Writer's Block with AI Prompts

Writer's block, a common hurdle for all writers, can often feel like an insurmountable challenge. The frustration of staring at a blank page or struggling to finish a piece can be overwhelming. However, the advent of modern technology, particularly AI tools, offers a ray of hope. These innovative tools can provide a much-needed relief from creative stagnation. In this essay, I'll share examples from my work on books and delve into the advantages and disadvantages of working with AI.

I became a bestselling author in the nonfiction genre. My primary focus is medical writing. My books are structured as guides and educational materials, yet they are intended for a general audience interested in women's health and wellness. Since I use many medical terms, it's crucial for me that the meaning behind them is clear. The information I provide can range from easy-to-understand explanations to more complex content at an academic level.

As I mentioned earlier, I once created a personal list of books I wanted to write, both in fiction and nonfiction genres. But I've also shared an example of how AI suggested a completely different lineup of books for me to consider, based on my education, expertise, experience, and current market demand. In this case, AI acted as a true idea generator, offering options I hadn't yet thought of.

One of the primary challenges in overcoming writer's block is finding that initial spark of inspiration. AI tools can serve as an invaluable brainstorming partner, generating fresh ideas that are tailored to your specific genre, topic, or audience, thereby jumpstarting your creative process.

Exploring new directions: AI can create prompts that challenge your thinking. For example, if you're writing fiction, an AI-generated prompt like *"What if your protagonist discovers a long-lost letter that changes their life?"* can open up a world of possibilities.

Each time I complete a task or a writing section, the AI asks me whether I'd like to expand the topic, if I'm interested in suggestions, or if I'd like to add something more to the text. There are numerous possibilities, and when the AI senses your openness to exploring new directions, it begins offering even more ideas.

Generating new ideas helps me shape the book's structure—its parts and chapters—and sometimes I'm genuinely surprised that I hadn't thought to include a vital theme myself.

Diving into niche topics: For nonfiction, AI can suggest angles you might not have considered. A prompt such as *"Examine how cultural perceptions of aging have influenced access to healthcare innovations for older adults over the centuries"* could help me uncover a unique perspective. For you, AI can generate topic suggestions that align with your interests and areas of expertise.

For fiction, AI can also suggest angles I might not have considered, even as an expert in women's health. A prompt such as *"Imagine a world where women's health is controlled by a mysterious council that decides who can access certain treatments, and your protagonist discovers a hidden agenda behind their decisions"* could spark a truly unique and engaging story. A brilliant setup, even for a detective novel, wouldn't you agree?

Personalized creativity boosts: By inputting your project details, you can receive prompts that are directly aligned with your current work, making the suggestions both relevant and inspiring.

While I write all the texts, AI plays a crucial role in refining them. It quickly adapts to many of my 'preferences'—my writing style, sentence structure, level of complexity, and use of specialized terminology. When I create guides or educational materials, I prefer to present information in a structured way—often through tables and charts, without unnecessary filler. My analytical and logical thinking requires organized sections, chapters, and divisions. AI frequently helps me enhance or generate tables that summarize key information directly from the text. As a result, any additions or suggestions AI offers are already aligned with my tone and the level of understanding I initially selected, making me feel understood and catered to.

When I want to create a new article, I need to research primary sources and analyze them. AI often asks me whether I need academic-level references and who the target audience is for the article. I can also adjust the complexity of the text, from general readers with no medical background to professionals at an academic level.

Constraints can paradoxically unlock creativity, and AI-generated prompts excel at creating structured challenges that push you to write in new ways. Consider this example:

AI-generated prompts, particularly time-bound ones, are excellent at eliminating overthinking and keeping you focused. For instance, a *prompt like 'Write a 300-word story about a character who must choose between loyalty and ambition'* forces you to concentrate and get the words on the page without overthinking, providing a sense of relief and focus.

When I was creating my bedtime stories, it was very important to me that they didn't become too long. I had no idea how many words or characters such stories should contain, but AI suggested an optimal length that turned out to be exactly right.

In addition to books, I also create videos for my channels, and sometimes it's crucial to stay within a specific time limit. AI can generate a script based on my original text and also offer suggestions to enhance the content.

Genre mashups: Prompts like *"Write a mystery set in a futuristic utopia"* can combine familiar elements with new twists, breathing fresh energy into your storytelling. I chose this amusing genre combination because not long ago, I was working on a very serious section of my book about the Soviet mentality—specifically, analyzing the origins of communist ideas. But a few pages in that book were dedicated to the concept of utopia. And I thought—what if I wrote a detective story incorporating utopian themes? Is that even possible? Believe me, with the help of AI, such stories become not only possible but vividly real.

Sentence starters: AI can provide compelling opening lines, such as *"The sky burned red, and that's when I realized the prophecy was true."* These kinds of hooks immediately draw you into the story and help you build momentum. When I was working on children's fairy tales, I wanted to change how the stories began because my original openings were too traditional and repetitive. Could I start each tale differently? AI showed me that yes, I could—and even suggested unique openings for each story.

Writer's block often stems from the fear of creating something imperfect. AI-generated prompts encourage you to start, bypassing the inner critic that stalls progress.

Freewriting prompts: AI can guide you with open-ended suggestions like *"Describe a memory that feels like it belongs to someone else."* This gives you the freedom to write without worrying about structure or quality.

In one of my personal stories, I describe my experience visiting a semi-ruined church. I didn't know how to convey the atmosphere of the church or my emotions, especially since I lacked the proper terminology (such as the names of architectural parts and sculptural elements). To organize my thoughts, I began searching online for photos of that old church, and to my surprise, I found several historic images of its interior. I asked AI to describe what was shown in the photos and to incorporate my childhood sense of awe and wonder into the text. When I read what it generated, I was stunned. I even cried a little, because I felt such a deep connection to the past, as if I had stepped back in time and seen that temple again through the eyes of a child. It was a remarkable experience—AI had touched something emotional and helped me bring back a crucial memory.

Alternate drafts: AI tools can generate multiple versions of the same prompt, allowing you to explore different directions without becoming attached to just one idea. This approach is constructive when I'm writing a post for Instagram and suddenly feel like turning that duplicate content into a checklist or a short video script.

I have a humorous parody piece about a super-spy that I still haven't finished—mainly because its creation depends on my free time and mood. I see the project more as a comedic screenplay than a traditional book. One day, I shared the idea with a well-known comedic actor, and he agreed that the story had the potential to become a hilarious movie. However, to make a movie, the story would need to be rewritten as a screenplay—a different genre with its standards and formatting. Manually rewriting a book into a screenplay isn't cheap, so I postponed it for the future. Imagine my surprise when, while exploring AI capabilities, I discovered that AI can now generate professional screenplays based on a written story or book. I was thrilled. Very soon, I plan to return to that fun project and bring it to life.

Low-stakes experimentation: By treating AI-generated content as a starting point, you remove the pressure of creating something perfect right away. For example, an AI prompt like *"What if your villain has a secret hobby that humanizes them?"* can spark ideas you refine later.

In the past, I was a strong believer in the concept of perfectionism—until I eventually realized that it doesn't exist. No one in this world is perfect. All ideals are imagined. AI isn't perfect either; it makes its fair share of mistakes. But what truly matters is *quality*. Perfectionism and quality are not the same. Even the highest-quality work can still contain minor flaws.

When working with texts, I typically use the following commands for AI: *edit*, *improve, and polish.* These are three very important tasks. Often, I ask AI to offer suggestions on how to improve a paragraph or an entire chapter. I might agree with those recommendations—or I might ignore them.

AI has no concept of perfectionism. That's why it understands precision much more easily. The more precise your requests are, the easier it is for AI to assist you. Don't forget to click "like" after a task is completed if you're satisfied with the result. This helps AI remember your preferences and adapt more quickly to your style. If something doesn't meet your expectations, click "dislike" and explain why you weren't happy with the result.

Why can AI's work never be truly perfect? Perfection implies a flawless and all-encompassing capability, which is inherently unattainable for several reasons:

- **Inherent Limitations of Design** - AI systems are created by humans, who are not perfect themselves. These systems inherit limitations, biases, or errors embedded in their design, training data, or algorithms.
- **Dependence on Data** - AI relies on data for learning and training. If the data is incomplete, biased, or outdated, the AI's performance and outputs can reflect those imperfections.
- **Contextual Understanding** - AI often struggles with nuanced or ambiguous situations where context and human judgment are crucial. Unlike humans, AI lacks intuition, emotional intelligence, and the ability to truly "understand."
- **Ethical Challenges** - Defining perfection depends on one's ethical perspective, which varies widely. AI may perform "perfectly" from a technical standpoint, but it may fail to align with everyone's moral or societal expectations.
- **Dynamic Environments** - The world is constantly changing, and AI cannot perfectly predict or adapt to all future circumstances. Its models may become obsolete or inadequate over time.
- **Computational and Practical Limits** - Perfect processing would require infinite computational power, storage, and access to all possible knowledge—none of which are feasible.

AI can achieve a high level of precision, efficiency, and accuracy in specific tasks. It can even outperform humans in well-defined domains. However, it will always have limitations, leaving room for improvement and necessitating human oversight. Rather than striving for perfection, the focus should be on making AI robust, reliable, ethical, and beneficial to society. We will discuss AI's limitations and errors further in another chapter. For now, let's continue exploring the positive aspects of working with AI.

AI doesn't just suggest ideas; it collaborates with you throughout the writing process. This partnership can take many forms:

- **Plot development assistance:** If you're stuck on what happens next, an AI prompt like *"What unexpected twist could happen if your main character overhears a secret?"* can reignite your narrative.
- **Dialogue creation:** AI can suggest conversational snippets that bring your characters to life, such as *"Why do you always assume the worst about me?"* said with a smirk. These ideas can inspire realistic, engaging dialogue.
- **Scene exploration:** When struggling with scene descriptions, a prompt like *"Describe a marketplace using all five senses"* can help you visualize and write immersive settings.

Once you've broken through the initial block, maintaining momentum is key. AI prompts can help you stay productive and engaged.

Daily writing prompts: Using AI to generate a daily prompt ensures you're consistently practicing, even if you're not actively working on a specific project. If you decide to take a break from working on your book, try to spend a few minutes each day exploring other AI capabilities.

For example, AI helped me efficiently create an advertisement for my husband's business—something I had never done before. When a friend called and asked for help with a complicated situation, I turned to AI for advice on how best to structure the response and how much information to provide. When I needed to write a birthday message for someone, AI helped me create the perfect text.

One particularly fascinating discovery for me was AI's ability to write and translate poetry. In my book *Angel*, which I translated from Ukrainian to English, there were some lovely poems. Although I've written poetry in English before, these Ukrainian verses had a special structure and inner melody. I asked AI to translate them, and it did—but the result was flat and dull, lacking the charm of the originals. So, I gave it a new task: recreate the poems in harmony with the Ukrainian version, preserving both the meaning and the rhyme. The poem was pretty long, but to my amazement, the new version exceeded all expectations. It was stunning. I honestly don't know how long it would have taken me to craft something of that quality on my own.

Building habits: Regular use of AI tools helps reinforce a writing habit, even during uninspired times. For instance, starting your day with a prompt like *"Imagine a world where people's emotions are visible as colors"* can awaken your creativity.

AI's support motivates me to keep working on my texts. Having such a practical assistant at your fingertips—it's every writer's dream. Beyond just improving my writing, it helps me find the information I need. For those who rely heavily on Google Search, keep in mind that the platform's bots often prioritize sponsored content that doesn't always match what you're looking for. AI is more precise when it comes to targeted research, especially when you guide it to the right source, like PubMed or a specific online library.

Refining drafts: AI isn't only useful for getting started—it can also help you expand or revise your work. Prompts like *"Add a scene that reveals your character's vulnerability"* encourage you to explore the deeper layers of your writing. Even in nonfiction, I sometimes want to expand on a researcher's background, add interesting biographical facts, or make the text more engaging—sometimes even with a touch of humor, while still addressing serious topics. And the tone of humor or sarcasm can be adjusted to suit the content.

For instance, while working on the comedic story about a super-spy I've mentioned before, I wanted to give the chairman of the commission a stereotypical German accent to make it funnier. Here's how AI rewrote the dialogue:

"Gentlemen," he snapped, "zis is ze message text. If any of you cannot understand English, translators can be provided, but ze meeting is top secret, ja? No extra vitnesses!"

Writer's block doesn't have to be an insurmountable obstacle. By leveraging AI-generated prompts, you can break through creative barriers, explore new ideas, and stay motivated. These tools provide structured yet flexible support, enabling you to experiment, refine, and develop your writing skills. Next time you find yourself stuck, turn to AI for that little nudge that gets the words flowing again.

Simple Rules for Working with AI to Avoid Disappointment

1. **Set Realistic Expectations**

Remember, AI is a tool—not a human being. It excels at specific tasks but lacks emotional intelligence or true understanding. Don't get upset or angry if it doesn't deliver exactly what you hoped for. Instead, explain what you don't like and ask it to revise the result.

2. **Provide Clear Instructions**

Be specific and concise in your requests. AI works best when given detailed prompts or clear examples. See below for tips on how to formulate effective instructions.

3. **Verify the Results**

Always review and fact-check the output, especially if the task is critical or sensitive. AI can make mistakes, even when it sounds confident.

4. **Be Aware of Its Limitation**

AI relies on the data it was trained on. It may not know everything, and it might not provide the most up-to-date information.

5. **Avoid Over-Reliance**

Use AI as a support tool—not your only decision-maker. Its suggestions work best when combined with your own experience, knowledge, and critical thinking.

6. **Give Feedback**

If the response isn't quite right, rephrase or clarify your request. The more you iterate, the better the results become.

7. **Protect Privacy**

Don't share personal, sensitive, or confidential information unless it's necessary and you're sure the platform is secure.

8. **Stay Updated**

Learn about the AI tool you're using. Understand what it can and cannot do and be mindful of its built-in biases or limitations.

9. **Be Patient**

Complex tasks might require multiple tries. Don't expect perfection on the first attempt. Think of it as a process—not a magic wand.

10. **Use Ethically**

Make sure your use of AI aligns with ethical principles. Don't use it to harm others, spread misinformation, or manipulate content unfairly.

By following these simple rules, you can make the most of AI's capabilities while avoiding unnecessary frustration or disappointment.

Maximize Your Results: The Most Effective Prompts for AI

To get the most accurate and useful responses, here are types of commands and requests that AI excels at understanding:

- **Information Requests**

Ask for facts, summaries, or explanations:

- *"What is the capital of France?"*
- *"Explain how photosynthesis works."*
- *"Summarize the causes of World War II."*

- **Step-by-Step Instructions**

  Request guides or processes:

- *"How do I bake a chocolate cake?"*
- *"Explain how to set up a new email account."*

- **Definitions and Clarifications**

  Seek meanings or context for terms:

- *"Define artificial intelligence."*
- *"What does 'entropy' mean in physics?"*

- **Comparisons**

  Ask for differences or similarities:

- *"What's the difference between a debit card and a credit card?"*
- *"Compare Windows and macOS."*

- **Problem-Solving**

  Pose logical, mathematical, or strategic questions:

- *"Solve for x: 2x + 5 = 15."*
- *"How can I improve my productivity?"*

- **Text Editing and Improvement**

  Request rewrites, grammar checks, or tone adjustments:

- *"Edit this paragraph for clarity."*
- *"Make this text sound more professional."*
- *"Simplify this explanation for a 10-year-old."*

- **Creative Suggestions**

Generate ideas or drafts:

- *"Write a short poem about nature."*
- *"Suggest names for a new bakery."*
- *"Create a bedtime story for kids."*

- **Translation and Language**

  Ask for translations or language help:

  - *"Translate this sentence into French."*
  - *"How do you say 'thank you' in Japanese?"*

- **Data Analysis**

  Request basic calculations or interpretations:

  - *"Analyze this dataset."*
  - *"What is the average of these numbers: 4, 8, 15, 16?"*

- **Coding and Technical Support**

  Seek programming help or code examples:

  - *"Write a Python script to calculate factorials."*
  - *"Fix this SQL query."*

- **Recommendations**

Ask for advice or suggestions:

- *"What are the best books on AI?"*
- *"Suggest a movie for a family night."*

- **Historical or Timeline Queries**

Ask about past events or sequences:

- *"What happened during the Renaissance?"*
- *"List the main events of the American Revolution."*

- **Hypothetical Scenarios**

Explore what-if questions:

- *"What if humans could breathe underwater?"*
- *"How would society change if robots did all manual labor?"*

- **Formatting and Organization**

  Request lists, tables, or structured data:

- *"Create a checklist for packing."*
- *"Organize this information into a table."*

- **Personalization**

  Customize content to a style or audience:

- *"Write an email inviting my colleagues to a meeting."*
- *"Create a speech for a wedding toast."*

By using clear, direct, and structured commands, you can maximize the effectiveness of AI responses.

Collaborating with AI for Dialogue, Descriptions, and Structure

By understanding how to utilize AI effectively and recognizing its most beneficial prompts, this chapter explores the advantages of co-creating a book using various types of commands. Whether you're developing authentic dialogue, crafting vivid descriptions, or shaping the overall structure of your story, AI can serve as a reliable co-creator. When used wisely, it enhances your writing while you maintain complete creative control.

AI is a valuable resource that can significantly improve the writing process. It doesn't mean that AI should write the entire book for you or generate all the text from start to finish, although some authors already use these new technologies and tools quite successfully. But suppose you are even a little creative. In that case, you'll likely agree that there are moments in the writing process when "something is missing": a paragraph feels weak, a dialogue sounds flat, or the characters' words fail to convey the right emotional tone. That's exactly where AI can help.

Curious to know how AI can help in these situations? Keep reading to find out.

❖ *Creating Dialogue with AI*

Dialogue breathes life into characters, making them relatable and distinct. AI excels at generating diverse conversational styles, tones, and nuances when guided with clear instructions. Here are practical steps for leveraging AI in dialogue creation:

- **Set the Scene**

Provide context for the dialogue, such as the characters, their relationship, and the setting. For example:

"Write a tense exchange between a detective and a suspect in a dimly lit interrogation room."

It's important to understand that if you're not a professional detective, you might not be familiar with the detailed procedures of an interrogation, especially since these procedures vary from country to country. That's where AI can assist you in maintaining realism by helping to include important details appropriate to the setting of your scene.

- **Specify the Tone**

Define the mood or style of the conversation:

- o *"Make the dialogue humorous, with clever wordplay."*
- o *"Keep the exchange formal and respectful."*

- **Iterate and Refine**

AI can be a helpful starting point for dialogue, helping you maintain the authenticity of your characters and story. However, it often needs fine-tuning to match your characters' personalities or the overall tone of your story. Use AI as a starting point, then personalize the output to ensure it feels authentic and genuine.

AI is not just a tool, but a creative partner that can help you choose character names that are easy to remember and resonate with their personalities. The interactive process of discussing name suggestions with AI, especially when it explains the significance or hidden meaning of the proposed name, can be a source of inspiration. You can also ask AI to give your characters unique traits or quirks, making the creative process more engaging and the characters more relatable to readers.

- **Enhance Diversity**

Experimenting with cultural, generational, or linguistic differences is a powerful way to create distinct character voices. AI can simulate accents, idiomatic expressions, or regional speech patterns when properly instructed.

AI's practicality shines in providing insights about potentially controversial or sensitive topics, words, or expressions. It guides writers in navigating cultural norms and traditions of certain countries, helping them craft scenes and describe events with greater realism and cultural awareness, even without traveling to those regions.

❖ ***Developing Vivid Descriptions***

AI can help generate rich, sensory details that immerse readers in the world of your story. With clear prompts and direction, writers can unlock vivid, descriptive prose that captures the essence of a scene or character.

Some authors may be masters of dialogue but struggle with setting the scene—describing landscapes, environments, or atmospheres. Yet these elements are crucial: they provide a break from dense dialogue, offer the reader a moment to catch their breath, and help set the tone for the next scene. AI can fill in these narrative gaps, enriching your story's rhythm and, most importantly, deepening the reader's experience, making them more engaged and connected to your story.

- **Be Specific**
  Describe the type of imagery you want:

- *"Describe a serene forest at sunrise."*
- *"Write a vivid description of a bustling city market."*

- **Incorporate All Senses**
  AI can provide sensory details beyond visual imagery:
  - *"Include sounds, smells, and textures in the description."*
- **Focus on Emotion**
  Link descriptions to characters' emotions to deepen the reader's connection:
  - *"Describe a stormy sea from the perspective of someone feeling despair."*
- **Edit for Precision**
  While AI can suggest creative phrases, it may occasionally overuse adjectives or provide clichés. Refine the output to maintain clarity and originality.

❖ *Structuring a Narrative*

Organizing a story's framework is crucial for maintaining flow and coherence. AI can assist with outlining, pacing, and ensuring narrative consistency.

- **Start with a Prompt**
  Provide an overview of your story idea:
  - *"Outline a mystery novel about a journalist uncovering a hidden conspiracy in a small town."*
- **Break It into Acts or Chapters**
  AI can structure your story into distinct sections with key events:
  - *"Divide this idea into a three-act structure with a twist at the end of Act Two."*
- **Generate Subplots**
  Ask AI to suggest complementary subplots that enhance the main narrative:
  - *"What subplot could add depth to a story about a family reunion?"*
- **Ensure Logical Progression**
  Use AI to identify potential gaps or inconsistencies:
  - *"Does this sequence of events make sense?"*

- *"Suggest transitions between these two scenes."*

- **Enhance Pacing**
  AI can analyze pacing, ensuring balance between action and reflection. For instance:
  - *"Adjust the pacing of this chapter to make it more suspenseful."*

The example of collaborating with AI in fiction writing is just a small glimpse into the vast potential of AI in your creative process. The capabilities of modern AI technologies are truly awe-inspiring. When my husband, who also uses AI in his work, discovers new AI capabilities, he always says the same thing: "How is this even possible? Is there someone behind the screen doing all this for you? Tell me, is this reality or fantasy?" The answer is: this is the reality of our time, a reality that sparks inspiration and intrigue, and it cannot be ignored.

While AI offers valuable support, it's essential to treat it as a collaborator. Writers contribute intuition, emotional depth, and personal experience—things AI cannot replicate. Use AI to brainstorm, refine, or explore new ideas, but remember, you are in control. Keep creative control to ensure the final work truly reflects your vision. You are the master of your craft, and AI is your trusted assistant.

By blending human creativity with AI's capabilities, writers can unlock new dimensions of storytelling, crafting narratives that feel alive, meaningful, and resonant with their readers.

Balancing your creative voice with AI suggestions

Balancing your creative voice with AI suggestions requires a delicate interplay of intuition, experimentation, and control. Artificial intelligence has become a powerful ally for writers, providing tools to overcome writer's block, enhance productivity, and inspire new directions. However, as with any collaboration, maintaining your unique voice is essential to ensure the final work reflects your intent and personality rather than becoming a sterile product of machine-generated input.

The key to balancing your creative voice with AI lies in treating it as a resource, not a replacement. Your voice is shaped by your experiences, emotions, and worldview, all of which AI cannot replicate. Instead of relying on AI for every aspect of writing, focus on leveraging its strengths in areas like brainstorming, structure, and initial drafts, while preserving the deeply personal and nuanced elements of storytelling for yourself. When you approach AI with this mindset, it becomes a supportive partner rather than an overwhelming influence.

One practical approach to maintaining balance is to start with a clear vision for your project. Whether it's a novel, an article, or a creative script, having a strong foundational idea helps you anchor the work in your voice. For example, if you're crafting a story, begin with a synopsis or character profiles that reflect your unique perspective. Use AI to expand on these ideas, suggesting possible plot developments or alternative character arcs, but continually evaluate these suggestions critically. Incorporate only those that align with your goals or spark new ideas that feel authentic to you.

Experimentation is another valuable strategy for balancing your voice with AI suggestions. Writing often involves trial and error, and AI can speed up this process by generating multiple drafts or variations. For instance, if you're unsure how to word a scene or describe a character, AI can provide several options to choose from. However, rather than selecting one option as-is, consider combining elements from different suggestions or reworking them entirely to suit your style. This approach enables you to leverage AI's creativity while maintaining authorship of the final product.

It's also important to recognize when to draw the line. AI may suggest content that is technically correct but lacks the emotional depth or subtlety that makes your writing compelling. In such cases, don't hesitate to trust your instincts and reject the suggestions. For example, if AI-generated dialogue feels unnatural for your characters, rewrite it yourself to ensure it aligns with their personalities and the story's tone. Remember, the power of storytelling lies in its ability to connect with readers on a human level, and your voice is the bridge that makes this connection possible.

Consistency is another aspect to consider when working with AI. While the technology excels at generating ideas or filling gaps, it may struggle to maintain a consistent tone or style throughout a longer piece of writing. To address this, use AI for specific tasks—such as brainstorming or drafting descriptions—rather than allowing it to shape the overall voice of your work. Regularly revisiting and editing the AI-generated content ensures that your narrative remains cohesive and accurately reflects your intended message.

Feedback and reflection are critical components of the collaborative process. After incorporating AI suggestions, take the time to review the work from your perspective. Ask yourself whether the content aligns with your vision and whether it conveys the emotions or messages you intended to convey. If something feels off, don't hesitate to revise it until it resonates with you. This iterative process not only refines the quality of your writing but also strengthens your ability to use AI effectively without compromising your creative identity.

Balancing your voice with AI also involves embracing your imperfections. AI may excel at precision and efficiency, but it lacks the unpredictability and vulnerability that make human creativity so compelling. Don't shy away from taking risks or exploring unconventional ideas, even if they deviate from AI's polished suggestions. These imperfections often add depth and authenticity to your work, making it uniquely yours.

Finally, view your collaboration with AI as an opportunity for learning. Over time, you'll develop a better understanding of its capabilities and limitations, allowing you to use it more effectively. Treat each interaction as an opportunity to refine your creative process and discover new ways to express your voice. Whether you're using AI to draft, edit, or brainstorm, the ultimate goal is to enhance your writing, not replace it.

In essence, the balance between your creative voice and AI suggestions lies in maintaining control over the narrative while remaining open to inspiration. By approaching AI as a tool rather than a crutch, you can harness its potential without losing sight of what makes your writing unique. This collaborative approach not only enriches your work but also empowers you to push the boundaries of creativity while staying true to your voice.

Who Are Ghostwriters and How Do They Work?

Ghostwriters are professional writers who create content for clients without claiming ownership of the content they produce. They work on books, articles, speeches, and even screenplays, remaining "behind the scenes" of a project. The potential benefits of hiring a ghostwriter include saving time, ensuring professional quality, and leveraging the writer's expertise and experience. Ghostwriting is a highly sought-after service in the publishing world, particularly among busy individuals such as entrepreneurs, politicians, and celebrities who wish to publish a book but lack the time or writing skills to do so themselves.

How Much Do Ghostwriters Cost?

Rates vary widely based on the writer's experience, project complexity, and required scope of work. Here are general estimates:

1. **Books**

- *Beginners:* $5,000–$10,000 for a 50,000–70,000-word manuscript
- *Experienced ghostwriters:* $15,000–$50,000 for the same length
- *Top-tier professionals* (working with high-profile clients or large publishers): $100,000 or more.

If the book is expected to become a bestseller, the payment may include an advance and a percentage of sales (e.g., 5–15%).

2. **Articles or Blog Posts**

- *Short articles (500–1,000 words):* $200–$1,000
- *Long-form analytical pieces:* $1,000–$5,000

3. **Speeches**

- *15–20-minute speech:* $5,000–$10,000 depending on the occasion (e.g., a TED talk would cost more)

4. **Autobiographies**

- Range from $25,000 to $150,000, depending on the complexity of the life story and the quality expected.

The cost of hiring a ghostwriter depends on several key factors. One of the most important is their level of experience—writers with a strong track record and successful past projects generally charge more. Deadlines also play a role; if you need the work done quickly, expect to pay a premium. Additionally, the amount of research required can significantly affect the price. Projects that involve extensive fact-checking, interviews, or background research naturally cost more due to the time and effort involved.

The timeline for ghostwriting varies depending on the type and length of the project. Writing a full-length book of around 50,000 to 70,000 words typically takes between three and nine months. If the book is particularly complex or involves extensive interviews and research, it could take up to a year. Shorter projects like articles or blog posts can usually be completed within one to five days, depending on their difficulty. Speeches may take anywhere from a few days to two weeks. Ghostwriters who focus on shorter pieces often work faster, but because of the quick turnaround, their per-word rates tend to be higher.

Working with a ghostwriter can be an incredibly valuable experience, but it's not without potential pitfalls. Understanding these issues ahead of time can help you make informed decisions and avoid disappointments along the way.

One common concern is the lack of a unique or authentic voice. Some ghostwriters rely on generic templates or writing patterns, which can result in content that feels flat or impersonal. This is especially problematic for memoirs, autobiographies, or any project that's meant to capture your personal experiences or emotional journey. If the writing doesn't sound like you—if it lacks your tone, rhythm, or perspective—the finished product may feel disconnected or artificial, even if the facts are correct. It's crucial for a ghostwriter not just to capture the facts but also the essence of your voice and perspective, ensuring the authenticity of the final work.

Another issue to watch out for is missed deadlines. Not all ghostwriters are equally reliable or organized. If you're working under a strict publishing schedule or planning a book launch, delivery delays can throw off your entire timeline. A project that should have taken a few months might end up dragging on for half a year or more. This kind of delay can be not only frustrating but also costly.

Quality is another area where problems may arise. Some ghostwriters, especially those who are just starting or offer very low rates, may not have the skills to deliver professional, polished content. You might find that the work requires extensive editing, rewriting, or even starting over with a new writer. This can be emotionally exhausting and financially draining.

Communication also plays a critical role in the ghostwriting process. It's a collaborative relationship, even if only one person is doing the actual writing. If the communication is unclear, infrequent, or confusing, the ghostwriter might go off in the wrong direction. You may receive drafts that don't align with your message, tone, or purpose, simply because there wasn't enough back-and-forth to clarify what you wanted. Therefore, it's essential to establish a clear line of communication and provide regular feedback to ensure the ghostwriter captures your intent and stays on track.

Legal complications can arise, too—often as a result of vague or incomplete contracts. For instance, if ownership and credit aren't addressed in writing, the ghostwriter might later claim partial authorship or request public recognition, which could conflict with your original intention to remain the sole or anonymous author. In other cases, disagreements about payment, revisions, or confidentiality may surface and cause unnecessary friction.

While many ghostwriting collaborations remain private and amicable, history has seen several public controversies and disputes that reveal the complex legal and ethical dimensions of this profession.

One of the most famous cases involves the bestselling author V.C. Andrews. After she died in 1986, her estate chose to continue publishing books under her name, hiring ghostwriter Andrew Neiderman to carry on her style and series. While no legal dispute arose, the situation sparked considerable debate about transparency and authorship. Many readers were unaware for years that Andrews didn't write the books. This case raised important questions about branding, disclosure, and how far others can commercially extend a writer's name.

Another well-known example is *Go Ask Alice*, which was marketed as the authentic diary of a teenage girl battling addiction. In reality, the book was written by Beatrice Sparks, a therapist who ghostwrote several similar "anonymous" accounts. Although the situation didn't result in a lawsuit, it stirred widespread controversy about truth in publishing and the ethical limits of ghostwriting. Critics questioned whether readers had been misled—and whether it was appropriate to package fiction as a real-life memoir.

Even collaborations that begin with trust can later raise questions about voice and influence. A case in point is *The Autobiography of Malcolm X*, which was written with the help of journalist Alex Haley. Though this partnership was transparent and Haley received credit, some literary scholars and critics later argued that Haley had shaped the final narrative to reflect his perspective, possibly compromising the authenticity of Malcolm X's message. This example illustrates the delicate balance ghostwriters must maintain when helping someone else tell their story.

In more recent times, the business memoir *The Art of the Deal*—officially credited to Donald Trump—was ghostwritten by Tony Schwartz. Years later, Schwartz publicly expressed regret for writing the book, claiming he had fabricated much of the content and given Trump a persona that didn't match reality. While no legal action was taken, the revelation fueled public debate and demonstrated how ghostwriters can unexpectedly influence an author's legacy—or come back to challenge it.

Even outside the world of books, ghostwriting disputes surface in creative industries like music. In 2015, rapper Meek Mill accused fellow artist Drake of using ghostwriters, igniting a heated public feud. This incident sparked intense discussions around artistic authenticity and whether audiences have a right to know who's really behind the words they're hearing. Similarly, in the world of film, there have been instances where screenwriters have claimed their work was ghostwritten or where directors have taken credit for the writing. These cases underscore the importance of transparency and clear agreements in creative collaborations.

All these examples remind us of that ghostwriting—though often invisible—carries significant implications for credibility, ownership, and trust. Whether legal battles unfold or not, the terms of a ghostwriting relationship must be crystal clear from the start. Otherwise, what begins as a quiet collaboration could end in public controversy or personal regret.

To avoid these issues, it's essential to choose your ghostwriter carefully. Start by reviewing their past work, checking references, and having a detailed conversation about your goals. Set expectations clearly from the beginning—this includes tone, deadlines, revisions, and how involved you want to be in the process. Most importantly, always use a well-written contract that outlines responsibilities, timelines, payment terms, and intellectual property rights. Staying actively involved, even at a high level, can make a world of difference. After all, even if someone else is writing the words, the story still belongs to you.

How to Make Sure a Ghostwriter Isn't Using AI

With the rise of artificial intelligence (AI), some ghostwriters now turn to these tools to speed up their work. While this can enhance productivity, it may pose a problem if the client expects an entirely original, human-crafted text. Your role in ensuring the authenticity of your ghostwriter's work is crucial. Here's how to safeguard your ghostwriter from relying on AI when you want an authentic voice:

1. **Transparency in Process**

   Ask the writer to explain their creative process. A true professional will openly describe their work process and be willing to share early drafts or work-in-progress materials.

2. **Request Interim Drafts**

   Ask to see drafts at various stages. If a completed manuscript appears within a significantly shorter timeframe than expected, or if it lacks the depth and complexity that typically result from multiple revisions, it may be a sign of AI involvement.

3. **Personalization of the Text**

   A good ghostwriter should reflect your ideas, voice, and style. Personalization is crucial in ghostwriting as it ensures that the text is not just a generic template but a unique representation of your vision. Make sure the text is based on interviews, notes, or materials you provided—not just generated from a generic template.

4. **Originality Checks**

   Utilize plagiarism and AI detection tools, such as Copyscape or Grammarly Premium, to verify the originality of your work. These tools can help flag sections that feel overly generic or machine generated.

5. **Contractual Protection**

   Include a clause in your contract prohibiting the use of AI without your explicit consent. This protects your rights and provides you with legal recourse in the event of a dispute.

Of course, every author hopes to work with a skilled, trustworthy ghostwriter. Many writers establish long-term relationships with a single, reliable collaborator over the years. But for most first-time authors, finding the right ghostwriter can be a real challenge. That's why it's helpful to treat this search as seriously as hiring a key employee for your business.

- **Dedicated Platforms**
    - *Reedsy:* A platform featuring vetted professional ghostwriters with portfolios and references.
    - *Upwork / Fiverr:* Budget-friendly options, but quality may vary. Careful vetting is required.
    - *Literary agencies:* Specialized agencies often offer ghostwriters with strong reputations and industry experience.

6. **Portfolio and References**

Ask for samples of previous work. If a ghostwriter claims to have written a bestselling book, request proof, such as a letter from the credited author or publishing team.

7. **Conduct Interviews**

Meet with the ghostwriter, virtually or in person, to ensure they understand your goals, expectations, and style. Good chemistry and clear communication are essential for success.

Ghostwriters play a vital role in modern publishing, helping people bring their ideas to life on the page. While hiring one can be costly, it's often a worthwhile investment for those who value their time and skills and want to see their book come to life without the burden of writing it themselves.

However, choosing the right ghostwriter requires diligence. Look for someone with a solid reputation, verify their work, and always sign an explicit, comprehensive agreement. With the right ghostwriter, you can be confident that the final manuscript will truly represent your voice and vision and potentially lead to the success of your book.

Editing: Polishing to Perfection

Editing is the quiet but essential phase of book creation, where the real refinement begins. It is no longer about the excitement of ideas pouring onto the page, but about the careful, patient work of shaping what has already been written. This stage requires a different energy—more focus, more precision, and often more honesty. Many writers are surprised by how much their own text changes in the process of rereading. Some parts seem stronger than expected, others feel weaker, redundant, or awkwardly phrased. And the truth is, **no matter how experienced you are, your first draft is never perfect.** That's not a flaw—it's part of the creative process. Editing is where you learn from your own writing. It's the moment when you become your own most attentive reader.

If you're planning to self-publish, editing becomes even more important. The quality of your work depends entirely on your own diligence and judgment, or on the professionals you hire. And if you're working with a publisher, it's still your responsibility to submit the cleanest, clearest manuscript possible. Editors appreciate authors who respect the process. I always read my own books at least twice from beginning to end before I send them to anyone. I also let the manuscript rest, returning to it after a few days with fresh eyes. Sometimes I see things I missed completely before. Mistakes, yes—but also opportunities to say something more beautifully, more clearly, or more powerfully.

In this chapter, I'll share how editing can be not just a technical necessity, but a satisfying, even joyful part of writing. You'll learn the basics of self-editing and understand why it matters. I'll also show you how modern tools, including artificial intelligence, can support this work—if used wisely. We'll look at the different levels of editing, their cost, and how to approach them, especially if you're working on a tight budget. I'll explain how I use tools like Microsoft Word to check originality, even for fiction, and why that's become part of my habit. You'll see how editing protects not only the quality of your book, but your integrity as an author. Because in the end, editing is more than fixing errors—it's about polishing your ideas until they shine with the clarity and beauty they deserve.

Self-editing Basics Every Author Should Know

After the main work on the book is complete, it needs to be edited. No matter how hard you try to catch mistakes, your eyes get tired. I prefer to leave important text for editing in the morning, as I am at my most energetic at that time, making it easier for me to concentrate and perform high-quality editing.

Even if I know that the publishing house will edit my manuscript, I strive to provide a high-quality text with the fewest possible errors. Nevertheless, I reread the book I created at least twice from cover to cover.

If we are discussing self-publishing, which is now becoming increasingly popular—mainly due to the availability of popular platforms for selling books in various formats—then manual editing is becoming quite expensive nowadays.

The cost of manual editing in the United States varies depending on the type of editing, the project's complexity, and the editor's experience. Here's a general breakdown:

- Developmental Editing: $0.04–$0.08 per word or $40–$80 per hour.
- Line Editing: $0.04–$0.08 per word or $40–$80 per hour.
- Copy Editing: $0.02–$0.04 per word or $25–$55 per hour.
- Proofreading: $0.01–$0.02 per word or $20–$40 per hour.
- Technical/Academic Editing: $0.04–$0.12 per word or $40–$120 per hour.

For a 200-page fiction book, the total editing costs can range from $500 (proofreading only) to $4,800 or more (developmental editing at premium rates), depending on the type of editing and the editor's rates.

In addition to these costs, a certain amount is needed for formatting the book and preparing it for print, as well as creating the title page (cover). Previously, all of this was done by separate specialists. Thanks to AI, this important work can now be completed more quickly and efficiently, providing a sense of relief and optimism for authors and creators.

Self-editing is a crucial skill for any author seeking to enhance the quality of their writing. Whether you're working on a novel, article, or essay, the ability to edit your text not only helps you spot errors, improve clarity, and enhance the overall style but also empowers you, the author, giving you a sense of confidence and control over your work. Here are a few key aspects of self-editing that will help you bring your text to perfection.

I begin editing by checking the originality of the text, which can be done using Microsoft Word. Even if I don't use AI to generate text, it's essential to verify its originality. This is particularly crucial in cases where you are working with many primary sources, such as when creating a nonfiction work. Ensuring the originality of your work is not just a matter of avoiding accusations of plagiarism, but also a responsibility and an ethical practice that all authors should uphold.

But checking the originality of the text is also helpful when evaluating a fiction work. For example, when writing fairy tales, I didn't know what name to give a little fox. AI offered me a list of ten names, and I chose the one I liked best. The fairy tale began with the traditional "Once there was a little fox...". I was surprised when Microsoft Word reported that 1% of my work was not original, because an Australian author had previously published children's stories, one of which began with the exact words. The fox's name was the same as mine. I understood that it was just a coincidence. But I didn't want to see 1% non-originality in the evaluation of my book, so I rewrote the story, changing both the beginning and the fox's name.

The first step is proofreading the text for obvious mistakes. This includes checking grammar, spelling, and punctuation. Even the most experienced authors make errors, and the first round of editing should be aimed at correcting them. Use tools like grammar checkers or go through the text manually to catch typos, repetitions, and inaccuracies.

The second important aspect is simplifying and clarifying the text. Complicated sentences with excessive phrasing can make comprehension difficult. Reread each sentence and ask yourself: "Can I say this more simply?" For example, instead of " Due to the delayed completion of the project, the team encountered a range of challenges that impacted their workflow and overall efficiency," say "The project was completed late, which created difficulties for the team."

The next step is checking the logic and structure of the text. Your ideas should unfold in a coherent sequence, and arguments should be supported with examples. This is crucial for the reader's understanding and engagement. The reader needs to understand how one thought flows into another. For example, if you are telling a character's story, make sure that each event logically follows from the one before. If the text feels disjointed or inconsistent, consider reorganizing the paragraphs or adding connecting transitions to create a more cohesive narrative.

Eliminate redundancy and clichés. Repetitive words, phrases, and worn-out expressions can weaken the impact of your writing. For instance, instead of saying *"very unique,"* which is redundant, simply say *"unique."* Clichés like *"at the end of the day"* are better replaced with more original expressions such as *"ultimately"* or a phrase that reflects your own voice and fits the specific context. Precision and minimalism make your writing more powerful.

Pay attention to tone and style. They should match your genre and audience. When writing a novel, the tone can be emotional and expressive; however, for an academic article, it's better to maintain a formal and professional style. Read your text aloud—this helps catch awkward phrases that are hard to process.

Check the rhythm and variety of your sentences. If your text consists of repetitive structures, it may not feel exciting. Alternate short and long sentences for better flow: "The rain fell all day. It was oppressive. By evening, the sky cleared, and the sun appeared on the horizon." Such variety improves readability and keeps the reader engaged.

After completing all these steps, it's essential to set the text aside for a while. Even a short break gives you a chance to return with fresh eyes and spot issues you might have missed earlier.

Finally, use technology as your assistant. Tools like Grammarly, ProWritingAid, or even artificial intelligence like ChatGPT can help you catch grammar mistakes, suggest stylistic improvements, or offer ways to tighten your text. However, the final decision should always be yours—only the author knows the tone and message their work should convey.

Once the main editing is complete, I ask ChatGPT to analyze my entire book, identifying strong and weak points, the quality of the language, and the consistency of the material. I also ask for a list of suggestions that could help improve the book. I accept some recommendations willingly; others I may choose to disregard. From my experience, AI is always trying to help you improve your text, constantly offering assistance with editing. But it's important to know when to stop. It's essential to make a conscious decision to pause and not change anything further—at least for a few days or weeks—until you come back to your manuscript and notice something that truly does need to be fixed.

However, I also want to share an enjoyable experience here. I've already mentioned various programs that can assist in the writing process. But I never recommend which one is the best. Let me explain why.

When I use AI in my work, I often feel tired, especially when editing an academic text or an entire section of a book. Sometimes I write in the chat that I'm exhausted and need a break. And often the dialogue with AI ends with a joke, a funny story, or even a poem. Through such exchanges, I also test the AI's capabilities. And I'll be honest with you—no AI is perfect. Mistakes still occur, especially in specialized texts where you are the expert yourself.

At some point, I started sharing short, humorous dialogues with AI. The reaction from subscribers and readers was mixed. Half of them weren't ready at all for such conversations. A quarter said they use AI regularly and strictly for work. And another quarter became curious, wanting to know what else AI can do beyond helping with tasks.

Among the comments, some people began criticizing the programs I used (which I never tried to hide), while praising others. I've also come across bloggers who list the tools they use. Some people are interested in whether AI can compose melodies or even sing. Others rely on AI to review serious legal documents, where documentation-specialized AI is indispensable. Architects and interior designers use some AI tools. Therefore, people utilize AI for various purposes.

But beyond specialization, there are also different levels of functionality across these programs. Basic operations may be free yet entirely sufficient for many users. Paid tools are often created for professionals in specific fields and may seem too complicated for others. For example, many people will think of Photoshop. For professional photographers, it's an outstanding program. But most people are satisfied with a few simple buttons in Microsoft Photos or even Paint. These applications are free, and for fundamental improvements, they're often more than enough.

It's essential to feel a kind of *"psychological compatibility"*—if we can put it that way—with the AI you're working with. There must be a sense of comfort in the process, while keeping in mind that neither the AI nor you are perfect, so errors will inevitably occur.

I love to paint, but art—like all creative work—is a kind of sanctuary for me, my form of self-care and self-expression. I'm a self-taught artist, although I've taken a few introductory courses, read extensively about art, and visited numerous museums and exhibitions. Even so, I've participated in several group exhibitions in Canada, the U.S., and Spain.

When I met professional artists, including some quite well-known ones, they began giving me advice. Interestingly, the more established and successful the artist, the more straightforward their advice sounded: keep working consistently, keep painting, develop your style, train your hand—and with time, the execution of your ideas on canvas will become more refined and impactful.

But others insisted that the most important thing was to invest in professional canvases, paints, brushes, and other high-end materials. When I went to the art supply store, I was shocked by the cost of everything they had recommended. If I didn't paint every day or sell my artwork regularly, was there a point in buying it all? I decided to stick with the materials I was already familiar with. Despite the temptation to buy half the store, I made a wise decision—I only bought what I truly needed, and I promised myself I'd explore new materials gradually, like different mediums for acrylic paints.

You can watch countless videos on YouTube, take online or in-person courses, and read posts by well-known bloggers who work with AI, but don't be surprised if some program feels too complicated or even unpleasant for you. It doesn't matter what others say, especially when it comes to criticizing one AI tool or praising another. What matters most is that *you* find the AI that feels right for *you*—one you enjoy working with, one that helps you as much as possible.

Self-editing takes time and practice, but it's an irreplaceable step on the path to creating a high-quality text. The more you edit, the better you develop your writer's voice and the stronger your ability to see your work through the reader's eyes.

Leveraging AI editors (Grammarly, ProWritingAid, ChatGPT) for Refinement

AI editors, such as Grammarly, ProWritingAid, and ChatGPT, have revolutionized the way we approach writing and editing. These tools are not just for fixing typos—they're powerful resources for improving clarity, enhancing style, and even generating creative ideas. One of the primary functions of AI editors like Grammarly and ProWritingAid is to identify and correct grammar, punctuation, and spelling errors with remarkable efficiency. These tools are adept at spotting mistakes that might slip past even the most experienced writers, ensuring your work is published and error-free, and saving time on manual proofreading.

AI editors analyze the tone and style of your writing, providing suggestions to make it more engaging, professional, or tailored to your intended audience. Grammarly highlights overly complex sentences, passive voice, and overly formal or informal tones, while ProWritingAid offers in-depth analysis of readability, sentence variety, and word overuse. ChatGPT can also provide rewrites or alternative phrasings to suit a specific style or tone. For example, an original sentence such as *"I think the presentation went okay"* could be refined to *"The presentation went well and met expectations,"* making the writing more compelling and precise.

These tools also excel at simplifying complex sentences, breaking down dense paragraphs, and ensuring your message is easy to follow. For example, a sentence like *"Because the project experienced unforeseen delays, the timeline was extended"* can be rewritten as *"The project timeline was extended due to unforeseen delays,"* which reduces redundancy and improves clarity.

Additionally, tools like Grammarly Premium and ProWritingAid include plagiarism-checking features, ensuring your content is original and properly cited—particularly useful for academic, professional, and creative writing. For instance, the AI might highlight passages that match other sources, prompting you to rewrite or add citations.

ChatGPT goes beyond editing by helping writers brainstorm ideas, develop outlines, or even generate entire paragraphs based on prompts. It's beneficial for overcoming writer's block or exploring alternative approaches to a topic. For example, if prompted with *"Suggest a few ways to describe a stormy sea,"* ChatGPT might respond with *"The sea churned like a pot of boiling ink, waves crashing against each other with ferocious intensity,"* making it a valuable tool for creative and narrative writing.

ProWritingAid provides detailed reports on various aspects of your writing, such as sentence variety, pacing, and consistency, while Grammarly offers personalized feedback tailored to your goals—such as enhancing formality or creativity. This customization ensures your writing meets your specific needs. For instance, you might set a Grammarly goal to enhance the conciseness of a formal report or use ProWritingAid to analyze pacing issues in a story and receive suggestions for where more action or dialogue could be added.

AI editors are also increasingly helpful for multilingual writing, offering suggestions to improve grammar and idiomatic usage in non-native languages. ChatGPT can rephrase or translate text, making it a valuable tool for global communication. For example, a sentence like *"I want my letter to sound polite"* can be rephrased as *"I would like my letter to convey politeness,"* ensuring grammatical accuracy and fluency.

By combining multiple tools, you can achieve higher-quality writing. For instance, start with Grammarly or ProWritingAid for basic grammar and style corrections, use ChatGPT for advanced rephrasing or brainstorming, and cross-check your final draft using both tools for additional insights.

However, it's important to remember that AI suggestions are not always perfect. They may not fully understand context or intended meaning, so reviewing edits carefully is essential to ensure alignment with your writing goals. Also, since these tools may misinterpret nuance, it's wise to double-check context-specific edits and ensure your tool adheres to privacy standards—especially for sensitive or confidential content.

Grammarly, ProWritingAid, and ChatGPT are powerful allies in refining your writing, whether it's an email, academic paper, or novel. By leveraging their unique strengths—grammar correction, stylistic enhancements, clarity improvements, and creative ideation—you can produce polished, professional, and engaging content. The key is to use these tools as collaborators while maintaining control over your voice and message.

Detecting AI-generated Text

Understanding the process of AI text generation is a crucial step in effectively detecting AI-generated content. AI writing tools, such as ChatGPT, Claude, or Gemini, are powered by large language models (LLMs) trained on massive datasets. These datasets comprise books, articles, websites, and other textual content, and the models operate based on statistical probabilities, predicting the most likely next word in a sequence given the input they receive. This knowledge enables you to recognize the distinctive features of AI-generated text.

The method of prediction gives AI its fluency and surface-level coherence. The text it generates often appears grammatically correct and well-structured. However, it's important to remember that this coherence is **synthetic**—it lacks the intentionality, emotional context, and subtle awareness that humans bring to language. This understanding enables you to distinguish between AI-generated text and human-written text.

As a result, AI-generated text tends to:

- Favor generic phrases and "safe" constructions.
- Avoid complexity unless prompted explicitly.
- Lack subtext, irony, or emotional progression.
- Struggle with abstract or ambiguous prompts that require lived experience or deep insight.

This foundational difference between how humans and machines write is the key to understanding why AI-generated writing, even when polished, often feels "off" to experienced readers. These subtle mismatches in tone, rhythm, emotional depth, and logic are what detection tools—and human editors—are trained to spot.

The ability to detect AI-generated content is not merely a technical curiosity—it's becoming a critical skill in education, publishing, journalism, content marketing, and even legal and scientific domains. As artificial intelligence becomes increasingly integrated into the creative and intellectual fields, concerns about **authenticity, accountability, and transparency** have also grown accordingly.

Let's explore several reasons why detecting AI-generated text matters:

• Academic Integrity and Education

In schools, colleges, and universities, students are increasingly using AI to draft essays, solve assignments, or even answer exams. While some institutions encourage the responsible use of AI for brainstorming or outlining, others strictly prohibit it. Educators need reliable ways to detect when a machine writes an essay—not to punish students arbitrarily, but to uphold the value of learning, critical thinking, and personal development. When AI-generated work is passed off as human effort, the result is **academic**

dishonesty, and detection becomes essential to prevent grade inflation and erosion of trust.

- **Publishing Ethics and Authorial Voice**

In the literary and nonfiction publishing world, readers expect a work to reflect the voice, experience, and values of the author whose name appears on the cover. This expectation becomes especially important in memoirs, personal essays, spiritual writings, and expert-driven books (e.g., medical, psychological, or historical works). If significant parts of such books are generated by AI and not disclosed, it raises questions about authorship, **intellectual honesty**, and the legitimacy of the content. Platforms like Amazon and Google Books are beginning to require disclosure of AI involvement, and failure to comply may lead to rejection, delisting, or loss of royalties.

- **Journalism and Truthfulness**

AI-written articles can introduce factual errors, misinterpret context, or spread misinformation—especially when not reviewed by trained journalists. In an era of widespread disinformation and propaganda, it is more crucial than ever to trace the origin of content, verify sources, and distinguish between fact-based reporting and synthetic content. Detecting AI text ensures that readers are not misled by content that only *appears* authoritative.

- **Professional Responsibility and Accountability**

In industries such as law, medicine, engineering, or policymaking, even minor errors in wording can have significant consequences. If AI produces a contract, legal argument, diagnosis explanation, or technical report, it must be identified, reviewed, and verified by a human expert. Detection tools help enforce these professional standards by ensuring that AI is used as a tool, not as a silent ghostwriter that bypasses human oversight.

- **Consumer Protection in E-Commerce and Marketing**

With the rise of AI-generated product descriptions, customer reviews, blog posts, and ad copy, consumers are being exposed to a growing volume of synthetic content. While AI can enhance efficiency, undisclosed use—mainly in emotionally manipulative or misleading ways—can erode consumer trust. Detecting such content helps ensure that what we read online has accountable authorship and meets ethical marketing standards.

- **Platform Compliance and Legal Risk**

Many content platforms, including self-publishing sites and freelance marketplaces, are adopting strict policies regarding the use of AI. These often include clauses requiring authors or contributors to disclose whether AI was used in any stage of content creation—from drafting to editing. Violating these terms can lead to demonetization, bans, or legal action. Detection tools are increasingly being used by platforms to enforce these policies automatically.

General Indicators of AI Text

Before diving into technical tools or statistical analysis, it's helpful to become familiar with the surface-level clues that often betray AI-generated content. These indicators may not be definitive proof, but they are practical red flags—especially for editors, educators, publishers, or anyone responsible for quality control.

Let's explore the most common and telling signs:

- **Repetitive Phrasing or Topic Looping**

AI language models tend to repeat words, phrases, or even ideas across paragraphs—especially in longer texts. This happens because the model prioritizes coherence and relevance by "staying on topic," often leading to overemphasis. A text might feel as if it's "spinning in place," circling back to the same concept using slightly different words.

This repetition often lacks strategic purpose. While human writers may repeat for rhetorical effect, AI repetition feels unintentional and mechanical. In narratives or persuasive writing, this can flatten emotional pacing and reduce impact.

• Overly Polished or Generic Fluency

Ironically, AI writing can appear *too smooth* at first glance. Sentences may be grammatically perfect and follow expected patterns, yet lack depth, variation, or a unique voice. It's the kind of writing that flows—but doesn't resonate. It feels like a composition that no real person would write, because it lacks the imperfections, surprises, and nuance of human thought.

• Flat Emotional Range

AI is capable of mimicking emotion, but often in a superficial way. Its emotional register tends to be either exaggerated or underdeveloped. For example, a loss story might transition directly from problem to resolution without any significant inner conflict, reflection, or transformation. The journey feels abrupt or too convenient, lacking the messiness and hesitation that usually accompany human experience.

In dialogue, AI characters might express feelings in overly direct or literal terms, avoiding subtlety or ambiguity. This flattens psychological realism.

• Unclear or Mismatched Tone

Because AI doesn't understand tone, it can slip into inappropriate registers. A casual blog post might suddenly sound academic; a romantic story might turn oddly sterile. These mismatches are often detectable to the human ear, which expects tonal consistency based on genre, audience, and emotional context.

AI models require explicit prompting to maintain a tone. Without this, they default to neutral or formal language—even when the subject calls for vibrancy, intimacy, or humor.

• Overuse of Transitions and Filler

AI-generated writing often leans heavily on connector words like "Moreover," "In conclusion," "On the other hand," or "It is important to note." These can be helpful—but when overused or placed awkwardly, they create an artificial rhythm. Sometimes the paragraph feels like it's following a template rather than a train of thought.

Human writers tend to transition more organically, often relying on intuition, rhythm, or imagery instead of formulaic linking.

- **Missing Specific Details or Lived Experience**

AI can summarize general knowledge but struggles to invent or recall the richness of sensory, cultural, or emotional memory. For instance, a passage might describe "a beautiful garden" or "a cold winter day" using standard vocabulary—but it rarely includes specific tactile impressions like the smell of dry leaves, the sting of icy wind on skin, or the awkward silence of a tense dinner.

- **Inconsistent Voice or Perspective**

In longer works, AI may shift perspective unintentionally (e.g., from third person to first person) or lose track of the tone it was initially instructed to use. This is because it doesn't "remember" as humans do—it relies on token length and context windows, which are limited in scope.

The result may be sudden changes in formality, unexplained shifts in narrative focus, and fluctuating sentence complexity or diction level. These general indicators are most useful when combined with your intuition and experience as a reader or writer. If a text feels too even, too safe, or emotionally detached, it may be generated by an AI. These signs don't replace technical tools—but they give you a human lens through which to begin your evaluation.

Linguistic Analysis

Linguistic analysis is one of the most intuitive and accessible methods for detecting AI-generated text. Unlike metadata or statistical methods, which require technical tools, linguistic patterns can often be identified through close reading and comparison. This type of analysis focuses on how a sentence is constructed: its rhythm, vocabulary, syntax, tone, and internal logic.

Language models are exceptionally good at mimicking fluency, but they still struggle with subtle qualities that characterize human writing—especially **voice, emotional pacing, narrative cohesion**, and **semantic precision**. Below are the key linguistic features to observe:

• **Repetition and Redundancy**

AI-generated text, especially in longer pieces, is prone to looping language—the unintentional repetition of words, phrases, or concepts. This happens because AI models prioritize coherence and topic relevance, which often results in the same idea being stated multiple times using similar structures.

• **Overuse of Formal or Neutral Tone**

AI models often default to a neutral, formal tone, regardless of context. While this can lend authority in professional settings, it usually comes across as emotionally flat, especially in narrative, persuasive, or conversational writing.

• **Lack of Contextual Understanding**

AI can generate grammatically correct responses that completely miss the meaning or context of the prompt. This is especially common when tasks involve cultural nuance, emotional intelligence, or domain-specific insight.

• **Unusual Sentence Structure**

AI often produces sentences that are grammatically correct but stylistically awkward. These may include overuse of passive voice, excessive subordination, or needlessly complex phrasing. These errors typically stem from the AI's attempt to maintain coherence across unfamiliar territory.

• **Semantic Incoherence or "Filler Logic"**

Sometimes, AI-generated text includes sentences that are grammatically sound but convey no meaningful information. These "filler" sentences feel like something is being said, but on closer inspection, they're vague or circular.

Linguistic analysis remains one of the most powerful tools for identifying AI-generated text. Because language models do not "understand" what they're saying, they frequently fall into repetitive structures, tonal inconsistencies, and superficial emotional gestures. Human writers, in contrast, embed intention, variation, and personal rhythm into their language.

By paying close attention to these stylistic and structural clues, editors and reviewers can often recognize AI content with surprising accuracy—even before applying technical tools.

Statistical Analysis

While linguistic analysis relies on human perception and close reading, statistical analysis uses measurable data to evaluate text patterns. These patterns—often invisible to casual readers—reveal underlying structures that distinguish machine-generated content from human-written prose. AI-generated text is shaped by algorithms trained to maximize *predictability* and *coherence*, resulting in a mathematical regularity that can be detected and quantified.

The most common statistical indicators include entropy, distribution uniformity, and unnatural word pairings. Let's explore how each can be used to flag AI content.

- **Entropy Detection**

Entropy in language refers to the level of randomness or unpredictability in word choice and sentence structure. Human writers, particularly skilled or creative ones, tend to vary their vocabulary, syntax, tone, and rhythm in a way that reflects personality, mood, or purpose. AI-generated text, by contrast, often exhibits lower entropy—meaning its structure is more predictable and conservative.

This happens because language models are trained to predict the most statistically likely next word. The output is often grammatically sound but overly safe and familiar. You may notice this in phrases that feel generic or in paragraphs that avoid risk, ambiguity, or original phrasing.

- **Uniform Distribution of Words**

AI-generated text often tries to balance word usage across a passage. It avoids repetition unless prompted, resulting in a flat, overly symmetrical rhythm. Human writers, however, use intentional variation: they may repeat a word for emphasis or mood, then break the pattern to create impact or emotional shift.

Word frequency analysis often reveals a more even distribution in AI-generated text, whereas human writing exhibits natural fluctuations and patterns. Excessive balance can make AI writing sound inoffensive but forgettable—what some call "blandly pleasant."

- **Unnatural Word Pairing and Semantic Tension**

AI models occasionally generate odd combinations of words—phrases that are grammatically correct but semantically jarring or emotionally contradictory. These often arise because the AI doesn't grasp deeper meaning; it simply matches probability distributions without understanding metaphors, tone, or sensory coherence.

Humans might use such paradoxes poetically, but when AI does it, it often feels unintentional and awkward. Human writers handle tension through metaphor, pacing, and implied meaning, not contradiction for its own sake.

- **Statistical Markers in Larger Documents**

AI writing patterns become evident in long-form documents. For example:

  - Sentence lengths tend to cluster around a narrow average (e.g., 12–15 words).
  - Paragraphs often follow identical structures: topic sentence → development → bland conclusion.
  - Vocabulary range is modest, often limited to 8th–10th grade reading level unless prompted otherwise.

Platforms like GPTZero, Writer.com's AI Content Detector, and OpenAI's classifier analyze these markers using backend models. Some tools even estimate the probability that a given text was generated by AI, often providing a corresponding confidence score.

Statistical analysis provides powerful, data-driven methods for detecting AI-generated text. While human writers introduce complexity, rhythm, unpredictability, and expressive tension, AI writing tends toward smooth, even, and safe outputs. By measuring entropy, word distributions, and phrase patterns, evaluators can flag synthetic text even when it appears well-written.

That said, statistical signals are strongest when combined with linguistic intuition and human review. AI detection, like any forensic process, benefits from multiple angles of inspection.

Specialized Detection Tools

While human intuition and statistical patterns can reveal many signs of AI-generated text, specialized detection tools bring technical precision and automated scale to the process. These tools are particularly useful in educational institutions, publishing platforms, and content moderation systems, where quick and consistent identification is essential.

Detection tools employ a range of technologies, including machine learning models, entropy measurement, stylistic fingerprinting, and metadata extraction. Each tool has its strengths and limitations, and its results should be interpreted in context rather than as absolute proof.

Let's explore the most well-known and widely used tools currently available:

- **OpenAI's AI Classifier**

Developed by the creators of ChatGPT, this tool was designed to distinguish between human-written and AI-generated text using a fine-tuned classifier trained on labeled data. The model assigns a probability score—ranging from "very unlikely AI" to "likely AI-generated."

• GPTZero

One of the most widely publicized detection tools, GPTZero, was explicitly created to identify AI-generated academic writing. It utilizes multiple indicators, including perplexity (a measure of how confusing a word is to a language model) and burstiness (the variance in sentence structure).

• Turnitin (AI Writing Detection)

Turnitin, a leader in plagiarism detection for decades, has integrated AI detection into its core services. Its updated algorithm compares student submissions against known AI patterns and identifies whether a machine likely wrote a paper.

• Copyleaks AI Content Detector

This platform offers both plagiarism detection and AI content classification. It supports multiple languages and is often used by publishers, universities, and corporate teams.

• Hugging Face Transformers & Analysis Models

Hugging Face provides access to a wide array of open-source language models and classifiers, including tools designed to detect whether a text aligns with known AI outputs.

• AI Text Classifiers Embedded in CMS and Platforms

Some publishing platforms and freelance marketplaces (such as Amazon KDP, Medium, Upwork, and Fiverr) are developing or embedding their AI detectors. These tools often work in the background and may flag suspicious content.

Tool Name	Purpose	Strengths	Limitations
OpenAI's AI Classifier	Detects whether text is AI- or human-generated using OpenAI's labeled training data	• Optimized for ChatGPT outputs • Simple UI • Built using OpenAI's internal data	• Low accuracy on short texts (<1,000 characters) • Struggles with edited AI content • No longer maintained as of 2024
GPTZero	Identifies AI-generated academic writing using perplexity and burstiness metrics	• Well-suited for academic use • Visual feedback and scoring • Analyzes structure and rhythm	• False positives with polished human writing • Less accurate for multilingual or mixed-source texts
Turnitin (AI Writing Detection)	Combines plagiarism and AI-use detection for student submissions	• Trusted by institutions • Integrated with LMS systems • Dual function: plagiarism + AI detection	• Subscription-only for institutions • Methodology undisclosed • Can be ambiguous with collaborative or hybrid content
Copyleaks AI Content Detector	Detects AI-generated and plagiarized content in academic, publishing, and enterprise contexts	• 30+ language support • Enterprise API • Business and academic suitability	• Paid for full features • Less accurate with short or rewritten content
Writer.com AI Content Detector	Ensures authenticity of marketing, editorial, and blog content	• Commercial writing focus • Prevents overuse of AI in drafts • Offers rewrite suggestions	• Less effective for long-form or literary works • Works best in English

Hugging Face Transformers & Classifiers	Developer-friendly AI alignment and detection tools for open-source experimentation	• Open-source transparency • Highly customizable • Ideal for research and model training	• Requires coding skills • Not designed for general users
AI Detectors in CMS & Marketplaces	Detects AI-generated content on platforms like Amazon KDP, Medium, Upwork, and Fiverr	• Native integration in publishing workflows • Flags before content goes live • Helps enforce platform rules	• Detection rules not visible to users • Thresholds and criteria may change without notice

Best Practices When Using Detection Tools

1. **Use Multiple Tools:**

It's crucial to avoid the pitfalls of bias or inconclusive results that can arise from relying on a single tool. A more comprehensive approach, such as combining platforms like GPTZero and Copyleaks, can significantly enhance the reliability of your assessment.

2. **Focus on Longer Samples:**

Most AI detectors struggle with short texts. Use blocks of at least 250–300 words for more accurate results.

3. **Contextual Judgment Matters:**

Detection scores should not be used in isolation to accuse, penalize, or reject content. Always pair them with human evaluation and a sense of proportion.

4. **Disclose When in Doubt:**

In professional settings, especially in academia, professional, or commercial environments where policies are tightening, it's crucial to maintain transparency. If AI is used in brainstorming, drafting, or rephrasing, it's best to mention this. This practice not only promotes transparency but also aligns with ethical standards. Specialized detection tools are becoming a cornerstone of ethical content review. As AI becomes more integrated into writing workflows, these tools help ensure accountability, transparency, and integrity. While none of them are perfect, they offer valuable support in evaluating authorship and identifying machine-generated patterns that even seasoned editors might miss.

Ultimately, the most effective approach is a hybrid one—using technology for detection and human judgment for interpretation.

Metadata and Time Analysis

In addition to analyzing language patterns and statistical properties, another approach to identifying AI-generated content involves non-linguistic evidence—specifically metadata and time-based indicators. These forensic clues exist beyond the words themselves and offer insight into *how*, *when*, and *with what tool* a text was produced.

While not always visible to the naked eye, these traces can play a significant role in formal investigations (e.g., in academia, legal proceedings, publishing disputes) or in automated content moderation systems.

- **Hidden Metadata and Embedded Markers**

Metadata refers to background information attached to a document or file. This might include timestamps, tool identifiers, author IDs, and formatting origins. In the context of AI-generated text, some systems embed markers—either deliberately (as a safeguard) or incidentally through tool use.

For example:

- o OpenAI has experimented with watermarking techniques designed to tag ChatGPT outputs with cryptographic signatures or subtle statistical quirks.

- Text generated via Google Docs, Notion AI, Jasper, or other platforms may contain file metadata indicating the creation tool or plugin used.
- Some content management systems (CMS) may automatically log the tools used for generation within their ecosystems.

In academic settings, a university may use internal software to verify whether a student's file was created in Microsoft Word or pasted from an online editor or AI tool. If file history shows that a 3,000-word essay was made in one minute and edited for only a few seconds, this can raise suspicion—even if the content looks polished.

When investigating suspected AI use, always request the original file. Please do not rely solely on pasted text, as it lacks crucial forensic data.

• **Time Analysis and Writing Speed**

AI systems can generate thousands of words in seconds. While this is part of their appeal for users, it can also serve as a powerful clue during authorship evaluation.

Time analysis involves reviewing how long it took to produce, format, and submit a text. While not definitive proof of AI use, implausibly fast creation speeds can serve as a strong signal—especially when paired with linguistic or stylistic red flags.

Common scenarios that raise suspicion:

- A student submits a 2,000-word essay less than five minutes after receiving the prompt.
- A freelance writer delivers five fully formatted, stylistically consistent articles in one hour.
- A newly registered account publishes an entire e-book within an hour of activation.

Google Docs, Microsoft Word (with autosave), and platforms like Notion track detailed editing timelines. Some publishing and learning platforms can track time-on-page and keystroke patterns. Internal logs on content platforms may show batch-pasted entries, indicating machine-generated origin.

Writers may use AI to create a first draft and then edit manually, making the creation timeline harder to judge. Proficient typists using templates may also produce content quickly, creating overlap with AI-style speed. Copying AI output into existing drafts or collaborating with co-authors can muddy the timeline.

- **Combining Metadata and Timing with Content Analysis**

While metadata and time data provide compelling circumstantial evidence, they are most effective when combined with linguistic and statistical review. For example:

- A file created in 45 seconds using an AI writing assistant, containing repetitive phrasing and low-entropy statistics, presents a strong case for AI authorship.
- A blog post submitted too quickly, with embedded markers matching GPT output and lacking personal anecdotes, raises multiple converging flags.
- In contrast, a file that took days to create, with varied stylistic elements and human revisions, is much harder to attribute to pure AI generation.

Metadata and time analysis offer a forensic lens on the authorship process—moving beyond the words on the page to examine *how* the text came into being. While not foolproof, these techniques are instrumental in institutional or legal settings where authorship matters.

Human Evaluation

While automated tools and statistical models are undoubtedly valuable, they cannot fully replace the irreplaceable value of human discernment. Skilled readers—editors, teachers, publishers, and experienced writers—possess a sensitivity to language that no algorithm can replicate. They notice subtle shifts in tone, rhythm, logic, and emotional depth that signal whether a person or a machine created a piece.

Human evaluation is especially critical in gray zones, where:

- AI was used only partially (e.g., to draft a paragraph or brainstorm headlines)
- A human writer has heavily edited machine-generated output
- The text's subject demands emotional insight, philosophical nuance, or lived experience.

Let's examine the unique advantages of human evaluation in AI detection:

- **Detection of Voice Inconsistency and Style Drift**

Human writers tend to have a recognizable voice—a distinct style of structuring thoughts, choosing words, and pacing sentences. AI-generated text often lacks this authorship fingerprint or changes tone inconsistently across sections.

A trained editor can identify sudden shifts in sentence complexity or tone, moments where the narrative feels emotionally disconnected, and a lack of rhythm, inner logic, or cohesion over time.

For example, in a memoir or personal essay, a human reviewer may notice that while some passages feel authentic and vivid, others sound hollow, vague, or overly formal. These inconsistencies may suggest AI involvement.

- **Evaluation of Emotional Realism and Narrative Depth**

One of AI's most significant weaknesses is the inability to portray complex emotions in a psychologically authentic way. While it can describe sadness, grief, joy, or trauma using correct language, it often does so without emotional texture or evolution.

A human evaluator can identify a lack of emotional progression (e.g., skipping from pain to resolution too quickly), the absence of metaphor, ambiguity, or introspective hesitation, as well as dialogues that feel flat or robotic. In fiction, creative nonfiction, or introspective writing, human evaluation is critical. AI tends to write about feelings—it does not *feel* them. Human reviewers instinctively recognize this gap.

- **Content-Specific Knowledge and Cultural Sensitivity**

AI often makes factual mistakes or cultural missteps that go unnoticed in machine-based detection tools. A human expert, however, can catch misused idioms or anachronistic phrases, as well as confusing or illogical explanations in technical writing, and cultural insensitivity or superficial treatment of complex topics.

For instance, a reader with domain expertise might realize that an AI-written article about a scientific discovery misrepresents the timeline, confuses terminology, or misunderstands the core hypothesis. These contextual errors often require subject-matter familiarity, not just grammar checks.

- **Recognition of Formulaic Structure**

AI-generated content often follows predictable patterns of rhetoric. It starts with a broad generalization, follows with neatly structured subpoints, and concludes with a summary that restates earlier points. There's nothing inherently wrong with this—but in specific genres, it can make the content feel sterile, mechanical, or overly structured.

Human evaluators can sense when structure feels too "template-like", when conclusions are vague or redundant, and when introductions lack originality or personality. Especially in essays, thought leadership, storytelling, or personal writing, readers often value narrative tension or the willingness to break convention—traits that AI lacks unless specifically instructed to do so.

- **Flexible Contextual Judgment**

AI detection tools are rule-based. Human judgment, however, can take context into account:

  - Was the text written by a child or a non-native speaker?
  - Was the tone deliberately neutral for the audience?
  - Could the author be intentionally mimicking a formal or AI style?

A good human evaluator does not rely solely on red flags. They evaluate proportionally, intuitively, and with fairness. They ask,

"Does this feel real?"—a question no algorithm can answer definitively.

Human evaluation remains the **gold standard** for detecting AI-generated content, particularly in nuanced, emotionally charged, or ethically sensitive domains. While detection tools can flag patterns and speed up review, only humans can truly understand what writing *feels like*, what it *means*, and whether it resonates with the complexity of human thought.

In the evolving relationship between human and machine, this ability to interpret meaning and emotion is our most significant advantage—and the most reliable compass when technology alone can't decide.

Emerging Techniques

As artificial intelligence becomes more sophisticated, so too must the methods for detecting its output. The traditional markers—like repetition, formal tone, and low entropy—are becoming less visible in newer, more refined AI models. As a result, researchers and developers are now pursuing next-generation techniques rooted in deep learning, computational forensics, and statistical modeling.

These emerging methods aim not just to *guess* whether AI generated a text, but to trace its origin, match it to specific models, or analyze hidden patterns that betray its synthetic nature. Let's explore the most promising developments:

- **Neural Network Forensics**

Neural network forensics is a growing field that studies the fingerprints left by AI models in their outputs. Much like a painter's brushstrokes or a composer's harmonic tendencies, each AI model tends to leave behind subtle but consistent patterns that reflect its training data, architecture, and internal rules.

For example, GPT-based models often favor specific sentence constructions or phrasings that are statistically overrepresented in their training data. Other models may exhibit unique punctuation habits, paragraph segmentation patterns, or a preference for specific transitional phrases.

Researchers are developing algorithms that compare the statistical "texture" of a document to the known signatures of popular models (like GPT-3, GPT-4, Claude, or LLaMA), detect patterns in **syntactic structure**, **semantic flow**, or even **semantic drift**—the gradual loss of meaning across paragraphs and use adversarial training to teach detectors how to distinguish between specific model outputs based on nuanced linguistic traits.

A forensic linguist examining leaked documents may be able to determine whether they were written by a human expert, an AI assistant, or a combination of both—by comparing the document to known model fingerprints.

- **Reverse Model Matching**

Reverse model matching involves comparing the unknown text against known AI outputs to determine the likely origin. Rather than relying on general features like entropy or tone, this technique employs a model-based comparison, asking: *Does this text statistically resemble content generated by GPT-4? By Claude? By an earlier model?*

This is especially useful when platforms suspect plagiarism or uncredited AI use, legal disputes arise over authorship or originality, or AI-generated misinformation is spreading across social media. Some platforms are developing internal libraries of generated content to use as baselines. Over time, this may evolve into model-specific databases, allowing for the detection not only of AI origin but *also which* model is likely to have produced a given text.

- **Stylometry Enhanced with Machine Learning**

Stylometry—the analysis of writing style—has been employed for centuries in literary studies, authorship attribution, and the detection of fraud. In the AI age, stylometry is being enhanced with machine learning to detect deviations from a known author's typical voice, abrupt changes in complexity, rhythm, or lexical choices, as well as inconsistencies in punctuation, verb tense, or idiomatic usage.

For example, if an academic paper submitted by a student drastically differs in style from their previous work, machine-assisted stylometry can highlight those contrasts. These tools can now be trained to distinguish machine-written variance from natural human evolution in writing style.

- **Multi-Layered Probability Scoring**

Emerging tools are moving away from binary judgments ("AI" or "human") and toward multi-dimensional scoring models that assess:

  - Language fluency
  - Lexical entropy
  - Stylistic uniformity
  - Semantic coherence
  - Contextual sensitivity
  - Emotional realism

These models output probability matrices rather than yes/no answers, offering a confidence range for each dimension. For example:

- 92% likely AI-generated based on entropy
- 75% likely AI due to low contextual responsiveness
- 30% likely human due to strong emotional nuance in specific paragraphs

This kind of nuanced scoring helps reviewers understand the degree of AI involvement, especially in hybrid or co-authored texts.

- **AI vs. AI: Detection by Counter-Models**

Interestingly, one of the most promising directions in AI detection is the use of counter-AI models specifically trained to recognize their kind. These detectors are adversarial models—built by training one neural network to generate content, and another to identify whether that content came from AI.

This adversarial approach is already being used in image detection (e.g., deepfake detection), and its adaptation to text is advancing rapidly. In the future, content platforms may deploy these detectors invisibly, analyzing all submissions in real-time and flagging those with high AI-generation probability.

Limitations and Ethical Considerations

The ability to detect AI-generated text has become more advanced, but it also brings a set of ethical, cultural, and practical challenges that can't be ignored. False positives remain a concern, particularly when the tools are applied to edited texts, non-native writing, or formulaic content such as legal briefs or technical manuals. These errors can have consequences if institutions rely on them too heavily, especially without transparency. People should always have the right to understand how decisions about authorship are made, especially when such judgments could affect careers, academic standing, or creative ownership. Digging into metadata, analyzing patterns of writing behavior, or tracking stylistic fingerprints without consent touches on privacy boundaries that must be treated with care.

As AI becomes a collaborator rather than a simple tool, our approaches to detection must evolve. It's not enough to look for superficial signs anymore—language models are too sophisticated for that. Instead, we're entering an era of more refined, model-aware techniques, such as neural forensics, adversarial analysis, and stylometry. But these tools aren't meant to punish. They serve a greater purpose: protecting the human aspects of creativity, the trust between writer and reader, and the integrity of authorship. Behind every flagged passage is a question about what it means to create, and how we recognize something as genuinely human.

The issue isn't the existence of AI-generated content—it's the loss of clarity when we no longer know who is speaking. That's why detection matters. It's not about control or gatekeeping, but about maintaining space for truth, voice, and intention in our written communication. Every time we detect AI-written content, we're not just identifying a technical artifact—we're asking whether the text reflects a person's mind or the invisible hand of a machine.

And while we embrace AI's role in drafting, revising, and inspiring, we must be cautious about its potential misuse. Not every AI-supported piece of writing is a deception, just as not every human-written piece is authentic. The point is not to draw rigid lines, but to reflect on the purpose behind the words. When AI is used with honesty and awareness, it becomes part of the creative process. When it's used to imitate or deceive, it undermines the very foundation of trust.

Detection becomes a quiet force for balance. It helps institutions uphold fairness, offers readers a tool for critical engagement, and invites writers to consider their methods more deeply. Most importantly, it defends the delicate, irreplaceable qualities of human storytelling—messy, emotional, surprising, and alive. In an age where AI can mimic tone and structure flawlessly, it's the human inconsistencies that shine through.

We must keep questioning. What counts as writing now? Is shaping, guiding, or editing less creative than composing every word from scratch? What about using AI like one might use a ghostwriter or editor? These are not questions with easy answers, and they shouldn't be rushed. They're invitations to stay curious. Because at the center of it all, writing is still about voice—not just the recognizable turn of phrase, but the pulse of a thought, the quiet flash of insight, the rhythm of feeling that machines can't truly imitate.

So rather than ending with certainty, this chapter ends with an invitation. As AI becomes part of our literary ecosystem, let's meet it with awareness, not fear. Let's hold space for questions. Let's stay honest about our tools and deliberate about our choices. And let's never forget what makes us human in the act of writing—not perfection, but presence.

Is AI Good or Bad for Authors?

This topic has sparked endless speculation and debate. But watching some people lash out—dragging even public figures into a war against AI—I can say with confidence that AI use is expanding. No matter how fiercely experts argue, the truth is that **AI is empowering many businesses to operate more efficiently, giving us greater control over our tasks and time.**

When I reflect on my education—and that of my children—I can confidently say that I regret the amount of time we wasted on absurd projects, irrelevant subjects, and endless tests. The many hours we spent studying the works of communist leaders in school proved useless in real life. My daughter once spent weeks constructing a model of an offshore oil rig—yet how did that help her? Why would she need to understand the structure of an oil platform? Some people hate writing essays. Others are not interested in physics.

When teachers express concern that students are using AI to complete their homework, it's important to remember that these students are not necessarily taking the easy way out. Instead, they're demonstrating their ability to master modern tools and access a wealth of information that was previously out of reach. We've been using computers for at least a third of a century, and yet there are still people who have no idea how to operate one. I spent hours learning to write neatly by hand, while my grandchildren learned to type on their iPads and other digital toys before even starting school. This is just one example of how AI is democratizing access to information, empowering people to learn and create in ways once unimaginable.

Some doctors feel offended that AI can now outperform them in diagnostic accuracy. But they conveniently ignore the high death rates caused by medical errors. In April 2025, the world witnessed the birth of the first baby conceived through a fully automated, AI-controlled IVF (In Vitro Fertilization) procedure. A 40-year-old woman in Guadalajara, Mexico, gave birth to a healthy baby boy. The fertilization process was performed using an AI-operated robotic system developed by Conceivable Life Sciences.

This system carried out all 23 steps of intracytoplasmic sperm injection (ICSI), including selecting and immobilizing sperm, and injecting it into eggs, all without human hands. The robot was remotely operated via a laptop from New York and Mexico. Out of five eggs, four fertilized successfully, and one led to the successful pregnancy.

This event does not mean the baby was genetically designed or artificially created. The child was conceived using traditional IVF with human egg and sperm—but the delicate fertilization process was automated using AI and robotics.

In a separate case, another AI breakthrough called STAR (Sperm Track and Recovery), developed at Columbia University, helped doctors locate a single viable sperm cell in a man with azoospermia (complete absence of sperm in semen). This led to a successful pregnancy after nearly 20 years of infertility.

These developments mark a significant step forward in reproductive medicine. AI is helping standardize delicate IVF procedures, reducing human error, and potentially making treatment more accessible and efficient. However, these technologies are still under evaluation and are not yet widely available.

There are countless examples where the limitations of the human brain—in creativity, construction, analysis, and logic—make it impossible to perform tasks that AI can complete in seconds. And yet, AI is a human creation. That's precisely why it's essential to acknowledge this reality and understand: AI is not a human brain, nor is it consciousness, nor is it some mystical being. It's a tool—a system that processes information, gathers signals, sorts, analyzes, and utilizes them faster and more efficiently than we ever could. And that's a wonderful thing.

There was a time when mobile phones didn't exist. Now, smartphones serve as both computers and cameras. The image quality of an ordinary mobile phone now surpasses that of the most expensive cameras used to produce images. I remember the submission requirements for photographs when you wanted to publish in a prestigious magazine: every image had to be submitted as a color slide. Early digital images were rejected outright, and many photographers were denied publication.

When the profession of graphic designer emerged, artificially created images and videos began to appear. These were widely used in advertising and film production. Today, many scenes in popular movies are entirely artificial. And yet no one protests that the movie isn't "real" just because it wasn't filmed in an actual location at an exact time. Countless video games are nothing more than complex products of digital programming—yet no one complains that they're not rooted in real-world experience.

So why is artificial intelligence met with such resistance by some people—especially among the older generation? Perhaps because the word *intelligence* has always been considered a uniquely human trait. Many scientists even deny that animals possess intelligence. Maybe the very name *artificial intelligence* was a misstep—perhaps even offensive to those who never developed or learned to use their intellect to its fullest. Just as typewriters, rotary phones, old televisions, and outdated refrigerators have disappeared, many of today's digital tools and programs will eventually be replaced by newer, better, and more advanced technologies.

AI-generated text, when used ethically and transparently, can be remarkably beneficial. The real question isn't whether it's inherently "good" or "bad"—but rather how it's used, in what context, and whether it aligns with ethical standards. Problems arise not from the tool itself, but from deception, plagiarism, or attempts to pass off machine output as entirely human work without disclosure.

AI isn't here to replace human creativity—it's here to enhance it. When integrated thoughtfully, it becomes a powerful partner in communication, education, research, and the arts. The key lies in intent, transparency, and the ability to adapt. And as with every new wave of technology throughout history, those who learn to work with it—not against it—will shape the future.

When AI-Generated text is beneficial:

1. **Efficiency and Productivity**

AI can handle repetitive tasks, draft initial content, or quickly summarize large amounts of information. This saves time for professionals like writers, researchers, and marketers.

2. **Accessibility**

AI helps make information accessible to a broader audience by generating translations, simplifying complex content, and tailoring material for different audiences.

3. **Creativity Boost**

AI can spark new ideas or suggest directions for writers experiencing creative blocks, inspiring us to explore new territories and think outside the box.

4. **Cost-Effective Content Creation**

For small businesses or individuals, AI provides a cost-efficient way to generate professional-quality content.

5. **Personalization at Scale**

AI can customize text for different users, such as tailored email campaigns or customer service responses, to provide a more personalized experience.

When AI-Generated text becomes problematic:

1. **Lack of Transparency**

Issues arise when AI-generated text is presented as entirely human-written, especially in contexts where authenticity or originality is critical (e.g., academic essays, journalism).

2. **Over-Reliance**

A heavy reliance on AI can stifle human creativity and critical thinking, rendering people less skilled at writing and problem-solving.

3. **Quality and Accuracy**

AI may produce factually incorrect, biased, or low-quality content, particularly when handling nuanced or sensitive topics.

4. **Ethical Violations**

Using AI-generated content without proper attribution or in contexts where originality is valued (e.g., art, literature) can raise ethical concerns.

5. **Job Displacement**

The overuse of AI in specific industries could lead to a decline in demand for human writers, editors, or translators.

The question isn't whether AI text is "bad," but instead how to use it responsibly and ethically. Here are some ways to strike a balance:

- **Be Transparent:** Disclose when AI was used, particularly in contexts such as academia, journalism, or the arts. Transparency fosters trust and helps avoid ethical dilemmas, making us feel reassured about the authenticity of the content we consume.
- **Combine Human and AI Efforts:** Utilize AI as a tool to support creativity and productivity, rather than as a replacement for human input.
- **Focus on Quality:** Continually review and refine AI-generated content to ensure accuracy, relevance, and alignment with your goals.
- **Educate and Empower Users:** Teach people how to use AI effectively and ethically to enhance their skills rather than replace them.
- **Value Human Creativity:** Remember that AI cannot replicate the depth of human emotion, intuition, or cultural context. Use it as a complement, not a substitute.

By approaching AI as a collaborator and maintaining ethical practices, we can harness its benefits while preserving the value of human creativity and authenticity.

When and How to Bring in a Professional Human Editor

In the era of advanced AI tools and automated grammar checkers, the irreplaceable value of professional human editors shines through. Writers across all disciplines, whether they are crafting a novel, academic paper, business report, or blog, can significantly enhance their work with the expertise of a professional editor. This guide explores the key considerations for when to engage and how to do so effectively.

Developmental editing, which focuses on the overall structure and big picture, is a key stage in the writing process. If you're working on a manuscript and are unsure about its structure, tone, or overall direction, a developmental editor can be invaluable. They can help shape the narrative or argument, identify gaps in content or logic, and ensure the work aligns with the intended audience's expectations. This professional guidance can significantly enhance the quality of your writing.

This stage is ideal for authors who have completed a draft but feel it's not yet cohesive or polished enough for publication. For example, when I was ready to write a book in English about the Soviet mentality, understanding the extreme complexity and multifaceted nature of the topic, it was essential for me to receive feedback not only from an expert in politics and history but also from someone with professional editing skills. That person turned out to be my friend, a lawyer by education and an exceptionally unique intellectual. He not only edited my text, correcting stylistic and grammatical errors, but also gave suggestions on where to expand the topic, where to rearrange paragraphs, and so on.

Once you've written the first draft, substantive editing focuses on refining the content itself. This stage ensures that

- ideas are clearly and logically presented,
- sections transition smoothly from one to the next,
- any redundancies or inconsistencies are eliminated.

Bringing in an editor at this stage is especially useful for technical or academic writing, where precision and clarity are critical.

It's fascinating to note that the potential of AI editing in this area is growing significantly each month, serving as a powerful supportive tool in the writing process.

One curious case happened when I was working on a book about girls' health. The topic was about genes that influence the formation of embryos along female and male lines. My text mentioned several genes. During editing, the AI suggested I add two more gene names that are important for the development of future boys and girls. And that's when I started to laugh.

When I created an academic book about hormone therapy a few years ago, I had used data from the only scientific article on that topic, and I even included its title in the list of references. I didn't use AI while working on that book. The article wasn't new and wasn't particularly popular in medical circles.

Then I started a dialogue with the AI, asking what it knew about the data it had provided, since I had read the source a few years ago. I asked the AI to give me the title of that article. Meanwhile, I began searching through my electronic files to locate it. Imagine my surprise when I saw the same article title appear in the AI window. Naturally, the AI did it faster than I did.

But what pleasantly surprised me at that moment was that the AI behaved like a professional editorial advisor, suggesting I include additional data in the context of the new book. I explained to the AI that the book on girls' health is not an academic project and, therefore, does not require such details or references to sources. In other words, I made it clear to the AI that my text is intended for a broad audience, most of whom do not have a medical background.

I will also share a critical point with you: you can request AI to edit from a professional perspective. What does this mean? You can assign a task by asking it to review a text "from the point of view of a doctor," "from the point of view of an engineer," "from the point of view of a police officer," and so on. For instance, if your text contains scenes related to specific professions, AI can provide valuable insights and suggestions from the perspective of professionals in those fields.

To illustrate this, I'll give a simple example. I am a doctor by training, and I can't calmly watch movies about doctors or scenes where doctors provide medical care. Why? Because I immediately notice a multitude of glaring mistakes. I see how blood pressure is mismeasured, how emergency care is provided inaccurately, how childbirth is shown unrealistically, and how medications are administered the wrong way. And then I get frustrated, wondering why the filmmakers didn't invest in a medical expert to teach the actors how to act realistically. There are very few films that get these details right. But this applies to any profession.

When editing a book, everything must be in harmony: the era, the interior descriptions, the characters' behavior, their actions, and so on. A literary character from the 1930s, for example, cannot be using a mobile phone—you'd agree with that. A professional editor's task is precisely to catch these kinds of inconsistencies. But most editors do not have education or training in other professions. That's why, today, thanks to AI, it's possible to improve the quality of texts without involving additional professionals.

Generally, everyone should proceed according to their means, as manual editing is not inexpensive. My work with some editors left me disappointed because their level of editing turned out to be lower than mine. Because of the unprofessionalism of a few, I lost money. To determine whether a particular editor meets your expectations, conduct a test—ask them to edit a few pages of your book. If you're satisfied with the editing, then you can continue working with that editor.

Before submission or publication, copyediting ensures that your work is polished and professional. This stage focuses on grammar, punctuation, and spelling, as well as sentence structure, word choice, and consistency in formatting, terminology, and style.

If your work is ready for submission, be it to a publisher, academic journal, or online audience, a copyeditor will help you make a strong impression.

Proofreading is the final step before publication. At this stage, an editor checks for typos and minor errors, as well as formatting issues that may have arisen during layout, and the accuracy of details such as page numbers, headers, and captions.

This stage is essential for printed materials or finalized digital formats where even small mistakes can detract from the work's professionalism.

How to Choose the Right Professional Editor

1. Determine the Type of Editing You Need. Identify your current stage in the writing process and the specific type of editing your work requires. Developmental editing requires a more collaborative approach, whereas copyediting or proofreading is more detail-oriented and technical.

2. Look for Relevant Expertise. Editors often specialize in particular fields or genres. For example:

- Fiction editors may focus on character development, pacing, and dialogue.
- Academic editors are familiar with citation styles and subject-specific nuances.
- Business editors excel at crafting clear and persuasive reports or proposals.

Choose an editor whose expertise aligns with your project's goals.

3. Review Credentials and Samples. A professional editor's portfolio and references can give you insight into their skills and reliability. Don't hesitate to ask for a sample edit or examples of past work to ensure their style matches your expectations.

4. Communicate Your Expectations Before hiring, clarify:

- Your timeline and deadlines.
- The scope of work (e.g., full manuscript, specific chapters, or sections).
- Your preferred style guide (e.g., APA, Chicago, MLA).

Effective communication ensures a smooth and productive collaboration.

Benefits of Hiring a Professional Human Editor

1. **A Fresh Perspective**. Even the most skilled writers can become too close to their work, making it difficult to spot errors or weaknesses. A professional editor brings an objective viewpoint, offering constructive feedback that improves the overall quality of your work.

2. **Enhanced Clarity and Readability** Editors excel at making complex ideas accessible to the intended audience. They can rework dense passages, clarify technical jargon, and ensure that the tone matches the purpose.

3. **Improved Professionalism**. Whether you're submitting a manuscript to a publisher or sending a report to stakeholders, a professionally edited document signals attention to detail and a commitment to quality.

4. **Time Savings**. While self-editing is essential, it can be time-consuming and may not catch all issues. A professional editor streamlines the process, allowing you to focus on other priorities.

In some cases, professional editing may not be necessary. For example:

- Early brainstorming sessions, where ideas are still being generated.
- Informal or personal writing with no intention of publication.
- Small-scale projects with limited budgets, where AI tools or peer reviews may suffice.

However, for critical or high-stakes writing, investing in a professional editor is often a worthwhile expense.

Knowing when and how to bring in a professional human editor can elevate your writing to new heights. By understanding your needs, selecting the right editor, and maintaining open communication, you can ensure that your work is polished, professional, and effectively achieves its purpose. Whether you're a seasoned author or a first-time writer, the guidance of a skilled editor can make all the difference.

Part 4: Designing for Success

When I decided to publish my book in 2010, the most difficult part turned out to be formatting the file—that is, preparing it for print, considering the book's dimensions, page order, and creating a proper cover. There were programs for this purpose, but they often required manual intervention from a specialist. Formatting a 200-page book could sometimes take up to a month. Thus, it was not enough to hire an editor to check the text—you also needed to find a specialist who could create a ready-to-publish book layout. This specialist, often referred to as a book designer, plays a crucial role in the book production process, ensuring that the book is visually appealing and meets industry standards. Even the most interesting book will go unnoticed if it is presented in a highly dull and unremarkable way.

Book Sizes and Cover Design Through the Ages

If you've ever had the chance to visit libraries (or museums) and see old books, you've likely noticed the differences in size and title pages. Fonts have also evolved, becoming more readable and user-friendly.

Let's take a brief look at the past, which always preserves some fascinating facts. Let's discuss book sizes, as you will also need to choose a size when publishing your book, including in electronic format. This choice is not just a technicality, but a crucial decision that can significantly impact the reader's experience and the book's marketability.

Book dimensions have undergone a fascinating evolution over the centuries, adapting to changes in technology, materials, and intended use. In ancient times and the Middle Ages, scrolls and codices were the predominant forms of writing. For instance, in Ancient Egypt, Greece, and Rome, texts were inscribed on papyrus scrolls. These could be several meters long, but their width was limited by the material (usually 20–30 cm). With the transition to codices (the prototype of the modern book), sizes varied from miniature to enormous—up to 70 cm (often in the case of Bibles). Miniature codices were used for prayer and travel, while large ones were usually kept in churches and on lecterns.

With the invention of the printing press in the 15th century, sizes began to standardize. During the Renaissance, three types of books emerged: octavo books, which were small pocket-sized editions (15–20 cm) suitable for personal reading; quarto books, which were medium-sized (20–30 cm) and popular with a broad audience; and folio books, which were large (30–40 cm) and typically featured religious or scholarly texts.

The first authentic pocket editions (10–15 cm) appeared in the 17th century with the rise of secular literature. Larger formats continued to be used for encyclopedias, maps, and religious texts.

The standard book sizes we still use today (12–25 cm) emerged in the 19th century, particularly for fiction, which was rapidly gaining popularity at the time.

In the mid-20th century, standard formats for books were introduced:

- **Pocket Book (10–18 cm):** Pocket-sized editions.
- **Trade Paperback (20–25 cm):** Popular editions, especially for fiction.
- **Coffee Table Books (30 cm and above):** Albums and photo books.

Electronic book formats, a significant milestone in the history of book production, emerged in the 19th century, coinciding with the development of digital tools for reading them. This digital revolution has not only changed the way we read but also the way books are produced and distributed.

- **E-books:** PDF or EPUB formats do not have physical dimensions but are optimized for screens (usually 6–10 inches).

- **Mini books:** A return of miniature editions for collectors.
- **Desktop books:** Large-format books for art and design enthusiasts.

We'll discuss formatting and choosing book sizes in more detail later in this section of the book.

Books with beautiful covers began to be actively published during the Renaissance (14th–16th centuries), when the development of printing and book design made it possible to mass-produce literature more efficiently.

In the Middle Ages (up to the 14th century), books were handwritten by monks and decorated with miniatures, ornaments, and gold leaf. Covers were made of leather, wood, and metal, and adorned with carvings or precious stones—but such books were rare and expensive.

In the Renaissance Period, the invention of the printing press (Gutenberg, 1440s) allowed for mass book production, but even then, covers were often decorated by hand. Leather bindings with embossing, patterns, and gilding became common.

In the 17th and 18th centuries, the growing availability of books to a broader audience led to the emergence of paper covers with illustrations. These books had simpler designs, though luxurious editions continued to feature gold embossing and artistic engravings.

The 19th century marked the flourishing of illustration. This period saw a real breakthrough. With the advancement of lithography and color printing, vibrant, illustrated covers became possible. Books began to be seen as works of art. Many renowned authors, such as Charles Dickens, published their works with exquisite covers.

The 20th century brought the commercialization and mass production of books. The emergence of inexpensive materials and offset printing technology made color covers a standard. During this time, cover design emerged as a powerful marketing tool, and book design evolved into a distinct art form.

Today, book covers are created using digital technologies. They are not only a way to attract attention but also a means of expressing the author's style or the theme of the book. Design is often tailored to specific markets and target audiences.

The Power of a Great Cover

The era of monotonous book covers is over. We live in a world of color photography, colorful digital images, and color television. There are now programs that can colorize old black-and-white photos and films. This has altered my perspective on the past. I was fascinated to see my ancestors in color. They became more real.

When you walk into a store, you look at products with your eyes—don't you? When shopping online, you also rely on your visual system. In other words, your first contact with a product is visual.

Now, let's experiment. Visit a public library and peruse the book covers in the section of your favorite genre. Many of the authors' names may be unfamiliar to you. What would you notice first when choosing a book to read? Some may pay attention to the title. But far more important is the cover, which has the power to either draw you in or push you away.

You can run the same experiment with e-books. Go to any online bookstore. All books are presented as images, not just titles. Which book catches your eye even before you read the title or the author's name? Of course, someone might say that the cover of their favorite author's book doesn't matter to them. That's a different kind of choice—one based on trust in that writer's work. However, suppose you aspire to become a writer, especially a bestselling author. In that case, it's crucial to bring your book as close to perfection as possible, including selecting or creating the ideal cover.

If you plan to print your books through publishing agencies, the task of creating a cover usually falls on them. Sometimes they consult the authors, sometimes they don't—it depends on the agency's attitude toward authors, their policies, and so on. Naturally, it's nice when the author's wishes and feedback are considered. In my case, they always sent the cover for approval, and sometimes I had to ask them to change details that were too obvious or distracting.

When it comes to selling books, **first impressions matter**. In a market saturated with millions of titles, your book cover is not just a design element—it's your most important marketing tool. It's the visual gateway to your story, message, or expertise, and it plays a pivotal role in attracting potential readers, setting the stage for the narrative that unfolds.

In today's digital and physical marketplaces, potential readers often make snap judgments about a book in mere seconds. Whether they're browsing online or perusing the shelves of a bookstore, the cover is the first thing they see. A striking, professional design can capture attention instantly, while a poorly designed cover may be ignored or dismissed, regardless of the content's quality inside.

A book cover is a visual shorthand for the story or subject matter. It's not just a design, it's a powerful tool that conveys the tone, genre, and quality of the work. For example, a thriller with a dark, mysterious cover signals suspense and intrigue, while a vibrant, colorful design for a children's book suggests fun and adventure. Aligning your cover with the expectations of your target audience is crucial for making a strong first impression.

For authors, particularly those building a career, the **book cover is an extension of their brand**. A cohesive and visually appealing cover design not only attracts readers to a single title but also builds recognition across multiple works. Think about authors like J.K. Rowling or Stephen King — their books are instantly recognizable because of consistent branding elements.

I created my brand logo in lavender color. To my great surprise, the publishing agency that began releasing my books used this color so that my followers and readers could easily recognize my books even by the color of the cover. For all the books, the cover color was harmonized with lavender or close to it.

Whether you're a debut author or a seasoned writer, your cover should reflect the essence of your unique voice and style. Elements such as typography, imagery, and color schemes contribute to creating a visual identity that readers can associate with your brand. For nonfiction authors, a strong cover can also enhance your credibility as an expert in your field, making it easier to market yourself and your book as authoritative resources.

In online bookstores, where covers are often displayed as thumbnails, an eye-catching design can make the difference between someone clicking on your book or scrolling past it. The **cover is a crucial factor in discoverability**—a well-designed cover that resonates with your target audience can improve click-through rates, leading to higher sales.

Moreover, covers are critical for marketing materials. They appear in advertisements, social media posts, email campaigns, and promotional banners. A visually compelling cover can make your marketing efforts more effective by drawing attention and encouraging engagement. Even word-of-mouth recommendations can be influenced by a memorable cover, as readers are more likely to share a book that looks appealing.

Your cover sets the tone for what readers can expect inside. A mismatch between the cover and the content can lead to disappointment and negative reviews, even if the book itself is well-written. For example, a romance novel with a cover that looks like a horror story might attract the wrong audience, leading to unmet expectations and lower ratings.

Investing in a professional designer who understands genre conventions and market trends is vital. They can create a cover that not only looks great but also aligns with reader expectations, ensuring your book finds its intended audience.

Fair or not, **readers often judge the quality of a book by its cover**. A polished, professional cover signals that the author cares about their work and has invested in delivering a high-quality product. Conversely, a poorly designed cover can give the impression of amateurism, regardless of the quality of the writing.

This perception extends to publishers and retailers as well. Independent bookstores, libraries, and even online platforms may be more likely to feature a book with a strong, professional cover, increasing its visibility and credibility.

And now a few tips on how to choose a cover for your book:

• **Research Your Genre:** Study successful books in your genre to identify common design elements and trends. This will help you understand the current trends in cover design within your genre.

• **Hire a Professional Designer:** While DIY options exist, a skilled designer can elevate your cover to a professional level. Often, cover templates or stock images are primitive. Authors who design their covers—or inexperienced designers—tend to choose images based on popularity: "this cover is trending, so let's go with it" (a phenomenon similar to YouTube thumbnails). And when you open a page of books within a specific genre, it sometimes becomes immediately apparent that the covers are very similar—practically clones of one another. This kind of cloning is noticeable in the *word puzzle books* section.

• **Keep It Simple:** Avoid cluttered designs; a clean, focused layout is more effective.

• **Test Your Cover:** Use surveys or focus groups to gather feedback on potential designs before finalizing. I often consult with people in my circle who have marketing experience.

• **Think About Thumbnails:** Ensure your cover looks good in smaller sizes, as it will often be displayed as a thumbnail online.

Your book cover is more than just an aesthetic choice; it's a strategic marketing tool that can significantly impact your book's success. By investing time and resources into creating a professional, audience-appropriate cover, you set the stage for higher sales, better discoverability, and a stronger connection with your readers. Remember, in the competitive world of publishing, your cover is your book's best chance to make a lasting impression.

AI-Based Design Platforms for Creating Stunning Covers

The rise of AI-based design platforms has revolutionized the way authors can create book covers. These tools provide accessible, cost-effective, and professional design options for authors, especially those who may not have access to traditional graphic designers. What's more, these platforms are designed to be user-friendly, making the design process less intimidating. Here are some popular AI-based platforms that can help you create stunning book covers:

- **Canva**: Canva's user-friendly interface and wide array of templates make it a popular choice for authors. Its AI tools suggest layouts, color schemes, and fonts tailored to your project, ensuring a professional look.
- **BookBrush**: Explicitly designed for authors, BookBrush offers templates and tools tailored to book marketing. Its AI-driven features analyze the characteristics of successful book covers in your genre and audience preferences, helping you customize covers that are more likely to attract your target readers.
- **Adobe Spark**, as part of the Adobe family, offers AI-assisted design tools that enable you to create visually appealing book covers with minimal effort.
- **Fotor**: Known for its AI-powered editing and design features, Fotor allows users to create high-quality book covers quickly. It includes customizable templates and one-click design enhancements.
- **VistaCreate (formerly Crello)**: This platform provides a comprehensive library of templates and AI-driven tools for creating visually striking content. Its intuitive interface makes it an excellent option for beginners.

By leveraging these AI-based tools, authors can achieve a professional and polished cover without extensive design experience. These platforms are equipped with AI-driven features that ensure the quality of your design, giving you confidence in the result. Many of these platforms also allow you to experiment with different styles and layouts, helping you find the perfect design for your book.

Tips for Creating a Compelling Cover:

- **Research Your Genre:** Study successful books in your genre, such as 'The Da Vinci Code' for mystery thrillers or 'To Kill a Mockingbird' for classic literature, to identify common design elements and trends that recur across the genre.
- **Hire a Professional Designer:** While DIY options exist, a skilled designer can elevate your cover to a professional level.
- **Keep It Simple:** Avoid cluttered designs; a clean, focused layout is more effective.
- **Test Your Cover:** Use surveys or focus groups to gather feedback on potential designs before finalizing.
- **Think About Thumbnails:** Ensure your cover looks good in smaller sizes, as it will often be displayed as a thumbnail online.

Your book cover is more than just an aesthetic choice; it's a strategic marketing tool that can significantly impact your book's success. By investing time and resources into creating a professional, audience-appropriate cover, you set the stage for higher sales, better discoverability, and a stronger connection with your readers. Remember, in the competitive world of publishing, your cover is your book's best chance to make a lasting impression.

Cover Design Best Practices: Trends, Fonts, and Colors

In today's publishing world—especially in a visually saturated digital marketplace—your book cover must not only reflect your story but compete with thousands of others for attention. This is where a thoughtful combination of **current trends, font selection, and color psychology** becomes essential.

Let's delve into the world of design trends, a realm that is constantly evolving and never ceases to amaze. The future of book cover design, set to unfold in 2025–2026, is both thrilling and demanding. Authors and designers are no longer just creating visually appealing designs—they're crafting invitations to an immersive experience. A cover today must instantly convey tone, genre, and promise, whether it's on a physical shelf or as a tiny thumbnail on a mobile screen.

One of the strongest trends we'll continue to see is the rise of artificial intelligence in the creative process. But rather than replacing human artists, AI is becoming more of a partner or tool. Designers are beginning to use AI not for final designs, but for ideation—for creating concepts, generating visual directions, or building mood boards. The covers that stand out will not be the ones that look synthetic or mass-produced, but the ones that blend AI innovation with human sensitivity. There's something unmistakable about a human touch—a flourish, an imperfection, or a stroke of intuition—that AI can't replicate yet.

Visually, two opposite trends are evolving in parallel. On one hand, there's the quiet confidence of minimalism. This is especially true in nonfiction and literary fiction, where covers are becoming cleaner, calmer, and more deliberate. Subtle colors like soft pinks, sage greens, or gentle grays dominate these designs. The fonts are refined, often serif or thin sans-serif, and everything breathes—there's space, there's restraint. These covers don't scream; they whisper, "Trust me. This is thoughtful, elegant, and worth your time."

On the other end of the spectrum, genre fiction is going all in—vivid, cinematic, unapologetically rich. Fantasy books might feature glowing elements, intricate borders, or lush backgrounds.

Thrillers go for bold contrast and tension. Romance plays with dreamy palettes and sensual imagery. Readers of these genres want to escape, to be swept away, and the cover is their first glimpse into that world. These books are not afraid to be a little dramatic. And in a crowded market, drama sells.

Typography is evolving, too. Bold, oversized fonts are showing up more often, with titles that dominate the entire cover. There's also a strong return of serif fonts—but not the safe, classic kind. We're seeing playful, exaggerated serifs that feel fresh and nostalgic all at once. Designers are mixing font styles in daring combinations: elegant with edgy, script with block, all caps with delicate cursive. The font is no longer just delivering the title—it's setting the emotional tone of the book before the first page is turned.

There's something else on the horizon, too—technology that makes the cover come alive. Augmented reality features are beginning to enter the world of books. Imagine pointing your phone at a book cover and seeing a trailer, a voice message from the author, or animated illustrations unfold on screen. This won't be everywhere yet, but it's starting to emerge, particularly in young adult fiction, graphic novels, and niche nonfiction. It's another way to blend print with digital, to make the book interactive without altering its physical form.

Color will continue to carry emotional weight, but its use is becoming more nuanced. The exact shade of red can feel dangerous on one cover and romantic on another. Designers are becoming more intentional with palettes—sometimes even breaking genre rules. You might see a mystery novel in pale yellow or a romance in icy blue. This is part of a larger movement of genre-blending, where the boundaries between categories are dissolving. Genre-blending is a trend where books are not confined to a single category, and this is reflected in the cover design. The same thing is happening in design. Covers are beginning to reflect more fluid storytelling. Some authors will take risks, and some of those risks will set new trends.

There's also a growing interest in the past. Vintage styles from the 70s, 80s, and 90s are making a comeback, but with a modern twist and a fresh polish. A horror novel might look like an old VHS case, with bold, retro fonts and grainy, nostalgic imagery A memoir might borrow from retro magazine design, with vibrant colors and playful typography. It's nostalgia with a clever twist—and readers seem to love the familiarity wrapped in something new.

And as always, book design will remain intricately linked to the reader's expectations. No matter how innovative or creative the cover is, it must align with what the audience subconsciously associates with the genre. This doesn't mean playing it safe—it means playing smart. Great design in the coming years will not be about copying trends, but about using them with intent. It's about knowing your readers, respecting their visual language, and offering them something that feels both familiar and fresh.

As we journey through 2025 and into 2026, the most compelling book covers will be those that strike a delicate balance: between art and marketing, between trend and timelessness, between technology and emotion. These covers won't just adorn a book—they'll open a door to a world of imagination and storytelling.

Formatting for Readers

When the manuscript is complete and edited, you receive a finalized document (file), which means the content of your book is ready for publication. But then come the practical questions: What size should the book be? What font should be used? How do you prepare the book for print or conversion into an e-book? In reality, this is an extremely meticulous task—possibly even more complex than writing and editing the book itself (though I may be wrong). To help you with these decisions, consider the genre of your book, the target audience, and the reading experience you want to create.

Formatting a book means aligning the text with specific standards and technical requirements for print or digital publication. This includes both the technical and visual design of the text to make it not just aesthetically pleasing and professionally presented, but also reader-friendly, ensuring a smooth and enjoyable reading experience for your audience.

If a traditional publishing house will publish your book, you can breathe a little easier—because the publisher will handle formatting. However, it's important to note that your preferences may not always align with theirs. A publisher might rearrange chapters, remove sections of text, or choose font colors that don't suit your taste. Clear communication is key in such situations.

For example, when my book *"1000 Questions and Answers in Gynecology"* was published in 2008, I was unpleasantly surprised by the formatting. The book ended up being pocket-sized, despite having around 350 A6-format pages. As a result, the font had to be made extremely small to fit everything in. It wasn't easy to read. The book turned out to be a miniature filled with a massive amount of content. Although it sold well and was popular, some readers complained that the font was uncomfortably small.

Another example of a disappointing design choice was in my 2018 book, *"Daughters and Mothers,"* which focuses on girls' health (in Russian). The editors decided to print the text in dark pink. While it may have seemed like a creative decision, it was ultimately a poor one. The lack of contrast between the paper and font color caused eye strain for many readers. Although the cover design was approved with my input, the font color was not. Small details like this can alienate readers.

If you're publishing through a self-publishing service or online platform, you'll need to follow the technical guidelines of that service. For instance, Amazon allows you to publish books in digital format, with both soft and hard covers. Lulu.com, Barnes & Noble Press, and several others offer similar options. But each platform has its file formatting requirements. Even Etsy, known for selling digital books and printables, has specific rules for file naming and size. That's why it's essential to read the platform's guidelines in advance—so you don't have to redo everything from scratch.

To avoid creating an overwhelming amount of text for every formatting step, I've put together a detailed table outlining each stage of the process:

Formatting Stage	Description
1. Text Alignment	• Justified text: Used to create a clean and professional look. • Paragraphs: Indented or spaced to mark the beginning of new paragraphs.
2. Fonts and Sizes	• Body text: Readable fonts (e.g., Times New Roman, Garamond, Georgia) in 10–12 pt. • Headings: Larger size or bold. • Italics and bold: For emphasis. • Line spacing: Typically 1.15–1.5 for print.
3. Text Structure	• Table of contents: Linked to headings. • Chapters and sections: Clearly divided. • Headers/footers: Page numbers, title, or author name.
4. Page Layout	• Margins: Proper top, bottom, left, and right for trimming and readability. • Page size: A5 or 6×9 inches. • Page numbers: Top/bottom, centered or aligned.
5. Paragraphs and Spacing	• Indentation: For better readability. • Spacing: Uniform space between paragraphs. • Hyphenation: Auto-hyphenation to avoid uneven lines.
6. Heading Formatting	• Hierarchy: Different styles for different levels (e.g., all caps for chapters, italics for subheadings). • Visual separation: Centering, spacing.
7. Working with Images	• Image placement: High-quality and properly aligned. • Captions: Added to images. • Charts/tables: Properly scaled and positioned.
8. E-book Formatting	• Responsive layout: Compatible with different screen sizes. • Hyperlinks: Clickable TOC and cross-references. • File formats: EPUB, MOBI, PDF.
9. Error Checking	• Proofreading: Correct grammar, punctuation, and spelling. • Typography: Check spaces, quotation marks, dashes, etc.
10. Preparing for Print	• Final check: Fonts, styles, page numbers. • Export: High-resolution PDF for print; EPUB/MOBI for digital formats.

Now, briefly about current formatting trends for different book genres. The sizes, page counts, fonts, and font sizes listed below refer primarily to printed editions, as they consider typographic standards, reading comfort, and formatting requirements for physical printing.

Here is an updated table that includes all the expanded genres:

Most Popular Genres	Popular Book Sizes	Typical Page Count	Common Fonts	Common Font Sizes
Novels (romance, detective, thrillers)	6 × 9 in (15.2 × 22.9 cm)	200–400 pages	Times New Roman	11–12 pt
Non-fiction (self-help, business, biographies)	5 × 8 in (12.7 × 20.3 cm)	150–300 pages	Garamond	10–12 pt
Fantasy and Science Fiction	5.5 × 8.5 in (14 × 21.6 cm)	300–500 pages	Georgia	11–12 pt
Children's Books (fairy tales, stories)	8 × 10 in (20.3 × 25.4 cm)	24–48 pages	Century Gothic	12–14 pt
Coloring Books	8.5 × 11 in (21.6 × 27.9 cm)	40–100 pages	Helvetica	12 pt
Word Puzzle Books	8.5 × 11 in (21.6 × 27.9 cm)	80–200 pages	Arial	11–12 pt
Graphic Novels	7 × 10 in (17.8 × 25.4 cm)	150–300 pages	Comic Sans (for titles)	11–12 pt
Poetry	5 × 8 in (12.7 × 20.3 cm)	80–150 pages	Baskerville	10–12 pt
Cookbooks	A4 (21 × 29.7 cm)	150–250 pages	Palatino	11–12 pt
Journals and Notebooks	A4 (21 × 29.7 cm)	100–200 pages	Calibri	12–14 pt
Young Adult (YA) Fiction	5.25 × 8 in (13.3 × 20.3 cm)	250–400 pages	Verdana	11–12 pt
Psychology Books	6 × 9 in (15.2 × 22.9 cm)	200–350 pages	Times New Roman	11–12 pt

Mystery and Horror	6 × 9 in (15.2 × 22.9 cm)	250–400 pages	Garamond	11–12 pt
Dystopian Fiction	5.25 × 8 in (13.3 × 20.3 cm)	250–350 pages	Georgia	11–12 pt
Erotica	5 × 8 in (12.7 × 20.3 cm)	150–300 pages	Palatino	11–12 pt
LitRPG	6 × 9 in (15.2 × 22.9 cm)	300–500 pages	Times New Roman	11–12 pt
Historical Fiction	6 × 9 in (15.2 × 22.9 cm)	250–450 pages	Garamond	11–12 pt
Essays and Short Prose	5 × 8 in (12.7 × 20.3 cm)	80–150 pages	Baskerville	10–12 pt
Popular Science	6 × 9 in (15.2 × 22.9 cm)	200–400 pages	Palatino	11–12 pt
Graphic Non-fiction	7 × 10 in (17.8 × 25.4 cm)	150–300 pages	Helvetica	11–12 pt
Psychological Thrillers	5.5 × 8.5 in (14 × 21.6 cm)	250–400 pages	Times New Roman	11–12 pt
Adventure Fiction	5.5 × 8.5 in (14 × 21.6 cm)	250–400 pages	Garamond	11–12 pt

Here is a table adapted for **e-books**, considering the specific features of digital formats:

Popular Modern Genres	**Most Common Screen Sizes (Responsive)**	**Popular Fonts**	**Recommended Font Sizes (pt)**
Novels (romance, detective, thrillers)	Responsive (6–10 inch screens, Kindle, iPad)	Georgia, Times New Roman	10–14

Non-fiction (self-help, business, biographies)	Responsive (6–10 inch screens)	Garamond, Helvetica	11–15
Fantasy and Science Fiction	Responsive (7–10 inch screens)	Palatino, Times New Roman	12–14
Children's Books (fairy tales, stories)	Tablets with larger screens	Comic Sans, Century Gothic	14–18
Coloring Books	Large screens (10 inches and up, tablets)	Arial, Verdana	12–16
Word Puzzle Books	Large screens (10 inches and up)	Calibri, Helvetica	12–16
Graphic Novels	Medium and large screens (7–12 inches)	Comic Sans, Verdana	12–14
Poetry	Responsive (6–10 inch screens)	Baskerville, Garamond	10–12
Cookbooks	Tablets and large screens (10 inches and up)	Helvetica, Georgia	12–16
Journals and Notebooks	Large screens (10–12 inches)	Calibri, Verdana	12–16
Young Adult (YA) Fiction	Responsive (7–10 inch screens)	Georgia, Palatino	11–14
Psychology Books	Responsive (6–10 inch screens)	Times New Roman, Garamond	11–14
Mystery and Horror	Responsive (6–10 inch screens)	Georgia, Palatino	11–14
Dystopian Fiction	Responsive (7–10 inch screens)	Times New Roman, Helvetica	11–14
Erotica	Responsive (6–8 inch screens)	Garamond, Baskerville	11–14
LitRPG	Responsive (7–10 inch screens)	Arial, Verdana	12–14
Historical Fiction	Responsive (6–10 inch screens)	Palatino, Times New Roman	11–14
Essays and Short Prose	Responsive (6–10 inch screens)	Baskerville, Garamond	10–12

Popular Science	Responsive (6–10 inch screens)	Helvetica, Times New Roman	11–14
Graphic Non-Fiction	Medium and large screens (7–12 inches)	Helvetica, Arial	12–14
Psychological Thrillers	Responsive (7–10 inch screens)	Times New Roman, Palatino	11–14
Adventure	Responsive (6–10 inch screens)	Georgia, Times New Roman	11–14

This table outlines the primary parameters for e-books, with screen size and text adaptability being key considerations.

There is a significant difference between formatting a book for print and digital formats. Not long ago, converting a book into an e-book without compromising the layout was quite tricky. The process often involved manual formatting to ensure the text and images appeared correctly on various e-reader devices. However, with the advancement of e-book creation tools and the standardization of e-book formats, this process has become much simpler and more automated.

Most e-book creation tools were initially designed for English (Latin alphabet) texts. Today, however, the landscape has undergone significant changes. Many programs have evolved to produce high-quality e-books in virtually any language, a testament to the continuous advancement in digital publishing tools.

There are at least 22 widely recognized e-book formats, though this number may grow over time. Most of these formats are now obsolete (e.g., LIT, PDB) or used only in specific cases. For instance, the LIT format, which Microsoft developed, is still used by some older e-readers. Similarly, the PDB format, initially designed for Palm Pilot devices, is still used by a niche group of users.

For general publishing and distribution, the most used formats today are:

- EPUB
- MOBI / AZW
- PDF
- CBZ / CBR (for comics)

Here is an extended table with additional e-book formats and their key characteristics:

E-Book Format	Popularity by Region	Translation Usability	Drawbacks
EPUB	USA, Europe, Asia	Very convenient: supports Unicode and is flexible for non-English texts.	Requires specialized software for creation and validation. Not all devices support it without conversion.
MOBI	USA, UK (Amazon Kindle)	Moderately convenient: supports major languages but has limited support for complex elements.	Outdated format with fewer formatting options compared to EPUB.
AZW3 (Kindle)	USA, UK, Canada (Kindle)	Convenient for English and some other languages; more difficult with less common languages.	Tied to the Amazon ecosystem. Limited compatibility with other devices.
PDF	Worldwide	Moderately convenient: supports all languages, but often locks text in image-like layers, making translation harder.	Not responsive to different screen sizes. Difficult to read on mobile devices.
RTF	USA, Europe	Convenient: easy to edit and translate, supports basic fonts and languages.	Limited formatting capabilities; unsuitable for complex layouts.
TXT	Worldwide	Very convenient: plain text is easy to translate with no language restrictions.	No formatting, no support for graphics or advanced design.
HTML	Worldwide	Convenient: supports all alphabets, highly	Requires coding knowledge for

		flexible for styling and translation.	editing. Depends on browsers or readers.
FB2	Russia, CIS countries	Convenient: popular for Russian and other CIS languages; supports styling.	Obsolete format with limited multimedia support.
DjVu	Eastern Europe, Asia	Difficult to translate since it's often used for scanned documents (no text layer).	Not suitable for editing or translation; poor support on modern devices.
DOCX	Worldwide (especially business use)	Very convenient: easy to translate, supports all languages and complex layouts.	Large file sizes; not optimized for mobile reading.
CBZ/CBR	USA, Europe (comics and graphic novels)	Moderately convenient: mainly used for images, not text.	Limited translation potential; designed for visual content.
IBA	USA (Apple iBooks)	Convenient within Apple Books; supports both text and multimedia.	Tied to the Apple ecosystem; limited cross-platform compatibility.
LIT	Obsolete (used by Microsoft)	Was convenient for text, but now rarely used.	Deprecated format; low compatibility with modern devices.
ODT	Europe, CIS countries	Very convenient: supports complex texts and is easy to edit.	Not designed for reading books; better suited for document editing.
KF8 (Kindle Format 8)	USA, UK (Amazon Kindle)	Convenient for multilingual texts and advanced formatting.	Tied to the Kindle ecosystem; limited compatibility with other platforms.
PRC	Worldwide	Convenient for simple texts and translations.	Limited formatting; low popularity.
XHTML	Worldwide	Convenient: supports all alphabets and complex formatting.	Requires coding skills; dependent on rendering software.

Thus, you can use the comparative data on e-book formats in your work to produce high-quality files.

The Importance of Embedding Text in Book Layouts

When we think about book design, we often focus on visuals, page layout, or typography — but one subtle and essential element is often overlooked: embedding text. More specifically, embedding fonts. This technical detail plays a crucial role in ensuring that your book appears exactly as you envisioned it, no matter where or how it's opened — whether on a printed page, a digital reader, or as a supplemental document to an audiobook.

At its core, *text embedding* refers to the process of including the actual font data within the file, so that the chosen typefaces accompany the document. Without embedding, your carefully selected fonts may be replaced by defaults, resulting in shifts in layout, spacing, and overall design. This can result in misaligned chapters, broken headers, or even unreadable text.

In the world of print publishing, embedding fonts isn't optional — it's essential. The file you send to the printer is usually a PDF, and if the fonts aren't embedded, the printer may substitute them with other fonts, which could dramatically alter the look of your book.

Imagine designing your pages with the elegant curves of Garamond, only to have them printed in Arial—the tone, texture, and rhythm of the page change entirely. This is the visual impact of font substitution. Embedded fonts preserve this visual harmony and help avoid technical errors, such as distorted characters or misplaced text blocks, during the printing process.

There's also a legal aspect: some fonts have licensing restrictions, and embedding is often required for lawful use in commercial printing. It's a detail easily overlooked, but it matters.

To check if your fonts are properly embedded, tools like Adobe Acrobat Pro are invaluable. Open your PDF, go to *file> Properties > Fonts*, and look for indicators like "Embedded" or "Embedded Subset." Printing a single proof copy is another smart move — it's the best way to ensure that everything looks just right before going to mass production.

With e-books, the challenge is a little different. Readers expect flexibility — the ability to change font size, background color, or even typeface. Still, at the same time, you want your book to retain its unique voice and visual identity.

Embedding fonts in e-books allows you to achieve both. It ensures your chapter titles, stylized headers, or multilingual text elements appear consistently across devices, whether on a Kindle, an iPad, or a smartphone. Custom fonts can be a beautiful way to reinforce your book's tone — playful, elegant, bold, or subtle.

However, not all platforms treat font embedding equally. The Amazon Kindle, for example, limits font customization to maintain compatibility with its system fonts, such as *Bookerly* or *Ember*. That means you need to test whether your formatting still works when your chosen fonts are overridden. Tools like Sigil, Calibre, and EPUBCheck are helpful here — they allow you to inspect font embedding and validate your files. Most importantly, always test your e-book on a variety of devices to see how it behaves in the real world.

Even though audiobooks are primarily auditory experiences, they often come with companion materials, such as transcripts, visual guides, or downloadable PDFs. These files, too, deserve careful formatting. Embedded fonts in such materials help ensure that your visual content aligns with your brand and remains accessible to all users, including those with visual impairments who may rely on larger text or specialized fonts, such as those designed for individuals with dyslexia.

Practical Tips for Proper Embedding

Whether you're working with a design team or creating your book solo, a few best practices can help ensure everything runs smoothly:

- **Use OpenType or TrueType fonts**, as they are widely supported and often come with built-in permissions for embedding.

- **Always review your licensing agreements**, particularly for commercial use — some fonts may be free for personal projects but restricted for publishing.
- **Use font subsetting** when possible. This technique embeds only the characters used in your document, keeping file sizes manageable without compromising the layout. Font subsetting is a valuable strategy to balance file size and design integrity.
- **Test extensively** across platforms — print a proof, load your file on various e-readers, and preview your PDFs on different devices.

In the grand scheme of book creation, embedding fonts may seem like a minor technicality — but it's one of those invisible details that uphold the integrity of your work. When done correctly, it protects the voice, tone, and aesthetic of your book. When neglected, it opens the door to visual inconsistency, technical glitches, and reader frustration.

So, whether you're preparing a hardcover memoir, a digital poetry collection, or a supplemental PDF for your latest audiobook, remember: embedded text is more than a design choice — it's a quiet guardian of your book's identity.

The Role of NCX and XML in Electronic TOC

In the world of digital publishing, the reader's experience is shaped not only by words and stories but by the unseen architecture that holds those words together. One of the most overlooked yet essential elements of an e-book's functionality is its ability to guide the reader through the content effortlessly — to allow them to tap a chapter title and be taken instantly to the right place, to scroll through a structured outline, or to find their way back with ease. This isn't magic. It's technology. At its heart is a file that most readers are unlikely to encounter: the NCX.

The NCX file, short for Navigation Control file for XML, acts as the digital spine of your e-book. It silently carries the book's structure — its chapters, sections, and subheadings — and presents that structure to the reading device. Whether a reader opens your book on a Kindle, a Kobo, an iPad, or a smartphone, the NCX ensures they can navigate through the book with confidence and clarity. It tells the device where everything is, how it's ordered, and how to interpret the layout in a way that's friendly, logical, and deeply human.

What makes this even more important is that most major digital platforms — Amazon Kindle, Apple Books, Google Play Books — won't accept an e-book without a valid NCX file. It's not just a matter of reader convenience; it's a matter of publishing compliance. Without it, your beautifully written, perfectly edited manuscript might fail technical validation and never reach your audience. However, when the NCX is present and well-formed, it becomes an invisible companion to the reader — one that never interrupts the flow but is always there when needed. It's like a skilled guide who knows the book inside out, leading the reader to their destination without them even realizing it.

Creating this functionality doesn't have to be difficult. Most modern tools now handle it automatically. If you're writing in Reedsy, you'll find that it builds a clickable table of contents seamlessly when you export your EPUB file. Calibre, a longtime favorite among independent authors, converts Word documents and manuscripts into various digital formats, embedding the NCX file in the process. Vellum, renowned for its elegant interface and polished results, enables the creation of visually appealing e-books with all necessary navigational tools in place, without requiring the user to write a single line of code.

Other tools make the process even more flexible. Kindle Create, for instance, is designed specifically for Amazon and provides built-in tools for generating the necessary navigation in MOBI and AZW formats. Sigil offers authors and editors manual control over the NCX structure, utilizing a friendly visual editor. Adobe InDesign, a professional design program often used in print publishing, can also be used to create EPUB files with a functional NCX — provided the layout has been built with consistent heading styles and a structured approach. And platforms like Pressbooks, popular in academic and educational settings, create the NCX automatically alongside the visible TOC during EPUB export. Other tools such as Jutoh, Scrivener, and iBooks Author also offer NCX creation features, providing authors and publishers with a wide range of options to suit their specific needs.

The role of NCX even extends beyond traditional e-books. As the publishing world becomes more multimedia-oriented, many authors include bonus materials — such as transcripts, visual guides, and reading companions — especially when releasing audiobooks. These materials are often delivered in PDF format. While PDFs don't use an NCX per se, the same principles apply: navigation, structure, consistency, and a respect for the reader's time and attention. Embedding fonts, maintaining style consistency, and offering hyperlinks or bookmarks inside the document can all mirror the role the NCX plays in EPUBs and MOBIs. In this way, the principles of NCX can be applied to various digital publishing formats, thereby enhancing the reader's experience across different media.

There's something elegant about this hidden layer of design. It doesn't announce itself. Most readers will likely remain unaware of it. But they'll feel it. They'll notice when a book is thoughtfully organized, when they can find what they need without frustration, when the flow of information feels natural rather than confusing. The NCX, though quiet and technical, supports the entire architecture of the reading experience.

It's easy to think that once the manuscript is written and edited, the hard work is done. However, crafting a digital book that feels effortless requires more than just good content — it necessitates structure, care, and an understanding of how people read. The NCX is not about bells and whistles. It's about respect. Respect for the reader, for the format, and for the message you want to deliver. It says: "I thought about how this book will live in someone's hands."

So, while you may never see it on a page, the NCX file is your book's quiet guardian. It doesn't carry emotion, narrative, or meaning in itself — but it holds everything that gives those things meaning together. And in a world where readers expect both substance and usability, that makes all the difference.

Creating Books for Every Platform: Print, E-Books, and Audiobooks

Publishing a book today is no longer a single-format affair. Readers experience stories in multiple ways — they flip through pages, scroll on screens, and press play on audiobooks. As an author, you're not just delivering content; you're shaping how people engage with it. Whether your words are printed on a page, displayed on an e-reader, or spoken aloud through headphones, the journey from manuscript to final product requires attention, care, and the right tools. And now, more than ever, artificial intelligence is stepping in to make that journey smoother, faster, and more accessible.

Let's start with the familiar: **print books**. There's a timeless quality to holding a physical book, feeling the paper, flipping pages, and seeing the design come together. But getting to that final, tangible form takes more than inspiration — it takes formatting. Traditionally, software like Adobe InDesign has given authors and designers meticulous control over layout, typography, and image placement. It's powerful, but also complex. Others begin with Microsoft Word, a tool many know well, which, while limited in design, is a comfortable starting point. Somewhere in between, programs like Affinity Publisher have made professional-quality formatting more affordable and intuitive. Then there are platforms like Scrivener, which authors love for its organizational tools, though formatting is often finished elsewhere.

AI doesn't replace these tools — it enhances them. InDesign, for instance, now uses AI to suggest layout refinements and automatically adjust image sizing, saving you precious time. Reedsy Book Editor gives indie authors a way to create print-ready files with professional templates, bypassing complex design work. Even Canva has quietly entered the book world, offering AI-assisted design suggestions for simpler projects like workbooks or journals. What used to take hours of manual layout can now happen in moments, with the software making intelligent choices based on design best practices.

When it comes to **e-books**, the challenge shifts from physical alignment to digital fluidity. Unlike a printed page, an e-book must adapt to screen size, font choices, and reading apps. Tools like Calibre have long helped authors convert manuscripts into multiple formats like EPUB and MOBI, ensuring a professional quality output. Kindle Create simplifies the process for Amazon's ecosystem, formatting text to match Kindle requirements. Vellum, while available only on Mac, is beloved for its clean, polished output. And for those willing to get technical, Sigil offers deep control over EPUB files.

But again, AI is weaving itself into these processes. Kindle Create analyzes your manuscript and suggests layouts. Reedsy applies formatting templates that adjust automatically. Draft2Digital uses AI to generate clean, consistent e-books with navigable chapters and accurate metadata. Even Calibre, though not overtly AI-driven, automates batch conversions and organizes large libraries of content — a quiet kind of intelligence that saves time and reduces mistakes.

Then there's the world of **audiobooks** — a format that brings stories to life through voice. Creating an audiobook is more than recording words; it's about performance, tone, pacing, and audio clarity. Tools like Audacity and GarageBand make it possible to record and edit narration at home. Pro Tools offers a studio-grade experience, while Reaper provides serious creators with depth at a lower cost.

This is where AI gets especially interesting. Descript lets you edit audio by editing text — delete a sentence from the transcript, and the audio disappears too. It even allows you to create corrections in your voice using AI-generated overdubs. For authors who can't hire a narrator, services like Google Cloud Text-to-Speech or Murf.ai now produce surprisingly natural AI voices. These are especially useful for non-fiction, tutorials, or tight budgets. Post-production has also become easier with AI plugins that handle noise reduction, volume leveling, and compliance checks automatically. Tools like ACX Check ensure your audiobook meets the strict technical standards of platforms like Audible or iTunes — without needing to be an audio engineer.

The result of all these tools, whether traditional or AI-powered, is the same: a book that's ready to meet readers and listeners wherever they are. AI doesn't take the soul out of the process — it handles the tasks that used to consume time and energy, giving you more control over your creative process. It quietly manages the technical side so that you can stay focused on the creative heart of your work.

That's the real magic. **Your job is still to write, to shape your voice, your message, your story.** But instead of wrestling with margins, coding footnotes, or re-recording a misread word, you get to hand off some of that weight to something that never sleeps, never loses patience, and learns how to make your book look and sound its best. In the end, AI doesn't steal your role — it strengthens it. It's not here to replace your voice, but to help it resonate more clearly, more widely, and more professionally than ever before.

Testing Your Book Layout for Readability and Compatibility

Once a book is formatted, many authors feel a sense of completion — the chapters are neatly arranged, the text looks clean, and everything seems to be in place. But there's one essential step that must not be overlooked before publication: testing the layout. This final phase is where everything you've designed meets reality. Whether your book is destined for print, digital readers, or headphones, layout testing ensures that your readers or listeners have the best possible experience with your work. It's about more than just appearance; it's about function, clarity, accessibility, and trust, and it's a commitment to your audience.

A book that looks perfect on your screen may behave very differently once printed, uploaded to Kindle, or converted into an audiobook. That's why this stage deserves as much attention as the writing itself. And while the tools and techniques vary depending on format, the goal remains the same: to deliver a polished, user-friendly experience across every platform. Layout testing is not just a necessity, but an opportunity for growth and improvement in your publishing journey.

In the world of printed books, layout testing is a deeply tactile experience. It's about ensuring that every element on the page sits exactly where it should, that the typography is comfortable for the eyes, and that nothing disappears into the gutter or runs too close to the edges. The process often begins with ordering a printed proof—something many authors feel both anxious and excited to do. Holding your book in your hands for the first time is a special moment, but it's also the first real test.

This printed proof allows you to examine alignment: Are the images centered correctly? Are margins consistent? Do page numbers appear where they should—and are they the same style throughout? Fonts must be readable without strain, especially in smaller formats. Testing different font sizes (such as 11- or 12-point Times New Roman or Garamond) helps ensure your text remains easy on the eyes during long reading sessions. Line spacing and paragraph indentation, though subtle, also affect readability in profound ways.

Equally important are the physical aspects—paper thickness, binding style, and whether illustrations extend to the edge of the page (a process called bleed). A hardcover book might behave differently from a softcover one, and if the paper is too thin, text from the reverse side might show through. These factors all influence how your book feels and how easily it can be read and enjoyed. For those working with tools like Adobe InDesign, built-in preflight functions can help identify potential printing issues before the proof is even ordered. Platforms like Amazon KDP offer both physical proofs and digital previews, although nothing quite replaces the value of seeing the real thing.

When it comes to e-books, the focus shifts to adaptability and interactivity. E-books are read on a wide variety of devices, from sleek e-readers and tablets to smartphones and desktop apps. This diversity underscores the need for a flexible layout that looks good and functions well on all these devices.

Testing an e-book involves running it through several devices and apps. A chapter that appears centered on one device might be misaligned on another. An image that appears sharp in Apple Books may look pixelated on Kindle. These inconsistencies can only be detected through hands-on testing. It's worth loading your EPUB or MOBI file onto multiple devices and adjusting font sizes, orientations, and screen brightness settings to see how your content responds.

Text should be reflowable wherever possible—especially for novels, essays, and nonfiction. That means it adjusts gracefully when a reader changes font size or switches to a different device. Fixed-layout formats are only suitable for specific types of content, such as children's picture books or textbooks with detailed formatting. Navigation is equally essential. The Table of Contents should be clickable and functional, leading the reader exactly where they expect to go. Hyperlinks, footnotes, and embedded media should also be tested, as a single broken link can undermine a reader's trust.

Images deserve special attention. Some e-readers display color, while others do not. A photograph that looks vibrant on a tablet may appear dull or muddled on an e-ink screen. Proper image scaling, compression, and testing in grayscale help prevent surprises. Tools like EPUBCheck help detect internal formatting errors, while Amazon's Kindle Previewer allows you to simulate how the book will behave across different Kindle models. Adobe Digital Editions offers another useful window into how your EPUBs will look in real-world reading conditions.

With audiobooks, testing takes on a new dimension. It's not about how something looks, but how it sounds—how it flows, how it feels, and how consistently the listener is guided through the experience. A beautifully written book can lose its magic if the audio is poorly paced, plagued by inconsistent volume, or broken up by awkward transitions.

Testing an audiobook begins with the sound itself. It's essential to ensure that the recordings meet the technical specifications set by platforms like ACX or Audible. These include standards for RMS levels (which determine average loudness), noise floor (background hiss or hum), and peak limits to avoid distortion. Any clipping, echo, or inconsistency in volume should be addressed before submission. Silence is also tested: leading and trailing pauses between sections must be just right—not too abrupt, not too long.

Structure is another critical factor. Each chapter should be its own file, clearly labeled in a way that follows platform conventions (such as Chapter_01.mp3). The narrator's voice should smoothly introduce each chapter, matching the tone and rhythm of the rest of the book. Mispronunciations, pacing changes, or inconsistent character voices can break the immersive spell of storytelling. These are best detected through active listening—ideally on the same devices your audience will use.

Playback testing on different apps and platforms helps reveal any unexpected issues. What sounds perfect on headphones may be muddy through a car stereo or distorted on a mobile speaker. Listen while walking, driving, cooking—situations where your audience may be engaging with the audiobook. Tools like ACX Audio Lab or Audible's preview function can further verify that your files meet all technical requirements.

In all formats—print, digital, and audio—testing your layout is a thoughtful act. It shows respect for your readers and confidence in your work. Simulating real-world use is essential. Read your print book under different lighting conditions. Scroll through your e-book on a bus or in bed. Listen to your audiobook while folding laundry or walking through a busy street. You'll learn things you never noticed before. And perhaps most importantly, ask others to experience your book as well. Feedback from beta readers, proof listeners, or fellow authors often reveals what our own eyes and ears can miss.

Testing isn't glamorous. It's not creative. But it is powerful. It's the final polish—the quiet step that transforms a good book into a great one. When done well, no one notices. And that's the point. A well-tested layout vanishes into the background, leaving only the story, the voice, and the message.

Ultimately, formatting is more than just structure, and testing is more than a mere checklist. It's about ensuring that every aspect of your book—every word, every pause, every page—is experienced with the ease, elegance, and impact you originally intended.

Part 5: Publishing in the Digital Age

The digital revolution in publishing has not only dismantled traditional barriers but also opened up a world of unprecedented opportunities. Authors, publishers, and independent creators can now reach global audiences through e-books, audiobooks, online articles, and other digital formats. This shift has democratized publishing, empowering creators and simplifying production, thereby transforming the industry.

Reflecting on my journey, if someone had told me just over ten years ago that I would be able to publish and sell my books and other works in digital form, I wouldn't have believed them. But today, this has become a reality—one that continues to inspire me with even greater possibilities for the future.

This shift is not merely a technological advancement; it is a fundamental reimagining of storytelling and knowledge sharing. From self-published novels on Amazon Kindle to interactive multimedia e-books and the rapidly expanding world of audiobooks powered by streaming platforms, the digital era has democratized publishing. It has not only simplified production, reduced costs, and provided direct access to readers worldwide, but also empowered creators, offering them the tools to reach a global audience.

However, along with these opportunities come new challenges. Authors and publishers must navigate an increasingly saturated market, adapt to constantly evolving technologies, and meet the diverse expectations of digitally literate readers. In this new world, success is often determined by an author's ability to master modern tools, effectively use distribution platforms, and build authentic connections with readers across multiple formats. The need for strategic adaptation is not just a choice, but a necessity in the digital age.

As we explore the evolving dynamics of publishing in the digital age, we'll take a closer look at how technology has reshaped the industry: the rise of self-publishing, the cultural shift brought about by audiobooks and e-books, and the strategies necessary to thrive in this rapidly changing landscape. Whether you're a seasoned publisher or just starting your journey as an author, understanding the nuances of this digital revolution is not only beneficial but also essential for making your voice heard in the global marketplace

Choosing the Right Platform

For today's authors, selecting the right publishing platform is as important as writing the book itself. The days when publishing meant chasing an agent or mailing manuscripts to traditional houses are long gone. Now, with just a few clicks, you can upload your manuscript to a digital platform and have it available to readers around the world within hours. But this unprecedented access comes with a question that every independent author eventually faces: Where should I publish my book?

The answer isn't as simple as it seems. Each platform offers its ecosystem, benefits, limitations, and business models. Understanding these differences is crucial and can mean the difference between a book that quietly disappears into the void and one that finds its readers, builds momentum, and earns revenue over time, making you feel informed and prepared for your publishing journey.

Overview of Amazon KDP, IngramSpark, Draft2Digital, and Others

The digital publishing landscape today is vast, vibrant, and often overwhelming for both new and seasoned authors. With so many tools and platforms available, choosing where to publish your book can feel like navigating a maze. But beneath the technical layers, each platform reflects a different philosophy of publishing—some prioritize reach, others focus on control, some reward exclusivity. In contrast, others celebrate openness and diversity of distribution.

Let's begin with the platform that has reshaped modern publishing: **Amazon Kindle Direct Publishing (KDP)**.

For most authors, KDP is the first stop—and for a good reason. It offers a fast, free, and user-friendly way to publish e-books and paperbacks directly to Amazon's massive global marketplace. Its dominance is hard to ignore: in many English-speaking countries, Amazon controls over 70% of the e-book market, making it a powerful gateway to readers. This means that by publishing on KDP, your book can potentially reach a large number of readers who prefer e-books, increasing its visibility and sales potential.

One of KDP's hallmark features is the option to enroll in KDP Select, which gives Amazon temporary exclusive digital rights to your e-book in exchange for marketing benefits. These include participation in Kindle Unlimited, Amazon's subscription reading service, as well as special promotional pricing tools such as Kindle Countdown Deals and free e-book giveaways. For many authors—especially in popular genres like romance, thrillers, fantasy, and self-help—this can mean a significant increase in visibility and income. The trade-off, however, is that you cannot distribute your e-book through other channels while enrolled in KDP Select, typically in 90-day increments.

Beyond e-books, KDP also allows you to create print-on-demand paperbacks, complete with ISBN assignment, cover templates, and distribution within Amazon's physical bookstore. This makes KDP a full-stack solution for many first-time and independent authors.

But while Amazon opens many doors, it also keeps some closed. Your book may thrive within its ecosystem but remain largely invisible outside it. This is where **IngramSpark** enters the conversation.

Run by Ingram, one of the world's largest book distributors, IngramSpark is best known for its broad reach in physical and online bookstores, libraries, and educational institutions. It's the preferred platform for authors who want their print books to be available in brick-and-mortar stores, university catalogs, and library databases.

IngramSpark also offers global distribution, high-quality printing options (including hardcover and color interiors), and professional-level metadata management.

However, the platform is less beginner-friendly than KDP. It requires more technical preparation, such as uploading your ISBNs and ensuring print-ready files that meet publishing standards. It also comes with setup fees, though these are often waived during promotions or with publishing memberships. Still, for authors who take the time to learn its systems, IngramSpark offers a level of professionalism and reach that goes far beyond Amazon.

A third major player, especially for e-book distribution, is **Draft2Digital (D2D)**. Known for its ease of use and strong customer service, D2D is often described as the "friendly middle ground" between Amazon and IngramSpark. It allows you to distribute your e-book to a wide array of stores—Apple Books, Barnes & Noble, Kobo, Tolino, Vivlio, and even library services like OverDrive and Bibliotheca—without the hassle of uploading to each store individually.

One of Draft2Digital's standout features is its automated back matter tools. 'Back matter' refers to the content at the end of an e-book, after the main story or text. This section is a valuable space for authors to promote their other works, update links to their other books, or manage series metadata without manually re-editing each file. This is a gift for busy authors with multiple titles or series, as it allows them to effectively cross-promote their other works within each e-book. D2D doesn't charge upfront fees; instead, it takes a small percentage of royalties from each sale, making it an accessible option for authors who want to go 'wide' with minimal risk.

Other platforms have carved out specialized niches. **Smashwords**, now merged with Draft2Digital, was one of the pioneers of e-book self-publishing and continues to serve a loyal base of indie authors. **BookBaby** offers full-service publishing packages, including editing and marketing, for those who prefer a more hands-off approach to publishing. **StreetLib**, based in Europe, focuses on achieving a global reach and providing multilingual distribution. Meanwhile, **PublishDrive** brings artificial intelligence into the equation with tools for sales analytics and pricing optimization, making it a good fit for data-savvy authors and publishers.

Ultimately, each platform addresses a distinct set of needs and priorities. Some authors find success by staying within the Amazon ecosystem, optimizing their presence there, and reaping the rewards of exclusivity. Others build long-term careers by 'going wide'—reaching readers across continents and formats by combining platforms like IngramSpark and Draft2Digital. 'Going wide' means distributing your book across multiple platforms, not just Amazon, to reach a broader audience.

There is no single correct answer—only what fits your goals, your genre, and your vision for the book. The beauty of the modern publishing world is that it allows you to experiment, adjust, and evolve as your journey unfolds, fostering an optimistic and forward-thinking approach to your publishing strategy.

The publishing landscape today is vast and evolving so rapidly that it's nearly impossible to pin down an exact number of available platforms. Still, we can confidently say that there are at least 40 to 50 major global platforms actively used for selling books. And when we begin to account for regional markets, niche platforms, and emerging tools, that number quickly climbs past 100. At first glance, this abundance can feel confusing — even overwhelming. But in truth, it's a gift. With the right guidance, this variety offers not only options but opportunities: a way to tailor your publishing journey to your book, your readers, and your vision.

Some platforms serve a broad, international audience; others are finely tuned to serve a particular region, a specific format, or even a defined community of readers. Your choices will depend on what you're creating — a novel, a photo book, an audiobook, a how-to guide — and who you're creating it for.

To help make sense of this rich but complex ecosystem, the following table organizes key platforms by their specialization — so you can begin to see where your work might fit best, and where your efforts are most likely to thrive.

Category	Platform	Specialization
1. Major Global Platforms	Amazon KDP	E-books, print books; audiobooks via Audible.
	Apple Books	E-books and audiobooks for Apple users.
	Google Play Books	E-books and audiobooks with global reach.
	Kobo Writing Life	E-books with global distribution through Rakuten Kobo.
	Barnes & Noble Press	Print and e-books, mainly for the U.S. market.
	Audible	Audiobooks; market leader; owned by Amazon.
	IngramSpark	Print-on-demand and e-book distribution to bookstores, libraries, and online retailers.
	Lulu	Self-publishing platform for print and e-books with global reach.
	Smashwords	E-book distribution to retailers like Apple Books, B&N, and libraries.
	Draft2Digital	Similar to Smashwords; easy e-book distribution across major outlets.
2. Niche & Regional Platforms	Biblio	Rare, collectible, and out-of-print books.
	Book Depository	Print books with free worldwide shipping; owned by Amazon.
	Alibris	Used, new, and rare books.
	ThriftBooks	Used books, especially U.S.-based.
	Books-A-Million	Online and physical book sales, primarily in the U.S.
	Scribd	Subscription-based access to e-books and audiobooks.
	OverDrive	Library and school distribution for e-books and audiobooks.
	Tolino	E-books; popular in Germany and other European countries.
	24Symbols	Subscription model for e-books.
	Bukua	E-book platform targeting emerging markets in Asia and Africa.
	Flipkart	Indian marketplace for e-books and physical books.
	StreetLib	Global e-book distribution with strength in Europe.

3. Social Media & Crowdfunding	Patreon	Subscription-based; authors offer content directly to supporters.
	Kickstarter	Crowdfunding platform; often used to launch books or offer special editions.
	Gumroad	Direct sales of digital books to readers.
	Etsy	For unique, handcrafted, or artistic editions of books.
4. Direct Sales Platforms	Payhip	Digital product sales, including e-books.
	Shopify	Full e-commerce setup for custom online bookstores.
	Sellfy	For selling digital and physical goods, including books.
	WooCommerce	WordPress plugin to sell books directly via author websites.
	BigCommerce	Advanced e-commerce platform for direct sales of books and merchandise.
5. Audiobook-Specific Platforms	Findaway Voices	Audiobook distribution to Audible, Apple Books, and more.
	Authors Republic	Audiobook distribution with wide global reach.
	Storytel	Subscription audiobook platform, popular in Europe and Asia.
	Libro.fm	Audiobook platform supporting independent bookstores.
	Chirp Books	Discounted audiobooks with no subscription required.
6. Academic & Specialty	Chegg	Textbook rentals and academic books.
	VitalSource	Professional and academic digital books.
	RedShelf	Digital textbook access for universities and students.
	Blurb	Specializes in self-published art/photo books, portfolios, and premium print books.
7. Subscription-Based Models	Kindle Unlimited	Amazon's e-book subscription service. Authors are paid per page read.
	Scribd	All-in-one subscription for e-books, audiobooks, and magazines.

	Storytel	Offers access to e-books and audiobooks via monthly subscriptions.
	Playster	Subscription model with access to books, audiobooks, and more.

To choose the right platform, you first need to understand the direction you want to take with your publishing. Are you aiming for global exposure, genre-specific reach, or full control through direct sales? Each path offers unique benefits—and challenges.

- **Global Reach**: Platforms like Amazon KDP, Apple Books, or IngramSpark are designed for worldwide distribution and visibility.
- **Genre-Specific**: Niche platforms like Smashwords (for e-books) or Chirp (for audiobooks) are excellent for targeting focused audiences.
- **Direct Sales**: If you want full control over pricing, branding, and distribution, platforms like Gumroad, Shopify, or Payhip offer independence and flexibility.

To help you make an informed decision, the following table provides a detailed comparison of major publishing platforms, including royalty rates, advantages, disadvantages, fees, and even the hidden pitfalls that many authors only discover after publishing.

Platform	**Royalties**	**Advantages**	**Disadvantages**	**Fees**	**Bestseller Potential**	**Hidden Pitfalls**
Amazon KDP	Up to 70% (eBooks $2.99–$9.99)	Largest market; global reach; user-friendly	Locked in Amazon's ecosystem; lacks hardcover/audio (unless via Audible)	Free	High (due to massive customer base)	Royalties drop under $2.99; KDP Select requires exclusivit

						y; download fees for large file sizes.
Apple Books	70% on all eBooks	Large audience; free upload	Requires Mac to publish; eBooks only	Free	Moderate–High for Apple users	Needs Mac + iTunes Producer; limited marketing tools; smaller global reach compared to Amazon.
Kobo Writing Life	70% ($2.99 and above)	Global reach; Kobo promotions	Smaller U.S. share; limited print options	Free	Moderate, strong in international markets	Limited U.S. traction; formatting errors when converting from other platforms; limited promo options.
Barnes & Noble Press	70% (above $0.99)	Easy to use; no exclusivity	Only available in B&N's ecosystem	Free	Moderate, strong in the U.S.	Weak outside U.S.; small customer base; lacks deep analytics and promo tools.
IngramSpark	45–65%	Hardcover options; wide distribution	Upload + revision fees; complex interface	$49 per print book	High (bookstores, libraries, online)	High upfront cost; interface difficult for

						beginners; additional print costs per sale.
Lulu	35–50%	Excellent print quality; bulk orders	Higher print costs; limited organic traffic	Free	Moderate, traffic-based	Print-on-demand can be costly; slow delivery; requires external marketing.
Draft2Digital	10% per sale	Easy to use; wide e-book distribution	No print books; limited customization	None	High, due to multiple channels	Takes 10% commission on all sales; limited promo tools; no print distribution.
Smashwords	60–80%	Multi-format support; author profile page	Complicated formatting rules	None	Moderate, broad reach	Rigid formatting rules; outdated interface; smaller audience than Amazon or Apple.
Google Play Books	70% (varies slightly by country)	Huge user base; flexible pricing	Unintuitive platform; limited author tools	Free	High, tied to Google ecosystem	Google may discount books arbitrarily; setup process is difficult; needs external traffic to succeed.

BookBaby	Varies	Full-service packages; good support	High cost; limited partner stores	Varies	Moderate (if marketed well)	Expensive for complete services; limited post-publication control; slow speed.
Blurb	Varies	Great for visual/photo books; Ingram option	High print cost; niche audience	Varies	Low–Moderate (niche appeal)	Expensive for buyers; best for art/photo books, not mainstream publishing.
StreetLib	10% of retail	International + multilingual support	Not widely known	Free	Moderate, growing abroad	Payout in euros may complicate earnings; limited sales analytics.
Publish Drive	10% of sales or subscription tiers	AI tools; global sales network	Subscription required for better features	From $14.99/month	High with scale	Monthly fees apply even if there are no sales; limited free tools; highly competitive.
Wattpad	Based on engagement/views	Huge user base; strong community	Hard to monetize; no print/bookstore access	Free	Moderate (for popular stories)	Only top stories earn money; piracy is common; no direct

						book sales options.
Reedsy	Varies (service-based)	Professional editing + design	No book selling; expensive	Varies	Low (not a sales platform)	Purely service-based; expensive for full packages; not for distribution.
OverDrive	Varies	Excellent for libraries	Hard for new authors to access	Varies	Niche, library-focused	Libraries prefer bestselling or reviewed books; low visibility for debut authors.
Scribd	Fixed share	High user engagement; subscription base	Reduced payouts; discoverability can be hard	Free	Moderate, volume-based	Royalties fixed regardless of book price; minimal insights into reader behavior.
Booktango	100%	No upfront cost; beginner-friendly	Very limited distribution; low support	Free	Low	Very outdated; minimal visibility; poor reputation for support.
iUniverse	Varies by package	Author support services	High costs; upselling common	From $999	Low, unless heavily marketed	Hidden fees; expensive upgrades; poor royalty structures.

Xlibris	Varies	All-in-one self-publishing	Expensive; sales-focused sales team	From $899	Low, depends on service tier	Aggressive upsells; low value for money; unclear royalty terms.

As you can see, there is no shortage of platforms today—each offering something slightly different depending on your goals, genre, audience, and resources. But with so many options, choosing the right one can feel overwhelming. That's why the key is not to rush into everything at once. Sometimes, the smartest strategy is to start small—with what feels most accessible and financially reasonable for you now.

Begin with a platform that matches your current needs and comfort level. Explore its features, understand how it handles royalties and promotions, and get a feel for the tools it offers. As your confidence and knowledge grow, you can experiment with more advanced or specialized platforms, or even combine several to reach wider audiences.

Remember, you never know where success is waiting for you. A book that performs modestly on one platform might suddenly take off on another—or find new life through a different format, like audio or direct sales. But before you invest significant time or money, take the time to research, test, and learn. Start with one step that feels manageable. With each experience, you'll build the insight and flexibility you need to navigate the publishing world wisely—and on your own terms.

Exclusivity vs. Wide Distribution

One of the most important decisions an author must make in today's publishing landscape is whether to publish exclusively on a single platform—usually Amazon—or distribute widely across multiple retailers and channels. This choice can have lasting implications for visibility, income, reader engagement, and overall career growth. And like most meaningful decisions in publishing, there's no universal answer—only trade-offs.

Let's begin with exclusivity, particularly through KDP Select, Amazon's program that requires your e-book to be available only through Kindle in exchange for specific benefits. Enrolling in KDP Select automatically places your e-book into Kindle Unlimited (KU), Amazon's subscription service that allows readers to borrow books and pay authors based on the number of pages read. This model can work exceptionally well for specific genres, especially where voracious reading is the norm—think romance, fantasy, thrillers, or litRPG.

The visibility boost is also hard to ignore. Amazon's internal recommendation algorithms often favor books in KDP Select. With access to Kindle Deals, free promotions, and Countdown Deals, authors can tap into discovery tools that would be hard to replicate elsewhere. For new authors or those writing in competitive genres, this can mean the difference between being overlooked and landing in front of thousands of potential readers.

But exclusivity comes with limitations. While Amazon is undoubtedly mighty, it's not the only bookstore in the world. Readers who prefer Apple Books, Kobo, or Nook—or who live in regions where Amazon isn't dominant—will never see your book. Libraries, too, may be shut out unless you separately publish the print version via IngramSpark or another platform. And even though KU pays per page read, that amount can fluctuate based on Amazon's internal calculations. In other words, you're placing a great deal of trust in a single platform's closed system.

This leads us to the alternative: wide distribution. To "go wide" means making your book available on as many platforms as possible, including Apple, Kobo, Google Play, Barnes & Noble, libraries, subscription services outside Amazon, and international storefronts. Tools like Draft2Digital, PublishDrive, and even direct uploads to select retailers make this process relatively smooth. You maintain greater ownership over your readership, more diverse income streams, and a buffer against policy changes or algorithm shifts from any one company.

Wide distribution often appeals to authors who are building a long-term career, seeking an international reach, or writing in niche or literary genres where Amazon's algorithms are less impactful. It's also ideal for authors who value direct sales—offering books through their website or platforms like Gumroad and Payhip—or for those who are growing a mailing list or reader community outside of Amazon's ecosystem.

However, going wide usually means slower growth in the beginning. You won't have access to KU's built-in audience, and you'll need to market more proactively across multiple platforms. Sales may be spread thinly across storefronts, requiring more time to learn how each one works, what promotions are available, and how readers behave differently on Kobo compared to, say, Apple Books.

Some authors attempt to balance both worlds by releasing their book exclusively on KDP for the first 90 days, utilizing promotional tools to gain traction, and then expanding their distribution later. Others separate their catalog, keeping some titles exclusive and others available to a broader audience. Still others opt for exclusivity only when writing in specific high-volume genres, using wide distribution for more experimental or evergreen content.

There is no one-size-fits-all model. It depends on your goals:

- Are you aiming for maximum visibility in the short term or steady, diversified income over the long term?
- Do you want to participate in Amazon's promotional ecosystem or build a presence in libraries and international markets?

Exclusivity is not inherently better or worse than wide distribution—it's simply a strategic choice. What matters most is that you make it consciously, based on your unique goals, your audience, and your vision for your publishing journey.

Using AI Insights to Choose the Best Platform

In an increasingly complex publishing world, intuition alone may not be enough to choose the right platform. This is where artificial intelligence quietly steps in—not as a decision-maker, but as an analytical partner. AI tools today can help authors move beyond guesswork and emotional bias to make choices based on real data, patterns, and strategic forecasting.

At first glance, selecting a publishing platform may seem like a simple comparison of royalties or distribution networks. But the nuances go deeper: genre behavior, reader preferences by region, price sensitivity, seasonal demand, keyword effectiveness, competitive saturation—each of these variables affects how well a book might perform on Amazon versus Apple Books, or through KDP Select versus wide distribution. AI thrives on precisely this kind of complexity.

Let's say you're writing cozy mysteries. An AI tool trained on genre trends can indicate that Kindle Unlimited readers consume this category in large quantities, suggesting that exclusivity with Amazon may yield the highest returns in the early stages. But if you're writing poetry or literary essays, those same tools might flag Apple Books and Kobo as stronger markets, with slower but more stable growth, and less dependence on page-read metrics.

Some AI-driven platforms—like K-Lytics, Publisher Rocket, or even Amazon's data tools—let you analyze thousands of book listings in real time. You can compare sales rank, keyword strength, reader reviews, and pricing patterns to make informed decisions. These insights help answer questions like:

- Where are similar books succeeding?
- Which genres are trending on different platforms?
- Is there room for your voice in a crowded niche, or would you be better off in a less saturated category?

Beyond market analysis, AI can assist in scenario testing. For instance, you can simulate what might happen if you price your e-book at $2.99 instead of $4.99, or release your audiobook first instead of your paperback. Some platforms even offer predictive tools that estimate future sales based on current metadata, genre signals, and comparable titles. While none of these predictions are perfect, they provide a new level of clarity in an otherwise uncertain field.

And AI doesn't just serve the numbers. It can help tailor your decision to your personal style and business model. Are you someone who thrives on personal connections and wants to build direct relationships with readers? Then, a wide distribution combined with email marketing might be your ideal path. Are you looking to be more hands-off and maximize income through passive income? Then Amazon's exclusivity programs may be a better fit for you—for now.

Ultimately, the most innovative use of AI is not to replace your intuition, but to amplify it. By blending your creative vision with intelligent analysis, you can make informed and inspired decisions for your publishing. And just as your books evolve, so can your platform strategy. The key is not to lock yourself into a static decision, but to remain curious, adaptable, and willing to adjust as your career—and the market—unfolds.

In this way, AI becomes not only a guide but a quiet partner on your publishing path. It won't write the book for you, and it won't choose your voice—but it can help you put that voice in the right hands, in the right place, at the right time.

Choosing the right publishing platform is more than a technical step—it's a declaration of how you want your book to live in the world. Whether you're drawn to the reach of Amazon, the flexibility of wide distribution, or the quiet power of data-backed AI insights, your choice becomes part of your book's identity. It shapes who will find it, how they'll experience it, and what kind of future it may have.

But just as important as *where* you publish is *how* you present your work. A compelling story or valuable idea can exist in many forms, and today's publishing landscape offers more options than ever before. Will your book be held in your hand as a printed paperback, or will it be read on an e-reader screen? Will it be heard as a voice in someone's ear while they walk or rest?

The next chapter opens this door: exploring the strengths and nuances of print books, e-books, and audiobooks—not as competing formats, but as different expressions of the same creative offering.

Print, E-books, and Audiobooks — One Story, Many Forms

There was a time when publishing a book meant only one thing: printed pages bound between two covers, stacked on bookstore shelves or mailed in boxes. That era hasn't disappeared—it's simply expanded. Today, a single book can exist simultaneously in multiple formats, each offering a unique way for readers to engage with the same content. For authors and publishers, understanding the differences between print, e-books, and audiobooks isn't just a technical matter—it's a creative decision.

Every format has its own personality. A printed book invites a tactile relationship; it's something to hold, flip through, underline. It's physical, rooted in a particular time and place—ideal for gifting, collecting, or reading without screens. In contrast, an e-book is agile. It fits into a pocket-sized device and can travel anywhere in the world in seconds. It's adjustable, searchable, and often more affordable. And then there's the audiobook, the most intimate format of all—heard through a narrator's voice, it brings language into the body through sound, often while the listener is doing something else entirely.

In this chapter, we won't argue for one format over another. Instead, we'll explore what each one can offer—to you as the author, and to your audience. We'll talk about when print might be your best option, when e-books make more sense, and why audiobooks are becoming not just a trend but a standard. You'll learn about the logistics behind each version—cost, tools, preparation—and what to expect when adapting your book into different formats.

Whether your goal is to make your story accessible, reach global markets, or offer readers a choice, knowing how to work with these three formats will expand your publishing possibilities. One story can live in many forms—and with a bit of strategy and care, each version can feel like it was made just for the person holding it, clicking through it, or listening in the dark.

Pricing Your Book — Finding the True Value of Your Work

Putting a price on a book is not just about choosing a number. It's about understanding what stands behind that number: the time, energy, money, and thought that went into creating it. It's also about knowing the expectations of your readers and the dynamics of the market. Pricing a book fairly and strategically is both an art and a calculation. And in the world of independent publishing, where the author often takes on the role of both creator and entrepreneur, it becomes an essential skill.

The first layer of pricing lies in understanding the true cost of the book. Many authors overlook this and think only of printing or platform fees, but the cost of a book begins long before it ever reaches a printer or a reader's device. If the book was written by the author herself (himself), it's important to estimate the value of her (his) time—days, months, or even years invested in crafting the manuscript. If a ghostwriter or a content editor was involved, their services are a significant financial investment and must be accounted for. Editing and proofreading, two stages crucial to the quality of the final product, also come with professional fees. A skilled editor who improves structure, tone, and clarity, followed by a proofreader who corrects mistakes, can cost hundreds or even thousands of dollars, depending on the length and complexity of the text.

The visual presentation is equally important. A compelling cover design that resonates with the intended audience often costs between $100 and $500. If the book includes illustrations, diagrams, or any other graphical elements, these too contribute to the production cost. Then there's formatting: a separate phase where the text is prepared for both print (usually in PDF format) and digital distribution (typically in EPUB and MOBI). This ensures your book meets technical standards and provides a smooth reading experience.

Print books, naturally, involve the added cost of actual production. The price per copy depends on page count, binding type, paper quality, and the size of the print run. Larger quantities generally lower the cost per unit, but also require upfront investment and storage or distribution plans. And if your book is sold through online platforms or bookstores, distribution costs—shipping, storage, platform commissions—must be factored in. Add to this your marketing efforts: ads on social media, promotional campaigns, printed materials, giveaways. All of these are real expenses that belong in the cost structure of your book.

Let's say, for example, that you invest $500 in editing, $200 in cover design, $100 in formatting, and $300 in marketing. If printing each book costs $5, and you're printing 100 copies, your total upfront cost is $1100, with $5 added to each physical copy. That's your starting point. But cost is only half the equation.

The second half lies in determining the selling price—one that not only recovers your investment but also yields a profit and aligns with what your target readers are willing to pay. This is where market analysis becomes vital. Prices vary by genre and format. E-books are often expected to be cheaper than print editions. Premium formats—like full-color hardcovers or illustrated editions—can command higher prices. A children's book aimed at young families may need to be priced accessibly, while a business guide promising tangible ROI for professionals may sustain a premium.

Knowing your audience helps enormously. Parents buying books for their children usually want affordable options since they purchase in volume. Romance readers often expect e-books under $5, while nonfiction readers may pay more if the content offers practical solutions. The format also matters: printed books typically range from $10 to $25, while e-books sit comfortably between $2.99 and $9.99. Audiobooks, which involve the cost of professional narration and audio editing, are often priced between $10 and $30, depending on length and subject.

And then there's the question of royalties. Platforms like Amazon KDP offer 70% royalty for e-books priced between $2.99 and $9.99, but only 35% outside of that range. Print royalties are lower once printing costs and distribution fees are deducted. Audiobooks sold through Audible or similar services provide royalties of 20% to 40%, often dependent on whether you've chosen an exclusive distribution contract. For example, if you price a paperback at $15 and your per-unit cost (including printing and logistics) is $8, your gross profit is $7—before the platform takes its share. That number might shrink further depending on sales channel fees.

Digital books, while cheaper to produce, still need pricing strategy. If your editing and design costs are already recouped through print, your digital edition might yield almost pure profit. Pricing your e-book at $4.99 on Amazon, for instance, could give you a royalty of $3.49 per sale—an attractive margin. The same goes for audiobooks: a $1000 investment in recording may sound high, but if you price the audiobook at $20 and earn $8 per copy through royalties, you break even after 125 sales and begin profiting beyond that point.

Publication Type	**Average Royalty Rate**	**Royalty Conditions**
Print Books	5–15%	– Traditional publishers: 5–10% of the retail price. – Self-publishing (Amazon KDP, IngramSpark): 40–60%, depending on the platform and distribution model.
E-books	35–70%	– Traditional publishers: 25–50% of *net revenue*. – Self-publishing: • 70% on Amazon KDP (for books priced $2.99–$9.99), • 35% for prices outside that range. – Other platforms (e.g., Smashwords, Draft2Digital): 50–70%.
Audiobooks	20–80%	– Audible/ACX: • 40% with exclusive agreement, • 20% with non-exclusive agreement. – Other platforms (Findaway Voices, Authors Republic): 20–80%, depending on terms and distribution.

		– Self-produced and sold audiobooks: up to 100% of profits after expenses.

Another important factor is flexibility. Book pricing is not static—it can and should evolve. Temporary discounts, promotional giveaways, and limited-time offers are useful tools for building momentum and attracting new readers. For some authors, giving away their first book in a series for free leads to higher sales of the sequels. Others experiment with pricing based on reader feedback or seasonal trends. And many successful authors test their prices, adjusting upward or downward depending on performance.

It's also worth considering that the perceived value of a book can be influenced by its price. A book priced too low may seem amateurish or unworthy of attention. A book priced too high might deter first-time readers. Finding the balance between value and accessibility is part intuition, part market awareness.

At its core, pricing a book is about recognizing the worth of your creation—honoring both the work that went into it and the impact you hope it will have. It is not simply a number on a screen or a tag on a shelf. It is the intersection of effort, artistry, economy, and psychology. And when you approach it with care, transparency, and a bit of courage, it becomes a vital part of your book's success.

Publishers: From Global Giants to Niche Innovators

The world of book publishing is vast and varied, encompassing everything from multinational corporations to small, independent presses. Choosing the right publisher — or understanding how they operate — is one of the most important steps for any author. But what exactly differentiates a "real" publisher from a "vanity press"? Who are the key players dominating the global market, and which lesser-known publishers specialize in your genre or audience?

Let's take a closer look at the publishing landscape today.

The Big Five: Giants of the Industry

At the top of the hierarchy are the so-called "Big Five" — powerful publishing houses that shape the literary market, control major imprints, and have extensive international distribution networks.

- **Penguin Random House (PRH)** is the world's largest trade publisher. Owned by the German media conglomerate Bertelsmann, PRH operates out of New York and houses iconic imprints such as **Knopf**, **Ballantine**, **Crown**, **Viking**, and **Berkley**.

- **Hachette Livre**, based in Paris and owned by the **Lagardère Group**, ranks second globally. It operates a wide range of imprints, including **Little, Brown and Company**, **Orbit**, and **Grand Central Publishing**.

- **HarperCollins**, owned by **News Corp**, is another major force, also headquartered in New York. Its diverse imprints include **Avon**, **William Morrow**, and **Harlequin**, the latter known worldwide for romance fiction.

- **Macmillan Publishers**, owned by **Holtzbrinck Publishing Group** in Germany, has a strong presence in both trade and academic publishing. Its well-known imprints include **St. Martin's Press**, **Tor Books**, and **Picador**.

- **Simon & Schuster**, now owned by the private equity firm **KKR**, completes the Big Five. It specializes in fiction and nonfiction across genres through imprints like **Scribner**, **Atria**, and **Gallery Books**.

These five publishers dominate the English-language book market, handling most bestsellers and offering substantial global reach — but they're not the only players worth knowing.

Medium-Sized and Notable Independent Publishers

Beyond the Big Five lies a diverse ecosystem of **mid-sized and independent publishers**, many of whom have carved out powerful niches by focusing on specific genres, topics, or audiences.

- **Scholastic** (USA) is a household name in children's and YA literature — best known for publishing *Harry Potter* in the United States, as well as *The Hunger Games* and *Captain Underpants*.
- **Bloomsbury Publishing** (UK) first gained international acclaim as the original publisher of *Harry Potter*, but its reputation spans academic, trade, and literary books.
- **Oxford University Press (OUP)** and **Cambridge University Press (CUP)** are the world's most prestigious university presses, both publishing high-caliber academic and educational works.
- **Wiley** (USA) is renowned for professional, academic, and scientific content, particularly in business, health, and technology.
- **Springer Nature** (Germany) specializes in scientific and medical publications, including journals, research monographs, and medical textbooks.
- **Hay House** (USA) has established itself as a leader in the self-help and spiritual space, publishing authors like Louise Hay and Dr. Wayne Dyer.
- **Workman Publishing** (USA) is known for its creative nonfiction and innovative formats — think calendars, cookbooks, and parenting guides.
- **Chronicle Books** (USA) focuses on visually stunning titles, including art books, cookbooks, and quirky gift books.
- **Europa Editions** (Italy/USA) is highly respected for bringing translated literary fiction to English-speaking audiences.

These publishers may not always offer the same reach as the Big Five, but they often provide greater editorial intimacy, creative freedom, and tailored marketing.

Independent and Niche Publishers

At the grassroots level, **small presses and boutique publishers** serve specific literary communities and genres that may be overlooked by larger houses. Their role is vital in maintaining diversity and innovation in publishing.

Some notable examples:

- **Graywolf Press** (USA): Specializes in literary fiction, essays, and poetry — known for nurturing award-winning voices.
- **Melville House** (USA): Publishes political nonfiction, literary fiction, and translations with a bold, intellectual edge.
- **Fantagraphics Books** (USA): A leader in comics and graphic novels, especially indie and avant-garde work.
- **Verso Books** (UK): One of the most prominent left-wing publishers, focusing on political theory, activism, and radical culture.

These publishers often champion voices that challenge convention, offering platforms for debut authors, experimental work, and underrepresented perspectives.

Academic and Educational Publishers

Academic publishing is a distinct world, governed by different economics and audience expectations. Unlike trade publishers, academic houses focus on peer-reviewed content, research monographs, and educational resources.

Key names in this field include:

- **Elsevier** (Netherlands): Dominant in science, technology, and medicine (STM), with a vast library of journals and academic books.
- **Taylor & Francis** (UK): Covers humanities, social sciences, and scientific research.
- **Pearson** (UK): Specializes in textbooks and learning tools for students across all education levels.
- **McGraw Hill** (USA): A go-to name for educational content in schools and universities, especially in STEM and business fields.

For scholars and educators, publishing with these companies is often tied to academic advancement, funding opportunities, and professional reputation.

Vanity Publishers vs. Traditional Publishers

A crucial distinction in publishing is that between **traditional publishers** and **vanity presses**.

- **Traditional publishers** invest their own money into editing, designing, printing, and marketing your book. They usually pay the author an advance and royalties. Selection is competitive, and acceptance signals professional endorsement.
- **Vanity publishers**, on the other hand, require authors to pay for publishing services while offering limited editorial support and minimal marketing. Despite charging high fees, they often produce subpar results — essentially selling authors the *appearance* of being published.

Vanity publishing can sometimes be disguised under euphemisms like "hybrid publishing" or "author services." It's essential to research carefully and read contracts before signing.

For easier reference, here is a summary of the most prominent publishers mentioned above. This table outlines their location, ownership, primary focus, and notable imprints. It can help authors better navigate the complex publishing landscape and identify potential matches for their work.

Publisher Name	Country	Ownership / Group	Main Focus	Notable Imprints / Notes
Penguin Random House	USA / Germany	Bertelsmann	Trade publishing	Knopf, Ballantine, Viking, Crown, Berkley
Hachette Livre	France	Lagardère Group	Trade publishing	Little, Brown, Orbit, Grand Central
HarperCollins	USA	News Corp	Fiction, nonfiction, romance	Avon, William Morrow, Harlequin
Macmillan Publishers	UK / Germany	Holtzbrinck Group	Academic, trade, children's books	Tor, St. Martin's Press, Picador
Simon & Schuster	USA	KKR (Private Equity)	Trade publishing	Scribner, Atria, Gallery Books
Scholastic	USA	Independent	Children's and YA books	Publisher of Harry Potter (US), The Hunger Games
Bloomsbury Publishing	UK	Independent	Trade and academic publishing	Original Harry Potter publisher
Oxford University Press (OUP)	UK	University of Oxford	Academic and reference works	World's largest university press
Cambridge University Press	UK	University of Cambridge	Academic and educational content	Historical academic powerhouse

Wiley	USA	Publicly traded	Academic and professional publishing	Strong in STEM, business, healthcare
Springer Nature	Germany	Private	Scientific, technical, and medical publishing	Includes Nature and Springer imprints
Hay House	USA	Independent	Self-help and spirituality	Louise Hay, Wayne Dyer
Workman Publishing	USA	Acquired by Hachette in 2021	Nonfiction, practical guides	Parenting, cooking, creativity
Chronicle Books	USA	McEvoy Group	Art books, cookbooks, gift books	Known for visual quality
Europa Editions	Italy / USA	Independent	Translated literary fiction	International literature
Graywolf Press	USA	Nonprofit	Literary fiction, poetry	Respected indie literary press
Melville House	USA	Independent	Political nonfiction, translations	Progressive and bold voices
Fantagraphics Books	USA	Independent	Graphic novels and comics	Indie comics pioneer
Verso Books	UK	Independent / Left Book Club	Radical politics and culture	Known for leftist academic writing
Elsevier	Netherlands	RELX Group	Scientific and medical publishing	Largest STM publisher
Taylor & Francis	UK	Informa	Academic journals and monographs	Wide range of disciplines
Pearson	UK	Publicly traded	Educational publishing	Textbooks, testing, digital learning
McGraw Hill	USA	Platinum Equity	Textbooks and	Strong K–12 and

			educational tools	university presence

Working with a traditional publisher still holds significant advantages, especially for authors who are not ready to manage the entire publishing and promotion process on their own. While self-publishing offers more control and potentially higher royalties, traditional publishing provides structure, credibility, and upfront investment.

One of the biggest benefits of signing with a publisher is cost coverage. Professional editing, cover design, layout, printing, distribution, and especially marketing—all of this is handled by the publisher at no upfront cost to the author. In return, authors receive a share of the profits in the form of royalties.

Although royalty rates with traditional publishers are often lower than in self-publishing, authors benefit from:

- Higher production quality
- Established distribution channels (bookstores, libraries, international markets)
- Credibility in media and awards eligibility
- Less personal financial risk

However, getting into a publishing house—especially one of the Big Five—is not easy. Most large publishers do not accept unsolicited manuscripts. This is where literary agents become essential allies.

What Is a Literary Agent and How Do They Work?

A literary agent is a professional who represents authors and their work to publishers, acting as a critical bridge between the creative world of writing and the business side of publishing. Their main job is to help authors navigate the complexities of the publishing industry, ensuring that each manuscript gets in front of the right editors and that each contract is as favorable as possible. For authors seeking to publish traditionally, a literary agent is often essential, as many major publishers—especially the largest ones—do not accept submissions unless they come through an agent.

The core role of a literary agent is to champion the author's work. Agents are experts in understanding the publishing landscape: they know which editors are looking for which types of books, and they know how to present a manuscript in a way that grabs attention. They don't just send off the manuscript; they pitch it thoughtfully and strategically, increasing its chances of being accepted. At every stage, from manuscript development to deal negotiation, the agent is on the author's side.

What Does a Literary Agent Do?

A literary agent's work spans many areas. One of their first responsibilities is **manuscript evaluation and feedback**. They carefully review the author's manuscript or proposal to determine its potential in the current market. If needed, they provide editorial suggestions—offering concrete revisions to improve the structure, voice, or appeal of the manuscript before it is submitted to publishers.

Once the manuscript is polished, the agent's role shifts to **finding the right publisher**. They use their insider knowledge and professional relationships to pinpoint publishers and editors who are most likely to be interested in a particular book. Because they are familiar with the editorial tastes and priorities of different publishing houses, they can match the manuscript with the people most likely to appreciate it.

Next comes **pitching to publishers**. This is more than just forwarding the manuscript. Agents submit it with personalized pitches that emphasize the book's strengths, marketability, and relevance to the publisher's catalog. The goal is to spark genuine interest and find an editor who will not only want to acquire the book but will also advocate for it within their publishing house.

When a publisher is ready to make an offer, the agent steps into their **contract negotiation** role. They work on behalf of the author to secure the best possible deal. This includes negotiating the size of the advance, royalty percentages, the handling of subsidiary rights (such as film, TV, or foreign rights), and protecting the author's long-term interests through careful attention to contract clauses.

Rights management is another important function. Many agents also handle subrights, which include translation rights, audiobook rights, and film/TV rights. In international or multimedia deals, they may collaborate with co-agents or specialized agents to maximize opportunities and income.

Beyond a single book deal, agents often serve as advisors in **career development**. They help authors build sustainable, long-term careers by advising on future book ideas, developing an author brand, and creating strategies for growing readership. When unexpected challenges arise—such as disagreements between the author and publisher—the agent provides **problem-solving** support, acting as a mediator and advocate to resolve conflicts effectively.

How Much Does a Literary Agent Charge?

Unlike other professionals who charge fixed rates or hourly fees, literary agents are paid on commission. This means they only earn money when the author earns money, making their success directly tied to the author's success.

The standard commission for domestic book deals is typically 15% of the author's earnings, which includes both the advance and future royalties. For instance, if an author receives a $10,000 advance, the agent's commission would be $1,500. When foreign publishers are involved, the commission is usually 20%, as it often includes the participation of a sub-agent who helps sell the book internationally.

For subrights—such as film, television, translation, or audiobook rights—the agent also takes a commission, generally between 15% and 20%, depending on the specific circumstances of the deal and whether co-agents or other specialists are involved.

Importantly, reputable agents do not charge upfront fees. They do not ask for payment to read or evaluate manuscripts. Their earnings come solely from commissions on sales. If a so-called agent asks for a reading fee, submission fee, or consulting fee before any sale has occurred, it is usually a red flag that should not be ignored.

In rare cases, an agent might deduct minor expenses related to selling the book—such as mailing physical manuscripts or making international phone calls—but these are typically small, reasonable, and clearly explained to the author.

Advantages of Having a Literary Agent

Having a literary agent offers numerous advantages. One of the most important is **access to publishers**. Many large publishing houses, including industry giants like HarperCollins and Penguin Random House, do not accept submissions from unagented authors. An agent opens these otherwise closed doors and gives your manuscript a real chance of being reviewed by decision-makers.

In addition, agents bring **strong negotiation skills** to the table. They know what is standard in the industry and what can be improved in a contract. As a result, they can push for higher advances, better royalty terms, and critical contract protections, such as reversion rights or control over future formats.

An agent also helps **save time**. Submitting to publishers, following up, and reviewing complex contracts can be overwhelming and time-consuming. With an agent handling these tasks, the author can stay focused on writing and creative work.

Agents provide **market expertise** as well. They are well-versed in trends and reader demands and can help shape your manuscript or proposal to align with what the market is currently buying—without compromising artistic integrity.

Most importantly, a good agent provides **career development support**. They help build your long-term path as a writer, offering perspective, honest feedback, and business strategy that goes far beyond a single deal.

Challenges of Working with a Literary Agent

Working with an agent is not without its challenges. One of the biggest is finding the right agent. Not every agent is right for every writer. Many agents specialize in specific genres or types of books, so authors must do careful research to ensure alignment before submitting a query.

Even with an agent, authors must face the reality of rejections. The publishing world is highly competitive, and many manuscripts are passed over before finding a home. Having an agent increases the odds but is no guarantee of a book deal.

The commission structure, though fair and aligned with success, means that authors share a portion of their income. While most authors see this as a worthwhile trade-off, it is a financial consideration.

There are also waiting periods to consider. Querying agents can take weeks or months, and even after signing with an agent, the process of submitting to publishers and waiting for responses can be slow. Patience is a necessary part of the journey.

How to Find a Literary Agent

The process of finding the right agent begins with thorough research. Resources such as the Association of Authors' Representatives (AAR), QueryTracker, and Writer's Market offer databases of reputable agents. Writers should look for agents who represent their genre and have a record of placing books with established publishers.

Next comes writing a compelling query letter. This short pitch should summarize the book's premise, describe its target audience, and highlight what makes the book unique. It's your first impression—and a critical one.

Authors must always follow submission guidelines precisely. Every agent or agency typically lists their preferences online, and failing to follow these instructions can result in instant rejection. Agents are busy professionals, and respecting their process is essential.

Finally, it's important to maintain patience. Rejections are common, and every successful author has likely received their share. Persistence, resilience, and a commitment to refining your craft and your pitch are key to eventually landing the right representation.

A literary agent is not just a gatekeeper to the traditional publishing world—they are a knowledgeable, invested partner in an author's career. While they take a commission on earnings, their expertise in editorial development, market positioning, contract negotiation, and rights management often leads to better deals, greater visibility, and long-term success. Finding the right literary agent takes time and perseverance, but for many authors, it is one of the most important relationships they will form in their publishing journey. The guidance, access, and protection an agent offers can be invaluable—and for writers who want to build a sustainable career, that partnership is often worth every effort it takes to achieve.

What Readers Want: Trends in Publishing Formats and What Actually Sells

Every author dreams of success. But beyond the dream lies a crucial question: *what do readers actually want?* Many writers spend years polishing a manuscript, only to find that the market is moving in a completely different direction. Sometimes, what readers are devouring today is far from what you're writing about. And while staying true to your voice is essential, there are moments when taking a step back and looking at publishing trends can open doors you didn't expect. It may even inspire you to explore a new genre, format, or approach you hadn't considered before.

Understanding the formats that are selling—and the genres that thrive within them—can help authors make smarter, more strategic decisions. Whether you're a first-time indie author or an experienced writer thinking of switching gears, these current trends can help guide your next move.

Format	Market Status	What Sells Best	Trends to Watch
E-Books	Mature but steady market. Growth has plateaued but remains popular for convenience and accessibility.	- Romance, Mystery, Thriller (fast-paced, addictive) - Self-help, Non-fiction (portable, practical) - Indie authors (low cost, global access via KDP)	- Subscription models (Kindle Unlimited, Scribd) - Interactive/enhanced e-books with multimedia, esp. for children and education
Print Books	Resilient and preferred for tactile experience, visuals, and collectibility.	- Children's books (durability, parent appeal) - Cookbooks, art/coffee table books (design-focused) - Hardcover fiction (collector value, first editions)	- Premium editions (foil covers, extras) - Eco-conscious publishing (recycled paper, soy ink) - Print-on-demand reducing waste and cost
Audiobooks	Fastest-growing segment; ideal for multitaskers and mobile lifestyles.	- Thrillers and suspense (immersive storytelling) - Memoirs/biographies (esp. author-narrated) - Self-help/business (for busy professionals)	- Subscription platforms (Audible, Storytel, Scribd) - Short-form and serialized audio content-AI-narration emerging, human narration still preferred
Hybrid/Niche Formats	Expanding creatively, serving	- Interactive/AR-enhanced books	- Serialized fiction (Kindle Vella, Radish)

	specific audiences and use cases.	(esp. for kids and education) - Adult coloring/puzzle books (mindfulness, stress relief)- Graphic novels and comics	- Customizable/personalized books (gifts, children's names, etc.)

Across formats, some genres consistently perform well, while others experience surges based on current trends or cultural shifts.

Fiction that sells: Romance, mystery/thriller, science fiction, and fantasy continue to dominate across all formats due to their passionate fanbases and endless market appetite.

Non-fiction that performs: Self-help, memoirs, business, and health/wellness titles maintain strong sales, especially in e-book and audiobook formats where practical information is easy to consume on the go.

Children's and YA books remain staples in both print and digital formats, with strong performance across school systems, parenting communities, and gift buyers.

What really drives book sales in today's world? It's not always what we expect. Sometimes, a book becomes successful simply because it speaks to a particular moment — a cultural mood, a question that's on everyone's mind, or a pain point people are quietly carrying. Topics like mental health, burnout, loneliness, identity, climate change, or trauma often surge into public consciousness, and books that touch these nerves tend to rise with them. It's not necessarily about following trends blindly, but about sensing the emotional undercurrent of the times.

And then, of course, there's the weight of a name. Recognition carries power. A book by someone like J.K. Rowling or Brandon Sanderson doesn't just land on shelves — it arrives with built-in trust, attention, and expectation. Readers already know what they're getting, or at least they believe they do, and that makes the decision to buy almost automatic. For new authors, that can feel discouraging at first — but it's also a reminder of what's possible when you build something slowly and with care.

What many new writers underestimate is how deeply community matters now. The idea of the distant, untouchable author has faded. Today, it's often the authors who show up — who answer comments, share their process, listen to their readers — who find surprising and lasting success. Especially in the world of self-publishing, that connection becomes part of the story. It's not just about writing a good book. It's about creating a space where readers want to follow you, return to you, and share your work because they feel something real behind it.

The publishing industry is not static—it's alive, shifting, and full of opportunity. Each format offers its own unique strengths: e-books for affordability and access, print books for sensory and visual appeal, audiobooks for convenience and immersion, and hybrid formats for creativity and personalization.

But success comes not only from understanding what's trending—it comes from knowing where your content fits, how your audience reads or listens, and being open to evolving as both a writer and entrepreneur. Don't be afraid to step outside your comfort zone. Sometimes, the genre or format you never considered might be exactly where your breakthrough begins.

Print-on-demand options and sustainability considerations

Print-on-demand (POD) has fundamentally changed the publishing industry, offering a flexible and accessible way for authors to produce and sell books without the risks associated with traditional print runs. Unlike traditional publishing, where books are printed in bulk and stored in warehouses, POD prints books only when an order is placed. This eliminates the need for large upfront investments and reduces the financial risks of unsold inventory. For many independent authors, self-publishers, and even small presses, POD has become the go-to solution for entering the publishing market.

One of the primary advantages of POD is its cost efficiency for small print runs. Traditional printing methods require large orders to justify the costs, but POD platforms like Amazon KDP, IngramSpark, and Lulu allow authors to print as few as one copy at a time. This is particularly beneficial for niche authors or those testing the market with a new title. POD also provides flexibility. Authors can update their files at any time, making it easy to release revised editions or correct errors without incurring significant costs.

Global distribution is another key benefit of POD. Platforms like IngramSpark operate printing facilities worldwide, enabling books to be printed closer to the customer. This shortens shipping times and reduces costs. For authors using Amazon KDP, their books are automatically available in the Amazon marketplace, one of the largest online retailers in the world. This global reach is invaluable for authors who might otherwise struggle to distribute their work.

However, while POD is often hailed as a cost-effective and innovative solution, it is not without its challenges—particularly when viewed through the lens of sustainability. On the surface, POD appears environmentally friendly since it minimizes overproduction and waste. Traditional publishing is notorious for overprinting books to meet anticipated demand, often resulting in unsold copies being destroyed or left to languish in storage. POD avoids this by printing only what is needed, reducing the likelihood of waste.

Yet, POD's environmental benefits come with caveats. Printing a single book at a time can be energy-intensive compared to large-scale offset printing. Digital printing, the method most used for POD, has a higher per-unit energy cost. Furthermore, while POD eliminates the need for warehouses, it relies heavily on individual shipping. Each book is typically shipped separately to the customer, leading to higher transportation emissions compared to bulk shipments in traditional publishing.

The materials used in POD also raise concerns. Many POD platforms use standard paper and ink that may not be sustainably sourced. Authors and publishers looking to prioritize sustainability can select eco-friendly options, such as paper certified by the Forest Stewardship Council (FSC) or inks made from renewable resources.

However, these options are not universally available on all platforms, and their costs may be prohibitive for some authors.

Packaging waste is another issue inherent in POD. Because books are shipped individually, the amount of cardboard, plastic, and other packaging materials adds up quickly. While some platforms are exploring biodegradable or recyclable packaging options, the industry as a whole has yet to adopt these solutions universally.

For authors committed to sustainability, there are steps they can take to mitigate the environmental impact of POD. Choosing platforms that print books closer to the buyer is one way to reduce emissions from long-distance shipping. IngramSpark, for example, has a network of regional printing facilities. Additionally, authors can encourage their readers to choose e-books or consolidate multiple orders to minimize packaging waste.

Print-on-demand is a double-edged sword when it comes to sustainability. It offers a way to reduce waste by eliminating unsold inventory but increases energy use and emissions in other parts of the process. Despite these challenges, POD remains a powerful tool for authors and publishers, offering opportunities to enter the market without the barriers posed by traditional methods. Balancing the benefits of POD with sustainability considerations requires thoughtful choices from both authors and POD platforms. As the industry evolves, integrating more sustainable practices into POD workflows will be crucial to its long-term viability as a publishing solution.

Part 6: Marketing Like a Pro

If you study the biographies of well-known people—writers, artists, musicians, and other creatives—you'll notice many common patterns. Most of them faced similar challenges long before they became successful. Unfortunately, fame often came too late—if not at the end of their lives, then only after their deaths. And fame, as we know, is often closely tied to income. As a result, many of the literary works from the past are now bringing in profits not for their creators, but for literary agencies and publishing conglomerates.

In today's world, the sheer volume of creative output—especially in literature—is staggering. Even the most original, extraordinary work can go unnoticed, never reaching its intended audience or offering its creator the recognition or financial return it deserves.

The isolation brought on by the COVID era pushed millions of people to spend more time online, living partially or even fully in virtual spaces. This shift gave rise to an explosion of bloggers and influencers who began to master the marketing ecosystems of platforms like Instagram, TikTok, and Facebook. Many of them started generating excellent income from home—creating digital products, building loyal audiences, and monetizing their content. Remarkably, even without formal education in business or economics, many began speaking confidently about marketing, targeting, and audience engagement—and teaching others how to use these tools to promote any kind of product.

But marketing is not just about pushing a product—like a book—or a service. True marketing is an art. It's the art of creating value for your audience and building lasting relationships. To master it, you must go beyond the basics. You must be willing to grow with the market, adapt to changes, and embrace modern tools and strategies. Below are a few essential steps that can help you elevate your marketing approach and start thinking like a professional.

Professional-level marketing begins with a deep understanding of your audience. If you're an author, who is your ideal reader? What are their needs, pain points, and desires? This process—defining the specific characteristics of your audience—is called targeting. In other words, it's about identifying your "target" readers, the core group most likely to connect with your work.

Personally, I always study the analytical data available on my subscribers, viewers, and readers—data that most social media platforms now offer for free. For instance, I've noticed that most of my audience is made up of women aged 25 to 40. But recently, I've also seen a shift toward the 45 to 50 age group. This tells me that my loyal readers are growing older with me—and it's something I consider when choosing new topics for future books, like menopause.

Analyze your own data. Use polls, track behavior on social media and your website. The better you know your readers, the more precisely and effectively you'll be able to speak to them.

Surveys are a wonderful free tool for understanding what your audience really wants. Whenever I consider a topic for a new book, I always conduct a poll on my platforms to ask my readers what they'd like me to write about next.

Your product or service must stand out in a crowded market. What makes you different? Why should a reader choose your book over someone else's? You need to develop a clear unique selling proposition—a simple, compelling way to communicate your strengths and the value you offer to your reader. Think of it as a concise description of your book as a product.

For example, I've written a book on women's health. A possible unique selling proposition might sound like this:

"*Unlock the secrets of longevity and energy through evidence-based principles!*

Our book Health Without Compromise: 7 Steps to Ideal Well-being is not just a collection of tips — it's a step-by-step guide grounded in the latest research in medicine, nutrition, and psychology. We offer a unique approach that combines personalized recommendations, practical exercises, and motivational techniques to help you not only improve your health but maintain those results for life.

Why do readers choose us?

- *Only verified information — every recommendation is backed by scientific studies.*
- *Personalized approach — quizzes and checklists help you adapt the guidance to your lifestyle.*
- *Simple and accessible — complex medical terms are explained in clear, everyday language.*
- *Long-term impact — the focus is on habit formation that will stay with you forever.*

Your health is your greatest asset. Start your transformation today with the book that will become your personal health coach."

And here's something else to remember: AI can help you craft descriptions like this. You can upload your book file and ask AI to create product descriptions, promotional blurbs, or engaging marketing content — from short taglines to full-page advertising copy. All the things that once required a professional marketer (with expensive hourly rates) can now be done with the help of artificial intelligence — and often, for free.

Modern marketing requires a multichannel presence. Social media, email newsletters, content marketing, SEO, paid advertising — all these need to work together as a unified system. Professionals know how to integrate these channels to amplify the effect of each one. There are even specialized tools and platforms that can bring these marketing components into one cohesive strategy.

But none of that works without content. Content is the foundation of all marketing. Useful, interesting, and high-quality content attracts an audience, holds their attention, and builds trust. Whether it's blog posts, videos, infographics, or social media updates, your content must solve problems and answer the questions your readers have. And this applies not only to your promotional materials — it applies to the book itself. The content *within* the book matters just as much as the content around it.

When Facebook first introduced advertising for businesses — for products and services — one of the most useful tools was its ad performance analytics. It allowed us to see, in real time, how efficiently money was being spent and how effectively new readers were being reached. I worked with a team to analyze campaigns, test different audiences, and optimize strategies. You can do the same. Use analytics tools like Google Analytics to track key metrics: conversions, engagement, ROI, and more. It's easier than you might think — especially with the help of tutorials and in-dashboard guidance. Even if these terms seem intimidating at first, modern analytics platforms present data visually — with charts, graphs, and tables that make it much easier to understand.

Marketing isn't just about selling — it's about creating loyalty. CRM (Customer Relationship Management) systems help you manage communication with readers, personalize your outreach, and build long-term relationships. Loyalty programs and bonuses can also be implemented, offering readers extra value while encouraging return visits and recommendations.

The world of marketing never stands still. New technologies, platforms, and trends emerge every year. Professionals stay alert — they study what's changing, test new tools, and adapt their strategies constantly. Today, video marketing, storytelling, and the use of artificial intelligence are becoming increasingly influential. Ignoring them means missing out.

And finally, to market like a pro is not just about learning tools — it's about mindset. Be curious. Be willing to experiment. Learn from your mistakes. Always put your reader, your client, at the heart of what you do. That's the only way to build something lasting. That's the only way to stand out.

Building Your Author Brand

Branding is more than a logo, a name, or a color palette. At its core, a brand is a feeling. It's the set of associations, emotions, and expectations that your name evokes the moment someone hears it or sees your work. A strong brand builds trust. It creates recognition. And perhaps most importantly, it forges an emotional connection between you and your audience — one that can last far beyond a single book.

In the world of publishing, where new titles appear by the thousands, a distinctive author brand is not a luxury — it's a necessity. It's what helps you rise above the noise, remain in the reader's memory, and turn a first-time buyer into a lifelong supporter.

So why does your brand matter?

Because readers don't just buy books — they invest in voices they trust. If you've built a reputation for thoughtful, reliable content — for example, as a health expert who explains complex topics in simple, empowering language — then your readers are far more likely to purchase your next book without hesitation. They're not just buying a title. They're following a person, a promise, a perspective they've come to value.

A recognizable brand is also your armor in a saturated market. With so many books competing for attention, yours must carry a signature. Maybe it's the striking clarity of your covers. Maybe it's the emotional honesty of your storytelling. Maybe it's your thoroughness, or the way you speak directly to your reader's deepest questions. Whatever it is — that recognizable fingerprint becomes your calling card. It tells your audience: "This is me. You've seen me before. And you'll want to see me again."

But branding isn't only about differentiation — it's also about intimacy. It's about building a space of familiarity and trust. When your work consistently resonates, when it uplifts, educates, comforts, or challenges in just the right way, your readers begin to feel like they know you. They return to your books not only for content, but for connection. Your work becomes part of their life — and they, in turn, become part of your community.

That's how loyalty begins. A reader who has had a meaningful experience with one book is far more likely to buy the next. And the next. In time, your name alone becomes a guarantee — a shorthand for quality and value. For some readers, your series or your style becomes a "must-have," something they seek out without needing to be persuaded.

When that kind of relationship is built, your brand begins to carry itself. Word spreads. Readers recommend your work to friends. They post about it, review it, quote it, and in doing so, introduce new people to your world — even those who've never heard of you before. If you write in a specific niche — health, for instance — and have already earned your readers' trust, your new releases will naturally draw attention, even from those outside your immediate circle.

To better understand how a personal brand can elevate an author's career, let's look at a few writers who have built powerful and recognizable identities. These examples illustrate how consistent voice, thematic focus, and emotional connection with readers can transform a name into a lasting literary brand.

J.K. Rowling

Rowling's name has become synonymous with magical storytelling, imaginative world-building, and emotionally resonant characters. The *Harry Potter* series is not just a set of books — it's a global phenomenon, extending into films, theme parks, and merchandise. Her brand evokes wonder, hope, and a sense of belonging, particularly for younger readers and fantasy lovers. Even when writing under a pseudonym (*Robert Galbraith*), her brand recognition quickly brought attention to her new work.

Stephen King

Stephen King is the ultimate example of genre consistency and prolific output. His brand stands for psychological horror, supernatural fiction, and suspense with deep human themes. Readers picking up a King novel know what emotional and thematic territory to expect. His personal story — a former teacher from Maine who overcame addiction and fear of failure — adds to his brand's authenticity and relatability.

Brené Brown

Though not a fiction writer, Brené Brown is a prime example of a nonfiction author with a powerful brand. Her books on vulnerability, shame, courage, and leadership (*Daring Greatly*, *The Gifts of Imperfection*) have created a strong, trust-based identity. Her brand is rooted in emotional depth, academic credibility, and motivational authenticity, appealing to both professionals and personal growth seekers.

Colleen Hoover

Colleen Hoover has built a massive and emotionally charged brand around contemporary romance and "BookTok"-friendly drama. Her stories combine intense relationships, emotional twists, and relatable themes that resonate with younger audiences. Her branding feels intimate, raw, and highly accessible — and she often connects with readers directly through social media, reinforcing that connection.

Malcolm Gladwell

Gladwell's brand is built on intellectual curiosity and unexpected insights. Books like *The Tipping Point*, *Outliers*, and *Blink* promise a unique way of looking at the world, often combining storytelling with social science. His brand appeals to critical thinkers, entrepreneurs, and lifelong learners who want to see hidden patterns in everyday life.

So how does one build such a brand?

First, it begins with clarity. You must know what makes your work *yours*. What is your voice? What sets your books apart? It could be the way you weave scientific knowledge with real-life stories. It could be your calm tone, your bold questions, or the warmth you offer your readers. Whatever it is, identify it — and lean into it.

Then, express that uniqueness visually. Covers, typography, color schemes — these are more than design choices. They're signals. They tell your reader what to expect, how to feel, and whether this book belongs on their shelf. A well-defined visual language, consistent across your titles, strengthens your identity. Just think of publishers like Mann, Ivanov & Ferber — their minimalist, striking style is instantly recognizable.

But a brand is not just built on image. It's also built on presence. The more visible and engaged you are — whether through interviews, events, social media, or blog posts — the more your audience will see you as a voice of authority. Many authors, particularly in personal development or wellness, build entire ecosystems around their work: YouTube channels, Instagram reels, podcasts. And they use these not only to promote but to connect.

Value, of course, is at the heart of any lasting brand. Your books must *do something* for the reader. They must offer insight, encouragement, clarity, or tools that matter. Whether you're writing about health, spirituality, relationships, or resilience, the question is the same: *What transformation am I giving my reader?*

And don't forget the human part. Interaction builds loyalty. Reply to comments. Host webinars. Ask questions. Create surveys. Readers want to feel seen — and when they do, they return with trust and gratitude.

A perfect example of effective author branding is Mike Viking's *Hygge* series. He didn't just describe Danish lifestyle trends — he invited readers into a whole philosophy of comfort and joy. The design, tone, and message were all in harmony, and the result was a set of international bestsellers that felt like a cozy invitation to slow down and savor life.

Ultimately, author branding isn't just a marketing tool. It's a strategy for connection, a foundation for long-term success. It helps you not only reach your audience but *stay* with them, becoming a voice they return to, rely on, and recommend. Whether you're just beginning or looking to evolve your image, your brand is the bridge between your message and your readers' hearts.

The Power of a Name — Why Authors Use Pseudonyms

Not every name on a book cover belongs to the person who wrote it. In fact, behind many iconic titles and bestselling novels lies a hidden truth: the author chose to remain unseen. The use of pseudonyms, or pen names, is an age-old literary tradition that continues to evolve in today's publishing world. From the classics to the contemporary, authors adopt pseudonyms for a variety of reasons — personal, strategic, and creative.

But why would someone choose to write under a different name?

Let's explore the motivations behind this choice, the advantages it offers, and the cultural impact of pseudonyms in the literary market.

One of the most common reasons authors use pseudonyms is to protect their privacy. In an age of constant exposure and surveillance, anonymity has become a rare luxury. Writers who delve into controversial or deeply personal topics — such as politics, religion, sexuality, or trauma — often prefer to keep their personal identity separate from their professional voice.

For these authors, a pseudonym is more than a mask. It is a shield. It protects their families, their careers, and their peace of mind. It creates a clear boundary between the inner self and the public stage.

In genres like erotica or confessional memoirs, pseudonyms are practically the norm. Readers may feel intimately connected to the writer's voice, while the author maintains a comfortable distance from the spotlight.

Many established authors use pseudonyms when transitioning into new genres. It's a way of entering a new market without carrying the weight of previous expectations. Readers often form strong associations with an author's name — a certain tone, theme, or promise. When that promise changes, it can lead to confusion or resistance.

Take J.K. Rowling, for example. After the global success of the *Harry Potter* series, Rowling decided to publish crime fiction under the name *Robert Galbraith*. The move allowed her to write freely, without the automatic comparisons or pressure of her previous brand. Interestingly, the books received modest attention until her identity was revealed — proving both the power of name recognition and the creative liberation a pseudonym can offer.

This approach is especially useful for authors who wish to explore darker, more experimental, or even more humorous content that would feel out of place under their original brand.

Sometimes, a name is chosen simply because it sounds better. Pseudonyms can be crafted to be more memorable, easier to pronounce, or more culturally adaptable than a writer's real name. In an international marketplace, a name that is short, catchy, and resonant can make a significant difference in recognition and sales.

Mark Twain, whose real name was Samuel Langhorne Clemens, chose his pen name from riverboat slang. The result? A name that became iconic in American literature — simple, vivid, and unforgettable.

Modern writers often think like marketers: their name is part of the brand. A well-chosen pseudonym can signal genre (e.g., romance, thriller, historical fiction), evoke emotion, or position the author within a particular literary tradition.

Throughout history, female authors have used male or gender-neutral pseudonyms to navigate sexist publishing norms. The Brontë sisters wrote as Currer, Ellis, and Acton Bell. Mary Ann Evans became George Eliot. Even today, gender bias persists in certain genres — especially science fiction, fantasy, and crime.

To appeal to broader audiences, some women writers choose names that conceal their gender. Others create initials that carry a tone of neutrality or gravitas.

Conversely, male authors who write for predominantly female audiences (for example, in the romance or young adult genres) often adopt female or gender-ambiguous pen names. Tom Sharpe published some of his early novels as Rebecca Blake to fit into a women's romance series. Harold Lewis Moore, a British World War II veteran, became known as Jessica Blair, author of dozens of historical love stories — a pseudonym his publishers insisted on to appeal to the target audience. Christopher Wood wrote under several aliases, including Timothy Lea (for erotic comedies) and Rosalind Erskine (for women's fiction).

A pseudonym thus becomes a bridge — a way to transcend assumptions and meet readers without prejudice.

Some authors write prolifically across multiple genres and use pseudonyms to separate their literary personas. One name might be used for literary fiction, another for horror, a third for children's books. This segmentation helps manage reader expectations and creates space for creative play.

Stephen King famously adopted the pseudonym Richard Bachman to test whether his success was due to talent or luck — and also to avoid saturating the market under his own name. The Bachman books offered a darker, more experimental tone and were well received, especially once his identity was revealed.

For writers juggling several projects, pseudonyms offer freedom, flexibility, and clarity. Readers know what kind of story they're picking up. Authors know they can explore without compromising their existing brand.

Modern Trends in Pseudonym Use

- **Social Media and Personal Branding**

With the rise of social media, authors are increasingly conscious of how their names function in digital spaces. Pseudonyms now serve not only to conceal but to attract — they are optimized for hashtags, search engines, and target demographics.

- **Secrecy as Strategy**

Sometimes, anonymity itself becomes part of the marketing. Readers are intrigued by the mystery: *Who is this author?* Why are they hiding? In a world saturated with noise, secrecy can cut through and spark curiosity.

- **Artistic Freedom and Emotional Safety**

Writing under a pseudonym allows for risk-taking. If a book fails, it doesn't tarnish the author's established reputation. If a topic is sensitive or deeply personal, the pseudonym can offer a sense of protection. It becomes a mask behind which truth can be spoken more freely.

Far from being a relic of the past, the pseudonym is alive and thriving in the modern literary world. It is a tool of strategy, creativity, and survival — a way for authors to navigate the ever-shifting landscape of public attention, genre conventions, and personal boundaries.

In a time when readers crave both transparency and mystery, the pseudonym offers a paradox: it hides and reveals at once. It allows authors to step into new worlds, experiment with form and voice, and reach new audiences — all while protecting something sacred: the self behind the words.

As publishing evolves and readers grow more curious about the people behind the prose, the pseudonym remains a powerful instrument — not of deception, but of design.

Let the Robots Help — How AI Can Be Your Favorite Assistant in Book Promotion

There's something oddly comforting about having a helper who doesn't sleep, doesn't complain, and is always ready to write, design, or brainstorm at 2 a.m. That's what artificial intelligence feels like for many modern writers today — not a threat, not a replacement, but an assistant. A very efficient one.

Book promotion used to be daunting. Between managing social media, writing newsletters, updating blogs, and crafting ads, you could spend more time marketing your book than writing the next one. That's where AI quietly stepped in and changed the game. No more staring at a blank screen, wondering what to post on Instagram or how to start your next blog article. With the right tools, AI can help you generate content that feels fresh, on-brand, and—yes—even a little bit human.

Social media is probably where most writers first test the waters. It's noisy out there, and keeping up with trends, hashtags, and witty captions can quickly drain your energy. But with tools like ChatGPT, Jasper, or Copy.ai, creating posts becomes more like play. Want a mysterious teaser for your thriller? Done. A heartfelt quote from your protagonist? Easy. You can even feed in a paragraph from your book and ask for three versions of a post — one poetic, one funny, one dramatic. Sometimes, AI surprises you with better word choices than you'd come up with at the end of a long writing day. And if you pair that with a design tool like Canva, which now has AI-powered suggestions and templates, you can walk away with a visual + text combo that looks like a professional marketing team made it.

Blogging, which once felt like an extra job you didn't sign up for, has also been reimagined. AI can take a simple topic like "how I chose the setting for my novel" and turn it into a 1,000-word article with subheadings, keywords, and a sprinkle of charm. Even if it doesn't get everything right, it gives you a solid draft — something to shape and refine. You can still infuse your voice, your story, your quirks — but now you don't have to build every sentence from scratch. And if SEO makes your eyes glaze over, tools like SurferSEO or Writesonic will gently (and automatically) optimize your post so it doesn't sink into the abyss of page three on Google.

Then there's advertising. Most writers would rather eat stale crackers in silence than write their own book ads. AI doesn't mind. It will craft a dozen taglines, ad copies, or promotional messages in under a minute. Whether you need a Facebook ad that sounds intriguing without being salesy, or a Google text ad that makes your book sound like a must-read, AI has you covered. And with machine learning platforms running A/B tests in the background — swapping images, headlines, calls-to-action — you don't even have to guess what works anymore. The data will tell you. You just keep writing.

AI can also play a role that's more interactive. Want to set up a chatbot on your website that answers questions about your books, shares discount codes, or recommends the next title in your series? Easy. Want to analyze reader reviews to find out what people love (or didn't love) about your latest novel? There's a tool for that. Even email marketing, which often feels like shouting into the void, becomes smarter with AI. Platforms like Mailchimp or HubSpot can segment your list automatically, suggesting who might want to receive a behind-the-scenes blog post and who's more likely to respond to a limited-time offer.

But let's be honest: there's still something sacred about the human touch. Readers don't follow you just for polished sentences and pretty graphics. They stay because they feel a connection — with your words, your energy, your honesty. That's why it's important not to let AI do all the talking. Use it as a tool but review everything. Tweak the phrasing. Inject humor. Show up occasionally as yourself, raw and real. That's what makes your brand magnetic, not just efficient.

In the end, artificial intelligence won't replace the messy, brilliant mind of a writer. But it can hold your hand through the parts that feel mechanical, repetitive, or intimidating. It lets you do more with less energy. It gives you space to breathe, create, and maybe even rest.

And sometimes, it even gives you a better headline than you could've come up with on your own.

Building an Author Website with the Help of AI — Where Technology Meets Personality

In the past, creating a website felt like a technical puzzle — one that required coding, plugins, and more patience than most writers could afford. Today, things are different. In this digital era, your website isn't just a static calling card. It's a living, breathing extension of your identity as a writer. A place where readers connect, explore your books, sign up for your newsletter, or pre-order your next release. And thanks to artificial intelligence, building that kind of vibrant space has never been easier.

You don't need to know how to code. You don't need to hire a team. You don't even need to start with a blank page. With AI-powered tools, you can build a beautiful, functional, and reader-friendly website in a matter of hours — and continually improve it with smart automation. Whether you're a first-time author or a multi-book creator with a growing brand, your website can become your central hub — your digital home.

So how exactly does AI help? Here's a closer look, step by step:

Step	What It Does	AI Tools You Can Use
Choosing the Right AI-Powered Website Builder	AI website builders simplify design by learning your preferences and building pages for you. No design skills required.	Wix ADI, Zyro, Framer AI
AI-Generated Content for Author Websites	From your homepage to your "About the Author" section, AI can draft bios, book blurbs, FAQs, and even blog posts tailored to your voice.	Copy.ai, ChatGPT
Personalized User Experience with AI	Add features like AI chatbots, voice search, and content that adapts to each visitor's behavior — making your site interactive and memorable.	Drift, ChatGPT chatbots, Dynamic content AI
AI-Driven SEO & Marketing	Ensure your site is discoverable by optimizing headlines, keywords, meta descriptions, and sending automated emails.	Surfer SEO, Yoast SEO, Mailchimp AI
AI-Generated Visuals & Multimedia	Bring your site to life with custom AI-generated graphics, book banners, animated trailers, and engaging video messages.	Canva AI, MidJourney, Synthesia

AI for Social Media Integration	Let your site sync with social media — and even schedule posts or respond to followers using AI-powered automation.	Buffer, Hootsuite, Lately AI
AI-Driven Analytics for Website Improvement	Understand how readers interact with your site and adjust layouts, calls-to-action, or headlines based on real data.	Google Analytics 4, Hotjar AI, Smartlook

Let's unpack this a bit, because behind each tool is a real benefit — and often, a real relief for overwhelmed authors.

You start with an AI website builder like Wix ADI or Zyro. Instead of dragging boxes around, you answer a few questions — What's your genre? What do you want on your homepage? Are you selling books directly or linking to Amazon? Based on your answers, the AI will design a layout for you, complete with fonts, colors, menus, and even placeholder content. You can edit anything, of course, but it gets you 80% of the way there in minutes.

Then there's the content. Not everyone likes writing about themselves, and even fewer people enjoy crafting catchy headlines or updating their blog regularly. That's where AI writing assistants come in. Tools like ChatGPT and Copy.ai can take the pressure off. You give a few prompts — "Write a short author bio in a witty tone" or "Summarize my fantasy novel in two paragraphs" — and you get content you can use or revise in your own words. This applies not only to static pages, but to newsletters, FAQ sections, book club discussion guides, and more.

Once the core of your website is ready, AI makes it feel alive. Visitors can be welcomed by an AI chatbot that answers questions like "Where can I buy your book?" or "Will there be a sequel?" With Drift or even a custom ChatGPT chatbot, your website becomes a two-way street — a place where fans feel seen and supported.

And what's a great site without being seen? That's where AI-powered SEO comes in. Tools like Surfer SEO and Yoast optimize your content behind the scenes — choosing the best keywords, refining sentence structure, and ensuring search engines actually find you. At the same time, AI-enhanced email platforms like Mailchimp can track who visits, what they click, and when they're most likely to open your emails — allowing you to send personalized messages that feel like private letters.

Visuals matter, too. If you don't have a designer, don't worry — Canva AI can create headers, banners, and promotional graphics that match your brand in seconds. Want a short book trailer or video intro? Synthesia uses AI avatars to deliver professional-looking videos without a studio. If you want illustrations, stylized scenes, or even abstract background images, MidJourney can bring your imagination to life.

And since your readers probably live on Instagram, TikTok, and beyond, AI can help there too. Your website can be connected to tools like Buffer or Lately AI that automatically create and post content across platforms — keeping your presence alive without constant manual effort. You can even schedule campaigns to promote new releases, pre-orders, or giveaways, all synced with your site.

Finally, the behind-the-scenes magic: AI analytics. Tools like Hotjar and Smartlook actually record how visitors navigate your site — where they pause, where they click, what they ignore. This isn't just data; it's feedback. It shows you what's working and what's not. Combined with Google Analytics 4, you'll know whether your newsletter sign-up form is visible enough, or if readers are leaving your book page too quickly. You adjust. You evolve.

Launching Your Book with Impact

A successful book launch is more than just announcing your release—it's about creating excitement, engaging your audience, and strategically positioning your book for maximum visibility. In today's digital age, authors have access to powerful tools and AI-driven strategies that can amplify their reach and ensure a strong debut.

From crafting compelling pre-launch campaigns to leveraging AI for targeted marketing, this chapter explores essential steps to make your book launch impactful. Whether you're a first-time author or an experienced writer, understanding how to build anticipation, attract the right audience, and sustain momentum will help your book stand out in a crowded marketplace.

In the following sections, we will delve into the key elements of a successful book launch, including AI-powered promotional tactics, social media strategies, reader engagement techniques, and post-launch actions that keep your book relevant long after its release.

Pre-launch Strategies: Building Buzz with ARCs, Beta Readers, and Influencers

The launch of a book is often seen as a single date — that moment it becomes available to the world. But in truth, a successful launch is built quietly, often months in advance. It begins in whispers: early readers, private feedback, a few photos of the cover here and there, maybe a quote shared on Instagram. The buzz grows in waves, and by the time the book officially arrives, it already lives in the minds and hearts of readers. That's the real work of pre-launch strategy — and it's as creative as writing the book itself.

Before publication, one of the most powerful tools a writer has is the Advanced Reader Copy, or ARC. These are early versions of the book, often unpolished or marked as review copies, that are shared before the official release. The goal isn't perfection — it's anticipation. ARCs are how reviews begin to roll in early, how your book finds its first champions, how social media starts murmuring your title. When someone says "I got to read this before it was even out," others listen. That's how buzz forms — organically, but deliberately.

Distributing ARCs isn't complicated, especially with modern platforms designed to help. NetGalley, Edelweiss+, and Booksprout connect authors directly with reviewers who specialize in early reads. Others prefer a more personal approach: writing to bloggers, contacting genre-specific influencers, or offering ARCs as exclusive gifts to email subscribers. Even social media giveaways work beautifully. And the best part? You're not just offering a copy — you're offering an invitation into your book's birth. That kind of access builds loyalty.

Of course, there's another group of early readers whose role is less about promotion and more about insight: beta readers. They're the ones who help you see your own story more clearly. Not editors, but thoughtful readers who spot the things you may have missed — the slow parts, the inconsistent character decisions, the moments that need just a bit more heart. Beta readers give you their perspective not as professionals, but as fans-in-the-making. If you choose well, they become your first real audience — and often, your earliest advocates.

Finding them doesn't require a formal process. Communities like Scribophile, Wattpad, or Goodreads host entire spaces devoted to beta reading. You can also reach out through Facebook groups, newsletters, or fellow authors you trust. The key isn't quantity — it's diversity and honesty. And if you want more specific feedback, give them guiding questions: Where did you feel most engaged? Did anything confuse you? Did you believe in the characters? Their answers won't replace your judgment, but they will shape your revisions — and strengthen your confidence.

And then there's the magic of influence — quite literally. We're living in a time when a single BookTok video can send an unknown title straight to the bestseller list. Influencers aren't just trendsetters; they're connectors. Whether they're blogging, posting polished flat-lays on Instagram, or raving about your characters on TikTok, their impact on visibility is enormous. Partnering with them isn't about begging for attention. It's about offering something meaningful, personal, and genuine. If they like your book, they'll share it. And when they do, their audiences listen.

Working with influencers doesn't have to feel transactional. Begin by engaging with their content. Follow them. Leave thoughtful comments. Share what you truly love. When it comes time to introduce your book, it's no longer a cold pitch — it's a conversation. Offer a free ARC, express that you'd be honored if they'd read it, and allow space for authenticity. The best endorsements aren't forced. They're enthusiastic, natural, maybe even a little poetic.

Some authors take it a step further by offering affiliate partnerships. This way, influencers receive a small commission for every book sold through their link — a thank-you for their time and platform. It's a win-win, especially for indie authors looking to expand their reach without large marketing budgets.

Throughout all these steps — the early reviews, the beta reading rounds, the influencer conversations — something begins to shift. The book is no longer just yours. It's in the world. It's being shaped not only by your words but by how people react to them. And this matters. When launch day arrives, your book isn't stepping out into silence. It's being welcomed.

And yes, AI can make this easier. It can help you track who's talking about your book, identify niche influencers, manage ARC logistics, even sort and analyze beta reader feedback. But the soul of the process remains human — the excitement of discovery, the joy of sharing something early, the intimacy of trust. That's what pre-launch is about.

So, if you're thinking your work ends when you type the last sentence, think again. That was the creation. This is the unfolding. This is where readers begin to gather, long before the doors officially open. And they're already waiting.

Which brings us to something worth pausing for: the way technology, specifically artificial intelligence, quietly supports all of this behind the scenes.

The pre-launch phase can feel overwhelming — juggling early copies, gathering feedback, following up with influencers, prepping blog posts, updating your website, and keeping readers engaged across platforms. But today, much of this work can be streamlined, if not lightened altogether, thanks to a host of AI-powered tools designed specifically for authors and creators.

You don't need to be tech-savvy or have a team. These tools are designed to work for you, not the other way around. They help you focus on the creative, human part of the launch — the connection with your readers — while taking care of the structure, visibility, and timing.

Here's a closer look at how AI can support your entire launch strategy from start to finish:

Category	AI Tools	Purpose
AI-Powered Website Builders	Wix ADI, Zyro, Framer AI	Create and customize a professional author website effortlessly.
AI for Content Creation	Copy.ai, ChatGPT, Jasper AI	Generate book descriptions, blog content, and social media captions.
AI for Beta Readers & Editing	Grammarly, ProWritingAid, Hemingway Editor	Improve manuscript readability and grammar before publishing.
AI for ARC Distribution	NetGalley, Booksprout, Edelweiss+	Distribute Advanced Reader Copies (ARCs) for early reviews.
AI for Influencer Outreach	BuzzSumo, Upfluence, Heepsy	Find and connect with influencers and book bloggers.
AI for Social Media Marketing	Buffer, Hootsuite, Lately AI	Schedule and automate social media promotions.
AI for SEO Optimization	Surfer SEO, Clearscope, RankMath	Optimize book descriptions and content for better search rankings.
AI for Email Marketing	Mailchimp AI, ConvertKit, ActiveCampaign AI	Automate personalized email campaigns for book promotion.
AI for Analytics & Performance Tracking	Google Analytics 4, Hotjar AI, Smartlook	Track reader engagement and website performance for improvements.

This isn't just about convenience. It's about precision. It's about clarity. These tools allow you to make thoughtful decisions based on real-time feedback, not just guesses. When you send out your ARCs through NetGalley or Booksprout, you're reaching real readers who are known for reviewing. When you search for influencers through platforms like BuzzSumo or Heepsy, you're narrowing your efforts to those who genuinely engage with your genre. When you automate your emails through ConvertKit or

Mailchimp, you're ensuring each reader gets the right message at the right time — no copy-paste fatigue necessary.

Even editing becomes more focused. Grammarly and ProWritingAid won't replace a good editor, but they will catch those small slips that can cloud a reader's first impression. And if you want to polish your prose before beta readers see it, Hemingway Editor is like a quiet friend reminding you to keep things clear, strong, and punchy.

Every part of the pre-launch journey can be touched, enhanced, or accelerated by AI — not to take away your voice, but to give you time and clarity to use it more fully.

So as your book inches closer to its debut, you don't have to feel like you're juggling everything alone. You're supported — not just by your early readers and excited followers, but by a quiet, intelligent network of tools working in the background, making sure that when your book finally arrives, it does so with grace, momentum, and the kind of presence that lasts.

And that's when the real magic begins.

After the Launch — How to Keep Your Book Alive in the World

The day your book comes out is exhilarating — the posts, the congratulations, the rush of seeing your work finally exist beyond your screen. But what comes next? After that initial burst of attention, a quiet sets in. Sales may slow, conversations taper off, and suddenly, you're not just an author — you're a marketer, a community builder, a strategist. Because launching the book was only the beginning. The real challenge is keeping it alive.

One of the most important lifelines for any book is reviews. They are more than social proof — they are algorithms' favorite currency. Platforms like Amazon and Goodreads reward books that have traction, and traction is often measured in stars and comments. Readers trust other readers. They check the reviews, read them carefully, look for honesty, emotion, resonance. But how do you get those reviews?

Start with the people who already read your book — your ARC readers, your email list, your beta readers. A simple reminder, kindly worded, is often enough. You can send a follow-up email or include a gentle nudge at the end of your book: "If you enjoyed this story, a short review means the world to me." No pressure, no incentives — just an invitation. And if you're looking to broaden the reach, tools like StoryOrigin or BookSirens connect you with readers who enjoy reviewing, particularly in your genre. Goodreads is also a quiet goldmine — not only for reader interaction but for subtle engagement, joining discussions, and making your presence known without shouting.

But even as you gather reviews, you can't let the momentum slip away. Your book is still new to thousands — perhaps millions — of potential readers. You just have to help them find it. This is where continued promotion plays a vital role. You might run a limited-time discount or a Kindle Deal to draw in price-conscious readers. Collaborate with other authors for a cross-promotion bundle — you promote their book, they promote yours. It's simple and surprisingly effective.

And don't underestimate the power of repurposing. That glowing review? Turn it into a quote graphic. That behind-the-scenes writing story? It's a newsletter or blog post. That deleted chapter you couldn't let go of? It might just make a great freebie to re-engage your mailing list. With AI tools like Jasper or Copy.ai, you can repackage content into posts, emails, ads, or even short videos. Smart, fast, on-brand.

Speaking of ads — they don't have to be overwhelming. AI-driven platforms like Facebook Ads Manager or Amazon Marketing Services help you target the right readers. You don't need a marketing degree. Just a sense of your audience, a strong hook, and the willingness to experiment. And yes, schedule your campaigns around seasonal events or relevant dates. A romance novel near Valentine's Day, a historical saga close to a national anniversary — context boosts visibility.

As your book finds its rhythm in the market, another opportunity opens up: you. You, as the voice behind the book, as the person who wrote something worth talking about. Podcasts, guest blog posts, virtual readings — these aren't just media gigs; they're extensions of the story. When readers hear your voice, understand your process, or see the passion behind your pages, they remember. And they often share.

AI tools can help you get there too. Platforms like Muck Rack and PressRush allow you to pitch to journalists and bloggers who cover your niche. And if your book touches on a timely topic or an evergreen theme, track its relevance using tools like Google Trends to know when — and where — to speak up.

But perhaps the most powerful post-launch strategy isn't promotional at all. It's relational. The authors who maintain long-term success aren't always the ones with the biggest budgets. They're the ones who build community. Who send newsletters that feel like letters, not campaigns. Who start private Facebook groups or cozy Discord chats. Who share writing updates, glimpses behind the curtain, questions, joys, doubts. These authors make readers feel part of something — and that kind of loyalty can't be bought.

AI lends a hand here too. Automated newsletters, chatbot-powered FAQs, personalized follow-ups — they all help you stay present without being exhausted. You can focus on writing, while your systems gently remind readers that you're still here, still creating, still reaching out.

So, if you're wondering what to do after the confetti of launch day settles, this is it: keep listening, keep sharing, keep showing up. Not all at once. Not every day. But consistently. Quietly. With intention.

Because a book doesn't disappear once it's published. If nurtured, if tended to with care, it can continue finding readers long after the headlines fade. And those readers will remember who brought the story into their lives.

AI-Driven Marketing Strategies

Marketing a book in the digital age requires more than traditional advertising—it demands precision, automation, and data-driven strategies to reach the right audience at the right time. Artificial Intelligence (AI) has revolutionized book marketing by offering tools that analyze reader behavior, optimize ad campaigns, and personalize promotional content for maximum impact.

In this chapter, we will explore how AI-powered marketing can help authors increase visibility, attract more readers, and sustain book sales long after the initial launch. From AI-driven social media campaigns to automated email marketing and predictive analytics, we will uncover practical ways to harness AI for effective book promotion. Whether you are an indie author or traditionally published, these strategies will provide you with the insights and tools needed to market your book more efficiently and successfully.

Using AI-Powered Ad Platforms for Targeted Campaigns

Advertising is a crucial component of book marketing, but without a targeted approach, ad spend can quickly become inefficient. AI-powered advertising platforms like Amazon Ads, Facebook Ads, Google Ads, and TikTok Ads leverage machine learning to optimize ad delivery, ensuring that the right audience sees your book at the right time.

Traditional advertising methods relied heavily on static targeting: selecting basic demographics like age, gender, or location. But modern AI systems go far deeper. They analyze users' past purchases, online behavior, reading habits, interaction patterns, browsing history, and even the time of day they're most active. This allows the platform to make real-time decisions about *when*, *where*, and *to whom* to show your ads.

For authors, this means:

- **Smarter budget allocation**: AI tools automatically increase spend on high-performing ads and cut losses on low-performing ones.
- **Dynamic creative optimization**: AI can test and adapt images, headlines, and copy to match what resonates with specific users.
- **Higher conversion rates**: By targeting readers who are already interested in similar genres or topics, your ads are more likely to result in actual sales.

Platform	Advantages	Disadvantages	Estimated Cost
Amazon Ads	- Directly targets book buyers on Amazon. - AI optimizes bids based on keyword performance. - Sponsored ads appear on book pages of similar authors.	- Competitive bidding can be expensive. - Limited audience outside Amazon. - Requires keyword research.	$0.10 – $2 per click (depends on competition and genre). Minimum daily budget: $1.
Facebook Ads	- AI-driven targeting based on user interests and reading habits. - Highly customizable audience segmentation. - Can drive traffic to external sites (Amazon, author website).	- Requires testing and optimization to be effective. - Lower conversion rates for direct book sales. - Can be costly if not optimized.	$0.50 – $2 per click. Minimum daily budget: $5.
Google Ads	- AI-driven search ads place your book in front of people searching for related topics. - Display and YouTube ads expand reach	- Not book-specific, so it requires precise targeting. - Higher competition for keywords.	$0.30 – $5 per click, depending on keywords. Minimum daily budget: $5.

	beyond social media. - Effective for branding and visibility.	- Can be expensive if targeting broad terms.	
TikTok Ads	- AI optimizes for engagement and viral potential. - Strong reach among younger audiences (Gen Z & Millennials). - Video ads can create a personal connection with potential readers.	- Requires engaging video content creation. - Less effective for niche or academic books. - Limited ad placement options compared to Amazon or Google.	$0.20 – $1 per click. Minimum daily budget: $20.
Instagram Ads	- AI optimizes ad placement in stories, reels, and feeds. - Highly visual, ideal for book covers and trailers. - Can target book lovers through interests and behavior.	- Best suited for visually appealing books. - Requires strong visuals and creative assets. - Similar to Facebook Ads but with fewer text-based ad options.	$0.50 – $2 per click. Minimum daily budget: $5.
Twitter Ads (X Ads)	- AI-based interest targeting helps reach niche communities. - Good for trending books and engaging discussions. - Can promote book-related threads and hashtags.	- Less effective for direct sales. - Short ad lifespan due to fast-moving feed. - Lower engagement rates compared to other platforms.	$0.50 – $3 per click. Minimum daily budget: $5.

These platforms connect to multiple ad accounts and use AI to:

- Optimize bids and budgets in real time.
- Generate reports with actionable insights.
- Automatically pause underperforming ads.

- Recommend new audience segments or creative tests.

This hands-off approach lets you focus on writing while AI works behind the scenes to grow your readership.

Choosing the Right AI-Powered Ad Platform for Your Book

Marketing a book in the digital age involves more than posting a few times on social media. To truly get your work in front of readers, authors now rely on paid advertising—and increasingly, AI-powered ad platforms are at the core of this strategy. But with so many choices available, how do you know which platform is right for your specific goal?

Let's break it down by purpose—because not every platform serves the same function. The key is understanding your objective: Are you trying to generate sales? Build name recognition? Get your book noticed in search results? Or stir up some online buzz?

If your primary focus is selling your book directly, especially if it's available on Kindle or in paperback through Amazon, then Amazon Ads should be your first port of call. These ads appear right where people are actively shopping—next to book listings, in search results, and on product pages. That's a huge advantage because your book is shown to people already in a buying mindset.

AI plays a decisive role in optimizing Amazon Ads, empowering authors with tools that automatically adjust bids, identify relevant keywords, and track performance. This intelligent automation reduces the guesswork and increases ROI, instilling a sense of control and confidence—especially useful if you have a limited budget.

But keep in mind: Amazon Ads work best when your book already has a strong product page—compelling cover, solid reviews, and a well-written blurb. Ads can drive traffic, but it's the product page that closes the sale.

If your book is new or you're an emerging author trying to build visibility, then focus on brand awareness and reader engagement. For this, platforms like Facebook, Instagram, and TikTok are unmatched.

These platforms are built for storytelling and emotional connection—perfect for authors who want to share their journey, highlight character stories, or offer sneak peeks. Through AI-powered targeting, you can show your ads to people based on interests, behaviors, age, reading preferences, and even past purchases.

For example, suppose you've written a fantasy novel. In that case, you can use Facebook Ads Manager's AI tools to target users who follow fantasy fan pages, authors like Brandon Sanderson or Sarah J. Maas, and even users who frequently interact with book trailers. Instagram's visual nature is ideal for displaying your cover, teaser videos, and behind-the-scenes content. TikTok, while newer, has a strong #BookTok community, and many indie authors have gone viral with creative, low-budget ads powered by AI insights into trending music, hashtags, and formats.

AI tools like AdCreative.ai or Smartly.io can even help generate multiple ad variations automatically, testing different images, taglines, and captions to see what resonates best with your audience.

People often turn to Google with questions: "Best books about grief," "how to write a novel," or "books for teenage girls." If your book fits into a niche or solves a specific problem—say, a self-help guide, a parenting book, or even historical nonfiction—then Google Ads can be your secret weapon.

Using AI-enhanced keyword targeting, you can ensure your book appears when people search for relevant topics. This is especially useful for nonfiction and practical books where readers are actively seeking information.

Google's algorithm can also optimize your ad placement and bidding strategy, showing your ads only to those most likely to click and buy. The platform's AI considers factors like time of day, location, device type, and more. Over time, the system "learns" and improves your ad's effectiveness automatically.

However, Google Ads can be more complex and expensive than social ads, and they require thoughtful keyword research. But that's where AI tools like SEMrush, SpyFu, or even Google's own Smart Campaigns can help, providing support and guidance to authors and boosting their confidence in navigating this platform.

When it comes to stirring up social buzz or inserting your book into trending conversations, Twitter Ads (now called X Ads) can be effective—if used wisely.

Twitter, now known as x, is where conversations happen in real time. Authors use it to engage in dialogue, react to news, or join viral threads. If your book touches on current events, controversial topics, or cultural commentary, Twitter Ads can help you get noticed fast, fostering a sense of community and engagement.

AI tools within the platform help you identify trending hashtags, track engagement metrics, and target specific demographics. And since tweets are short and easy to consume, even a small ad budget can stretch far—especially if your ad prompts discussion or sparks emotion.

Just remember: X is not about selling directly; it's about *participating* in a conversation. It's ideal for non-traditional books, memoirs, or anything that might provoke curiosity or debate.

No single platform guarantees success. The best ad strategies involve testing multiple platforms, analyzing what works, and reallocating budget accordingly. That's where AI tools like Adzooma and Revealbot come in.

These platforms connect to multiple ad accounts—Google, Facebook, Instagram, and more—and use AI to analyze your campaigns. They tell you which ads have the highest click-through rate, where people drop off, and how your return on ad spend (ROAS) stacks up. They can also automatically adjust your budget in real time—boosting spend on high-performers and reducing it on low-performers without you needing to monitor every hour.

This is crucial for authors who wear many hats. Instead of manually managing each platform, you can let AI handle the math while you focus on writing and connecting with readers.

Automating Email Marketing with AI

Email marketing remains a powerful and cost-effective tool for authors seeking to build relationships with readers, consistently promote their books, and drive long-term sales. Yet, the process of managing an email list—writing personalized messages, segmenting audiences, and timing campaigns—can become overwhelming and time-consuming. This is especially true as your list grows.

That's where artificial intelligence (AI) steps in. AI-powered email marketing platforms now offer smart automation, precision targeting, and real-time optimization. With minimal input, these tools liberate you from the burden of managing every detail, helping you deliver the right message to the right reader at precisely the right time—without burning out or spending hours on manual tasks.

Manually dividing your email list into categories like "new readers," "frequent buyers," or "inactive subscribers" is not only tedious—it's ineffective at scale. AI can analyze detailed subscriber behavior, such as open rates, click-throughs, past purchases, downloads, or browsing activity on your author website.

This data is then used to sort subscribers into meaningful groups, for example, automatically:

- **New Subscribers**: These readers are unfamiliar with your brand. AI can trigger a 'welcome sequence' that introduces them to your books, values, or backstory—building trust from day one. This personal touch makes them feel understood and valued.
- **Engaged Readers**: These are loyal followers who open most of your emails or have purchased a book recently. AI can identify them and push tailored promotions, pre-launch teasers, or exclusive bonus content to deepen the relationship.

- **Inactive Subscribers**: These users haven't opened your emails for weeks or months. AI tools can craft subject lines that recapture their attention and personalize messages to reignite interest.

Platforms like Mailchimp AI, ActiveCampaign, and HubSpot AI do this automatically, freeing you from the guesswork and ensuring each group gets content that truly matters to them.

Instead of writing and scheduling emails manually, you can now design sequences once and let AI handle the rest. These are structured series of emails triggered by specific reader actions or milestones, such as. This efficient process saves you time and effort.

- Welcome Series: When someone joins your list, they get 3–5 introductory emails over a few days. AI can adjust the pace and content based on whether the reader clicks or responds.
- Pre-Launch Campaigns: Want to build anticipation for a new release? AI sequences can share excerpts, character teasers, early reviews, and preorder links timed perfectly ahead of launch day.
- Post-Purchase Follow-Ups: After someone buys a book, AI sends a thank-you message, suggests related titles, or requests a review—at the moment when the reader is most engaged.
- Re-Engagement Campaigns: When readers stop opening your emails, AI can automatically send fresh, personalized content, survey links, or exclusive offers to bring them back.

Tools like ConvertKit and Drip AI make it easy to set these up with "if-this-then-that" logic and built-in templates designed for authors.

The subject line is the first thing your audience sees—and it determines whether they open or delete your email. AI tools analyze thousands of subject lines across industries and apply that data to generate personalized, high-performing options.

For instance, instead of writing "New book coming soon," AI might suggest "A New Adventure Awaits You – Sneak Peek Inside!"—based on your reader's interest in fantasy or romance.

In addition, AI can optimize the body of your email by adjusting tone, layout, length, and even the placement of your call-to-action (CTA). For example, if a reader has a history of responding well to casual language, AI can adjust the tone of your email to match. Some tools, like Phrasee and Copy.ai, go further by generating complete email drafts or dynamic text blocks that change depending on reader behavior. This means that the content of your email is always tailored to your reader's preferences, increasing the likelihood of engagement.

Not everyone checks their inbox at the same time. AI tracks individual reader habits—some open emails in the morning, while others prefer to open them late at night or on weekends. Rather than blasting your entire list at once, AI-powered platforms can automatically stagger delivery so that each email lands at the optimal time for each reader.

This dramatically increases open and click-through rates, since your message appears when readers are most likely to engage. Tools like Mailchimp AI and ActiveCampaign offer this as a built-in feature.

Benefit	How AI Helps
Saves Time	Automates email sequences and personalization.
Increases Engagement	Sends emails at optimal times and improves content relevance.
Boosts Sales & Reviews	AI recommends personalized book offers and encourages reviews.
Improves Deliverability	AI filters out inactive subscribers to maintain a high sender reputation.
Enhances Targeting	Analyzes user data to segment readers effectively.

Best AI Email Marketing Tools for Authors

There are several powerful AI tools available to help authors run smarter email campaigns. Mailchimp AI is a great all-rounder, ideal for beginners and experienced users, offering segmentation and automated campaigns. ConvertKit is simple and popular among indie authors, with tools for automation and tagging readers by interest.

For authors with large or complex email lists, ActiveCampaign AI offers advanced features like behavior tracking and AI-generated subject lines. Drip AI is best suited for authors who sell books or products directly on their websites, thanks to its personalized funnels.

If you're managing multiple books or projects, HubSpot AI offers CRM features and content suggestions to keep everything organized. Lastly, Phrasee specializes in crafting optimized subject lines and email content, perfect for authors who want to boost open and click-through rates.

AI Tool	Key Features	Best For
Mailchimp AI	Audience segmentation, predictive analytics, automated campaigns	Beginner to advanced authors
ConvertKit	AI-powered email sequences, reader tagging, automation	Indie authors & content creators
ActiveCampaign AI	Advanced automation, behavioral tracking, AI-generated subject lines	Authors with large email lists
Drip AI	Personalized email campaigns, AI-driven sales funnels	Authors selling directly via their website
HubSpot AI	AI-powered CRM integration, content recommendations	Authors with multiple books and business ventures
Phrasee	AI-generated subject lines & content optimization	Authors focusing on engagement & open rates

AI tools do more than automate your emails—they help make every message smarter, more personal, and more likely to get results. Here are four ways authors can use AI to level up their email marketing and connect with readers more effectively:

One of the greatest advantages of using AI is its ability to make every email feel tailor-made for the person receiving it. Instead of sending the same generic message to your entire list, AI studies what each reader is interested in—what they've clicked, bought, or read—and customizes the content they receive.

For example, suppose someone recently purchased your mystery novel. In that case, AI can automatically recommend your other mystery titles in the following email, or offer them a special deal on a related short story. This kind of personalization makes readers feel seen and valued, increasing the chances that they'll stay engaged with your emails—and keep coming back for more.

Getting reader reviews is essential for every author, especially independent ones. But asking for reviews manually can be awkward or easy to forget. With AI, you don't have to worry about timing or tracking who bought what—everything is handled for you, giving you more time to focus on your writing.

You can set up an email that goes out automatically a few days after someone purchases your book. The AI ensures that it's sent at the right time—after the reader has likely finished the book, but while it's still fresh in their mind. The message might say something simple like:

"Enjoyed [Book Title]? We'd love to hear your thoughts! Leave a quick review here."

It's gentle, well-timed, and can lead to a steady stream of feedback that builds your credibility and boosts your visibility on platforms like Amazon or Goodreads.

Not sure what subject line will grab attention? Or whether your readers prefer short and sweet emails, or longer, more detailed ones? That's where A/B testing comes in—and AI can do it all automatically.

AI tools can create and test two or more versions of your email—changing the subject line, layout, CTA (call to action), or even the time it's sent. Then, based on early results, it sends the best-performing version to the rest of your list.

For instance, AI might test "New Book Alert!" against "Your Next Favorite Read is Here" and determine that one gets 40% more opens. Over time, this kind of testing helps refine your messaging so that every email performs better than the last.

Many authors struggle to keep their newsletters interesting and consistent. With AI, you don't have to guess what your readers want to hear from you—because the technology figures it out for you.

AI analyzes past interactions—what articles or books your readers clicked on, which topics they responded to, what they skipped—and uses that data to tailor each newsletter. This means one subscriber might receive writing tips and a free chapter download, while another sees upcoming book events or personalized recommendations. With this level of understanding, you can confidently deliver content that resonates with your readers.

Imagine your newsletter being automatically filled with content that each reader wants to read. That's the power of AI-curated emails—and it helps keep your audience engaged and looking forward to your next message.

AI isn't just a trendy tool—it's a true game changer for authors who want to grow their audience without burning out. By handing over the repetitive and time-consuming parts of email marketing to AI, you free up your energy to focus on what you love most: writing. This efficiency enables you to produce higher-quality content without the stress of managing every aspect of your marketing.

AI helps you stay connected with your readers, send messages they'll care about, and keep your books top of mind—without constantly managing your email list or trying to guess what works.

Whether you're a new author building your first list or an experienced writer managing a growing fanbase, AI can help you personalize every campaign, reach the right people, and steadily build your book's success over time.

Analyzing Reader Data to Refine Your Marketing Approach

Understanding your readers is key to successful book marketing. Instead of relying on guesswork, AI-powered data analytics can provide deep insights into reader behavior, preferences, and engagement patterns. By leveraging this data, authors can refine their marketing strategies, optimize ad spend, and create more targeted campaigns that lead to higher sales and stronger reader connections.

Reader data helps authors answer essential marketing questions, such as:

- Who are my most engaged readers?
- What marketing channels drive the most book sales?
- Which types of content resonate best with my audience?
- When is the best time to promote my book for maximum visibility?

By analyzing data from website visits, email engagement, social media interactions, and ad performance, authors can fine-tune their approach to reach the right readers with the right message at the right time.

Data Point	What It Reveals	AI Tools for Analysis
Website Traffic & Behavior	Identifies which book pages get the most attention and how visitors navigate your site.	Google Analytics 4, Hotjar AI, Smartlook
Email Open & Click Rates	Measures engagement levels and determines which emails drive action.	Mailchimp AI, ConvertKit, ActiveCampaign
Social Media Engagement	Reveals which posts and ads get the most likes, shares, and comments.	Buffer, Hootsuite AI, Sprout Social

Ad Performance Data	Shows which ads generate the highest conversion rates and ROI.	Facebook Ads Manager AI, Amazon Ads, Google Ads AI
Reader Demographics	Helps refine targeting based on age, location, interests, and reading habits.	Google Audience Insights, Amazon KDP Reports
Book Sales Trends	Tracks which books perform best in different time frames and markets.	KDP Analytics, Book Report, Publisher Rocket

As an author, refining your marketing strategy is essential—not just to reach more readers, but to make sure your time, effort, and budget are being used wisely. AI-powered tools now give you the ability to fine-tune your campaigns with precision, taking the guesswork out of when, where, and how to promote your books.

AI offers a decisive advantage to authors by personalizing marketing campaigns. These tools analyze individual reader interactions with your content, such as email open rates, click behavior, or purchase history, and adapt future messaging based on these patterns. For instance, if you find that readers who enjoy mystery novels tend to open emails more on weekends, you can schedule your promotions accordingly. Platforms like ActiveCampaign AI automate this process, segmenting your audience based on behavior and ensuring each reader receives the content they're most likely to respond to—be it a book recommendation, a discount code, or an early peek at your next release.

AI also helps you spend your advertising budget more wisely, making your marketing efforts more efficient and effective. Instead of throwing money at broad, untargeted ads, AI tools dig deep into performance data and identify the keywords, audiences, and platforms that give you the best results. For example, if your Amazon Ads dashboard reveals that campaigns aimed at 'thriller lovers' are generating significantly more clicks and purchases than broader categories, you can reallocate your budget accordingly. On platforms like Facebook and Instagram, AI automatically adjusts bidding in real time to help you get the most conversions for the least cost—making your marketing more efficient and more effective.

AI-powered analytics extend beyond ads to shape your entire content strategy. These tools reveal the type of content your readers engage with most, whether it's blog posts, social media reels, author interviews, or video snippets. If your Instagram insights show that short video clips about your books outperform static images, it's a clear signal to adjust your content focus. AI facilitates these adjustments swiftly and confidently, ensuring you don't waste time on formats that don't resonate with your audience.

Finally, AI helps you look ahead. Tools like Google Trends, Bookstat, and other data-driven platforms can analyze wider market behavior to help you predict what readers might be looking for next. Suppose there's a growing spike in interest around dystopian fiction, for instance. In that case, you might consider incorporating those themes into your upcoming work—or, at the very least, tailoring your next campaign to appeal to fans of that genre. With this kind of insight, you're no longer just reacting to trends—you're anticipating them and staying ahead of the curve.

In short, AI doesn't just help you execute your marketing—it enables you to shape it strategically. By understanding your readers better, spending smarter, and planning with real data, you can make every aspect of your book promotion more strategic, more focused, and more successful.

Once you've gathered insights from AI tools, the next step is making strategic adjustments:

Insight from Data	Marketing Adjustment
High engagement on book trailers but low engagement on blog posts.	Focus on more video content for book promotions.
Email subscribers from a particular region have the highest open rates.	Target ads and promotions to that region.
Ads targeting a broad audience have low conversion rates.	Narrow the target audience to a more specific niche.
Readers engage more with discount emails than new release announcements.	Incorporate more limited-time discounts in campaigns.

By consistently analyzing reader data, authors can create more innovative, more effective marketing campaigns. AI tools, with their efficiency in automating this process, offer valuable insights that improve audience targeting, content strategy, and ad efficiency. The key is not just collecting data but using it to refine and optimize your marketing approach—ensuring that your book continues to reach the right readers and drive long-term success.

Part 7: Scaling Your Success

Publishing a book is an achievement, but turning that success into a long-term, sustainable career requires strategy, consistency, and innovation. As an author, scaling your success means not only expanding your readership and optimizing your marketing efforts, but also diversifying your revenue streams. This can lead to significant financial growth and the building of a lasting brand.

In this section, we will explore how AI-powered tools and strategic planning can help authors make more informed and strategic marketing decisions. These tools can automate growth, reach broader audiences, and maximize book sales beyond the initial launch. Whether you're looking to expand into foreign markets, leverage AI-driven analytics, or build a loyal community of readers, the insights in this part will provide a roadmap for long-term success.

From advanced book marketing techniques to AI-powered content creation and monetization strategies, this part will equip you with the tools not just to publish a book, but to build a thriving author business. Let's dive into the next level of success and explore how AI can help you scale your career as an author.

Expanding Your Reach

I create my work in three primary languages: English, Ukrainian, and Russian. My printed books in Russian and Ukrainian have become bestsellers. When the possibility of publishing these books in other countries came up, one honest conversation changed my perspective. It was with a representative of a well-known Italian publishing house, whom I met at an international book fair in Moscow. He said, quite frankly, that if my books were available in English, they would gladly publish them—not just in Italy, but in many other countries as well.

Now let's look at some numbers. The approximate number of people who speak Russian worldwide is around 260 million. About 150 million of them are native speakers, while the rest use Russian as a second language or for international communication. Ukrainian is spoken by roughly 41 to 45 million people globally, with 37 million of them identifying it as their mother tongue. The rest use it primarily in countries with Ukrainian diaspora communities.

Being a bestselling author within such a large linguistic audience already means a great deal. After all, we're not talking about just a few thousand people—we're talking about tens of millions who can potentially become readers. So, the question arises: with such a vast potential audience, do I even need to expand further?

For some writers, recognition outside their home country might not be a priority. Take this example: According to the United Nations Population Fund (UNFPA), as of April 2023, India had a population of approximately 1.4286 billion people, while China had around 1.4257 billion. UN projections estimate that by 2050, India's population could reach 1.668 billion, while China's may decline to 1.317 billion. If a writer becomes a bestseller in just one of these countries, imagine the royalty income they could receive. In such cases, international recognition might seem unnecessary—the home market alone offers tremendous rewards. And that's a personal choice every author must make.

However, for many—even well-known writers—a lack of foreign language skills and the absence of translations into other languages can be a significant barrier to entering the international market.

English, spoken by approximately 1.5 billion people worldwide, is one of the most widespread languages globally. Of these, around 360 to 400 million people are native speakers, while more than 1.1 billion use it as a second or foreign language. English is the official language in 67 countries and serves as the dominant language of international communication in business, science, and culture.

When you look at those numbers, it's hard not to reflect: among this enormous global audience, your future readers might be waiting.

The most widely spoken languages in the world—both by native speakers and those who use them as a second language—include:

1. **English** (around 1.5 billion speakers) – the global language of communication, widely used in science, business, and culture.
2. **Chinese (Mandarin)** (about 1.1 billion native speakers) – the most spoken language in the world by number of native speakers.
3. **Hindi** (around 600 million) – a primary language in India.
4. **Spanish** (approximately 500 million) – the official language in most Latin American countries and Spain.
5. **French** (about 280 million) – spoken in Africa, Europe, Canada, and beyond.
6. **Arabic** (around 310 million) – official language in 25 countries and the language of the Quran.
7. **Bengali** (approximately 270 million) – primarily used in Bangladesh and eastern India.
8. **Portuguese** (about 260 million) – spoken in Portugal, Brazil, and former Portuguese colonies.
9. **Russian** (roughly 260 million) is the most widely spoken language across Eurasia.
10. **Urdu** (around 230 million) – a primary language in Pakistan and some regions of India.

These ten languages cover most of the world's population due to the number of speakers, their use in international communication, and their global reach. Now, imagine if your books were translated into just ten of the roughly 7,000 languages that exist today. What would your potential readership look like?

But let's return to my conversation with the Italian publisher. Why was it so important to him that my books be in English? As it turns out, translating from English into other languages—including Italian—is far easier and significantly cheaper than translating from less commonly used languages, especially those that don't use the Latin alphabet. Both Russian and Ukrainian are written in Cyrillic.

Here's something fundamental I'd like to share with you: many AI tools, computer programs, and publishing technologies are developed first and foremost in English—for English-speaking users and English-language texts. Even Microsoft Word, which is now used globally, was originally designed in English.

From a practical standpoint, publishers find it much easier to hire professional translators who work with English as a source language. It's not only more convenient, but the translation costs are also significantly lower when translating *from* English compared to translating from a language like Russian or Ukrainian.

When I first started considering the idea of translating my books into English—about five years ago—it felt like an impossible goal. The cost of manual translation in U.S. dollars varies depending on the language pair, volume, and complexity of the text. Here are some rough estimates:

- General texts: $0.04–$0.12 per word
- Specialized or technical texts: $0.10–$0.25 per word
- Let's say your book is 50,000 words.
- At $0.10 per word, the cost would be $5,000
- At $0.25 per word, it would be $12,500

And if the text requires high accuracy or involves complex terms, you can expect to pay closer to the higher end of that range. When I calculated the approximate cost of translating even just one of my books, the total ranged between $8,500 and $21,500. This book has almost 100 000 words! If I wanted to translate all my bestsellers, I would have had to sell my house to afford it.

Translation rates vary by country and region, but from a publisher's perspective, translation is often seen as a burden that significantly increases the production cost of a book. Even when working with translators under hourly contracts or long-term agreements, the additional expense can quickly make a book project financially unviable. And when the overall production costs go up, publishers may cut back on other important areas—such as advertising. That reduces the book's visibility and profitability.

That's when I began searching for more affordable, supportive tools to help me translate my books. Naturally, I started with Google Translate. But as many of you know, standard machine translators have significant limitations. They often deliver awkward, inaccurate, or outright incorrect results—especially when working with languages that don't use the Latin alphabet.

My attempts to use other programs were also disappointing. Most of them fell short when it came to structure, tone, and grammar—and I found myself spending even more time trying to fix the automated translations than if I'd started from scratch.

But technology evolves rapidly. Today, AI-powered translation tools are becoming faster, more reliable, and—most importantly—far more affordable. I've now begun using these new tools to translate my books into different languages, and I'll be happy to share my experience with you.

Leveraging AI for Translations to Reach Global Markets

Modern technology has completely transformed the way we approach translation, making it faster, more accessible, and more affordable than ever. Artificial Intelligence (AI), powered by machine learning and natural language processing, can now translate text into dozens of languages within seconds. Tools like ChatGPT, for example, can work with over 150 languages from around the world.

When I work on my books, I often use source material written in foreign languages. In these cases, AI helps me quickly understand the content by translating it into English. And when I include quotes from various sources, accurate translation becomes even more important. That's where AI plays a critical role in preserving meaning across languages.

I also began using AI to create high-quality subtitles for my videos, as well as to generate video titles in over 60 languages. With the help of YouTube analytics and AI insights, I was able to identify which countries offered the best viewership and the highest revenue potential through monetized content. If you run a monetized video channel and earn income through YouTube, you'll understand how important this can be. AI-driven translations helped me significantly increase view counts and broaden my audience.

Still, despite these apparent advantages, automatic translation does have its limitations—though I wouldn't necessarily call them "flaws." Successful translation using AI depends largely on your understanding of how these programs work and how to interact with them effectively.

Here's a helpful tip: you don't have to repeat your command for every paragraph or sentence you want translated or edited. AI tools, including ChatGPT, can remember previous instructions. So instead of repeating the whole command, you can say *"do the same"* or even just *"same"*, and the AI will follow your previous instructions in the correct order.

AI, with its remarkable speed, can be used to translate a wide range of content—from everyday messages to complex technical documents. A manual translation might take days or weeks, while AI can complete the task in minutes. This is especially empowering when you need a quick understanding of a text written in a language you don't speak, making you more efficient in your work.

In addition to speed, AI brings greater accessibility to global communication. Online platforms like Google Translate and DeepL allow people across the world to interact with one another, breaking down language barriers. This sense of connection is essential in the age of globalization, where international collaboration is standard practice in business, science, and culture.

That said, translation accuracy is still a challenge. Although AI algorithms are improving rapidly, they don't always convey the exact tone or context of a message. Idioms, cultural references, and complex grammar structures often lead to errors or distortions in meaning. In professional or official contexts, these issues can create misunderstandings if the translation isn't reviewed and refined. It's important to understand these limitations and be prepared to address them when using AI for translation.

From my personal experience, I've learned that there are different levels of translation quality—and I'll share more about that shortly. But first, here's an essential piece of advice: always translate in small portions, typically no more than 2,000–3,000 characters at a time. The larger the text block, the more likely it is that errors will occur.

When you receive a translation from an AI tool, what you're getting is a first draft—a raw version that is usually literal and doesn't account for natural English stylistics. Every language has its unique features: idioms, expressions, and words with subtle meanings that only native or fluent speakers truly understand. That's why these early translations may contain inaccuracies or awkward phrasing.

Another common issue is that AI can sometimes struggle with grammatical gender (masculine, feminine, neuter) and plural forms—mainly when translating from languages like Russian or Ukrainian. But this isn't a serious flaw. If you're translating into a language you know reasonably well, even if it's not your native tongue, you'll be able to spot many of these mistakes. And you can always ask AI to help you review and improve the quality of the translation.

To achieve a professional-level result, it's crucial to avoid rushing to copy or use the raw output. Instead, keep refining it. Ask the AI to edit, improve, polish, check grammar and spelling, or to simplify or elevate the tone of the text. You can also ask for a more academic or formal translation, depending on your needs. You'll immediately see the difference. AI recognizes the contrast between a rough translation and a professional one—but it won't improve the result unless you guide it to do so. That's your role: to manage the tool intelligently and clearly, taking responsibility for the quality of your work.

You can also use a hybrid approach: begin with an AI-generated translation and then have it reviewed or refined by a professional translator. This combines the speed of technology with human insight and nuance—something that's especially important for complex texts such as legal documents, medical literature, or creative writing. A human translator can understand the emotional tone, cultural context, and target audience in a way machines still cannot fully replicate. This approach can significantly improve the quality of your translation, especially for texts that require a high level of accuracy and nuance.

Another powerful use of AI in translation is the creation of specialized term databases. For instance, in medical or technical writing, specific terms appear frequently. AI can learn and automatically apply these terms with accuracy and consistency, helping professionals avoid errors and work more efficiently.

In the past, I used to create term lists for my books manually. At the end of each book, I would include glossaries or appendices with key terms and their definitions. But no matter how carefully I worked, it was still easy to miss some words. Now, AI has simplified this process tremendously. After finishing a chapter or a section of a book, I ask the AI to scan the entire text and generate a list of terms with definitions—in alphabetical order. Within seconds, the glossary is ready.

AI also assists me in translating foreign names and surnames, which is more important than many people realize. A poorly translated name can confuse the reader or make a translated text seem less professional. When used correctly, AI helps ensure consistency and accuracy in the treatment of names, which strengthens the overall quality of the translation.

However, when it comes to literary works—like novels or poetry—AI is not yet a perfect solution. These texts rely heavily on the emotional atmosphere, the author's voice, and subtle stylistic choices. Capturing those nuances still requires the depth of human understanding that modern algorithms haven't fully mastered. That's why translating creative literature remains, for now, the domain of experienced human translators.

That said, AI can still play a supporting role here. Beyond simple translation tools, there are also AI editing programs that can be trained to recognize the style and tone of the original text. With the proper guidance, these tools can learn to preserve emotional depth and replicate the author's voice in translation. The key is to work in small sections—paragraph by paragraph—especially when the content is rich in emotion or literary complexity.

There's also an essential ethical consideration when using AI for translation: data privacy and confidentiality. When you upload text to an online translation service, you run the risk of that data being stored, analyzed, or even shared with third parties. This is especially critical for businesses or organizations handling sensitive material. In such cases, it's better to use secure or offline AI solutions that don't rely on cloud servers or internet connections. These tools allow for confidential processing while still benefiting from the power of AI.

Despite its current limitations, the future of AI in translation is auspicious. Algorithms are becoming more sophisticated, able to understand meaning, structure, and context better. We may soon see systems capable of recognizing emotional tone, adjusting for regional dialects, and even localizing humor or cultural references. But even then, the human factor will remain essential—especially in cases where emotional impact, nuance, or cultural sensitivity are required.

In short, AI has translated faster, more accurately, and more conveniently than ever before. But it does not replace the value of a professional translator—especially when high quality, cultural accuracy, or emotional precision is necessary. The best results often come from combining the strengths of both: using AI for speed and consistency and relying on human expertise for refinement and depth.

This combined approach is convenient for authors, researchers, professionals, and organizations who want to operate globally without sacrificing quality. With the right balance, AI becomes not just a tool for translation—but a gateway to new audiences, new markets, and new opportunities.

Creating spin-offs, sequels, or related books

Embarking on the creation of spin-offs, sequels, or related books is not just a task but an exhilarating and fulfilling journey for writers. It's a chance to expand the world they've built and strengthen connections with an existing audience hungry for more. Whether it's delving into a character's untold story, exploring a new perspective, or imagining the aftermath of events, the possibilities are endless. Below, I'll delve into the key elements of crafting successful spin-offs, sequels, or related books, igniting your passion for this creative endeavor.

Before embarking on a sequel or spin-off, it's essential to analyze what made your original story resonate with readers. Was it the compelling characters, the immersive world, or the unique narrative style? Understanding the core appeal ensures that your follow-up work remains true to the elements that captivated your audience while giving you room to innovate.

For instance, in J.K. Rowling's *Harry Potter* series, the wizarding world itself became a central draw for fans. This opened opportunities for related works like *Fantastic Beasts and Where to Find Them,* which expanded on the lore and backstory without replicating the original story. Similarly, the Star Wars franchise has successfully expanded its universe with spin-offs like The Mandalorian, which retained the franchise's iconic tone and aesthetic while introducing new characters and stories.

A sequel should build on the original's foundation while introducing new challenges and conflicts. This ensures the story doesn't feel like a repetition of past events. For instance, in *The Hunger Games* series, Suzanne Collins introduced a more complex rebellion in *Catching Fire* and *Mockingjay,* escalating the stakes for Katniss and her world.

Characters should grow and change in response to the events of the first book. A sequel provides an opportunity to deepen their arcs, explore their flaws, and reveal new dimensions of their personalities.

Readers who loved the original story will expect consistency in tone, setting, and character motivations. Minor inconsistencies can break the immersion, so it's crucial to maintain logical coherence.

While continuity is essential, a sequel shouldn't be overly predictable. Twists, unexpected developments, and new themes can keep readers engaged.

Spin-offs offer the freedom to explore side characters, different timelines, or alternate perspectives. These stories can stand alone or tie back to the original work in meaningful ways. Here's how to approach spin-offs effectively:

A compelling spin-off often centers on a character or aspect of the original story that left readers curious. For example, Leigh Bardugo's *Six of Crows* duology spun off from her *Grisha Trilogy,* focusing on a new set of characters and their heist adventures in the same universe.

A spin-off allows you to shift the narrative lens, offering readers a fresh way to experience the world. This could involve telling the antagonist's backstory, exploring a different region, or focusing on a supporting character's journey.

While it's important to reward loyal fans with Easter eggs and connections, a spin-off should also appeal to new readers who haven't experienced the original story. Easter eggs are subtle references or callbacks to the original story that can enhance the reading experience for fans. They should be engaging and self-contained, adding to the story without relying too heavily on the original.

Related books, such as prequels, companion guides, or anthologies, enrich the original story by providing additional context or depth. These books often cater to superfans who crave a deeper understanding of the world or characters. A successful prequel adds depth without detracting from the mystery or impact of the original story. A collection of short stories set in the same universe can explore minor characters, alternate outcomes, or untold tales, providing fans with a variety of new experiences.

One of the most significant challenges in creating sequels, spin-offs, or related books is striking the right balance between familiarity and innovation. However, it's crucial to remember that leaning too heavily on the original can make the new work feel redundant, while deviating too far may alienate loyal fans. The key is to preserve the essence of the original while introducing new ideas, conflicts, and characters, giving you the confidence to make bold, creative decisions.

For instance, *Star Wars* has maintained its enduring appeal through spin-offs like *The Mandalorian,* which retained the franchise's iconic tone and aesthetic while introducing new characters and stories.

Readers can be invaluable allies in shaping your spin-offs or sequels. Pay attention to fan discussions, reviews, and feedback to identify which elements they loved most. Interactive platforms like social media or newsletters can also help you gauge interest in potential ideas.

However, it's essential to maintain your creative vision. While reader feedback can inspire, decisions about the story should ultimately align with your artistic goals and the narrative's integrity.

Expanding your universe comes with challenges, including:

- **Creative Burnout:** Revisiting the same world repeatedly can be draining. To stay inspired, explore new genres, themes, or storytelling techniques within the familiar framework.
- **Overcomplicating the Plot:** To add depth, it's easy to overcomplicate the story. Keep the narrative focused and cohesive.
- **Satisfying Expectations:** Fans often have strong opinions about sequels or spin-offs, which can create pressure. Stay true to your vision while being mindful of their expectations.

Creating spin-offs, sequels, or related books is a powerful way to breathe new life into your stories and connect with readers on a deeper level. By honoring the original's strengths, evolving your characters and world, and balancing innovation with familiarity, you can craft follow-up works that are both satisfying and fresh. Whether continuing a beloved saga or offering a new perspective, the possibilities are endless for writers willing to take the leap into their expanded universes.

Monetizing Through Courses, Workshops, and Speaking Engagements

For authors looking to expand their revenue streams beyond book sales, courses, workshops, and speaking engagements offer excellent opportunities to leverage expertise and connect with audiences in new ways. With the help of AI-powered tools, authors can streamline content creation, automate course management, and find speaking opportunities that align with their niche.

Empower yourself as an author by turning your knowledge into profit through online courses. These courses not only monetize your expertise but also provide real educational value to your audience. Whether your niche is health, self-development, business, or creativity, transforming your content into a course reinforces your authority and opens up a new income stream.

AI simplifies and accelerates the process of creating course materials, instilling authors with a sense of confidence and capability. Start by outlining your course content with tools like ChatGPT, Jasper AI, or Notion AI, which generate structured lesson plans based on your book's central themes. Once you have a plan, you can either create video or written lessons. Tools like Synthesia let you produce professional-looking videos with AI avatars—so you don't even have to be on camera. If you prefer text, you can convert your book or audio into course material using transcription services like Otter.ai.

Designing course materials is also simple with AI-powered design tools. Canva AI helps create attractive slides, downloadable PDFs, and workbooks. When you're ready to launch, you can host your course on platforms like Teachable, Udemy, or Kajabi. These services offer built-in AI features to automate tasks like pricing, email follow-ups, and student engagement. To boost sales and connect with learners, AI chatbots and email automation tools like ConvertKit or ActiveCampaign AI can send targeted messages, answer questions, and convert interest into enrollment. For instance, if you've written a book on creative writing, you could build a course teaching writers how to craft believable characters and strong plotlines—guided by AI every step of the way.

Live workshops are an excellent way to engage with your audience and earn income, while also fostering a sense of connection and engagement. Unlike pre-recorded courses, workshops offer direct interaction, real-time feedback, and opportunities to build community. They work exceptionally well for authors looking to deepen their reader relationships.

AI can assist in every part of workshop planning and management. You can use tools like Google Trends or BuzzSumo to figure out what topics your audience is searching for. Once you know the focus, create professional slides with tools like Canva AI or Beautiful.ai, which can design eye-catching presentations in minutes. To streamline logistics, AI integrations with platforms like Eventbrite and Zoom handle registrations, reminders, and follow-up emails. During the live event, AI chatbots can answer FAQs in real time so that you can stay focused on teaching.

Workshops are easy to monetize. You can charge a participation fee, offer VIP upgrades with private consultations, or bundle workshop access with your book or online course for greater value. For example, if you write about health and wellness, you could host an interactive AI-assisted webinar on managing stress, complete with live demos and downloadable guides.

Speaking engagements offer another powerful way to grow your author brand while generating income. Public speaking positions you as an expert, builds trust with new audiences, and opens doors to more partnerships, media appearances, and book sales. Whether you're speaking at literary festivals, business conferences, or virtual summits, these events help elevate your visibility.

AI can help you find and prepare for speaking opportunities. Platforms like GigSalad, SpeakerHub, or Podchaser AI connect you with event organizers looking for voices like yours. Once you're booked, tools like ChatGPT and Jasper AI can help you draft speeches tailored to the theme and audience. AI also enables predictive audience analysis, giving you insights into demographics and interests so your talk resonates more deeply. You don't even need to travel—virtual event platforms like Hopin and BigMarker let you speak to global audiences from home.

To monetize your appearances, you can charge a speaking fee, offer signed copies of your book, or add post-event workshops for extra value. If you've written a self-help book, for example, you could land paid speaking slots at leadership events using AI platforms that match experts with organizers.

Altogether, branching out into online courses, workshops, and speaking events allows authors to move beyond book sales and build a multifaceted business. These strategies not only generate income but also expand your reach, deepen your reader relationships, and position you as a thought leader in your field. Thanks to AI, the process is more straightforward, faster, and more scalable—giving you more time to focus on what you do best: creating, teaching, and inspiring.

Building Passive Income Streams

When people hear the term' passive income,' many immediately think of MLM (multi-level marketing) companies—and often, the negative experiences that come with them. That's understandable, as only a small number of people make significant earnings in network marketing. However, what these systems do teach—regardless of their outcomes—is the core principle behind income generation: leveraging time and duplication. This means creating a system or product that can be replicated or sold multiple times, thereby increasing your income without necessarily increasing your effort.

With **active income** in writing, you exchange your time and effort—essentially, pieces of your life—for a product or service. You either sell the result yourself or someone pays you a wage for the time you worked. But time is a limited resource. We all have only 24 hours in a day, so no matter how efficient you are, once you sell a product or deliver a service, you need to start all over again to keep income flowing. It becomes a repeating cycle.

Time ⇒ Product/Service ⇒ Money

Passive income, on the other hand, is when you create something once and continue earning from it repeatedly. Books are a perfect example. You write it once, but it can be sold an unlimited number of times—without needing to recreate it. A single investment of time and energy can generate ongoing income through repeated sales or increasing value over time.

Here are just a few examples of how passive income can be built:

- Pre-recorded online courses, seminars, and webinars, which can be sold repeatedly.
- Royalties from books, audiobooks, or video content.
- Licensing or franchising which can bring in both active and passive income.
- Creating a product and scaling it for mass distribution.
- Rental income from property, equipment, or digital tools.
- Investing in other businesses—such as stock portfolios or real estate—that bring steady returns without daily effort.

For many authors, the goal isn't just to publish a book—it's to build a sustainable income that not only continues to grow over time but also has the potential to increase significantly. Passive income streams offer the freedom to step away from the constant hustle, so you can focus on writing more, connecting with your readers, or even launching new creative projects.

In this chapter, we'll explore how modern technology—especially AI-powered automation—cannot only support but also significantly accelerate the process of building passive income. From book royalties and subscription models to digital content, online teaching, and affiliate marketing, you'll learn how to leverage these tools to diversify your revenue streams and build a stable foundation for your writing career.

You'll also discover how to use AI tools to repurpose your content, automate marketing, and engage with your audience, so your creative work continues to generate income while you sleep. These tools can help you turn your knowledge and ideas into multiple streams of revenue that function in the background—quietly but effectively supporting your financial independence as an author.

Let's take a closer look at the strategies that will help you build a passive income ecosystem that works for you—not the other way around. Remember, the ultimate goal is not just passive income, but financial independence that allows you to focus on what truly matters to you as an author.

Repurposing Content for Blogs, YouTube, or Podcasts

Writing a book is a significant achievement, but once it's published, many authors face the same question: What's next? While book sales can generate revenue and build an audience, the content you've created doesn't have to remain confined to the pages of your book. One of the most empowering ways to expand your reach, attract new readers, and create additional income streams is by taking control and repurposing your content into different formats—blog posts, YouTube videos, and even podcasts.

By leveraging digital platforms and AI-powered tools, authors can efficiently transform their written material into engaging multimedia content that meets audiences where they are. Some people love reading long-form blog articles, others prefer short, visually rich video content, while another segment enjoys listening to in-depth discussions while commuting or exercising. Repurposing allows you to connect with all these audiences, understanding and meeting their preferences without constantly creating new material from scratch.

A blog can be a powerful tool for keeping your ideas alive long after your book's release. Not only does it provide an opportunity to break down complex topics into digestible articles, but it also helps with search engine visibility, allowing new readers to discover your work organically. Every day, thousands of people search Google for information, and a well-written blog post can introduce them to your expertise, making you more visible and discoverable.

Converting a book into blog content doesn't mean copying and pasting entire chapters online. Instead, consider extracting key ideas and reworking them into stand-alone articles. A single book chapter might turn into multiple blog posts, each focusing on a specific theme or insight. For example, if you've written a book on productivity, a chapter on time management could evolve into several blog posts: one on eliminating distractions, another on creating morning routines, and yet another on setting realistic goals.

AI-powered tools can make this process even easier. Platforms like ChatGPT and Jasper AI can summarize long sections of text, generate blog post outlines, and even suggest compelling headlines based on trending keywords. Meanwhile, SEO optimization tools like Surfer SEO and Clearscope can analyze which topics are currently in demand, helping you structure your content in a way that maximizes visibility.

The beauty of blogging is that it keeps your book relevant and positions you as an authority in your niche. Readers who discover your blog may eventually decide to buy your book, and those who have already read your work will appreciate the additional insights you share.

Video content is more engaging than ever, and YouTube has become the go-to platform for people searching for both entertainment and information. If your book is packed with insights, turning those key lessons into short, engaging video content can help attract a broader audience. Unlike blog posts, which rely on written text, video content adds a personal touch—viewers get to see and hear you, creating a stronger emotional connection.

For authors who are comfortable speaking on camera, the process is relatively straightforward: take the key points from a book chapter, outline a short script, and record a video where you explain the concepts in your own words. But for those who aren't keen on appearing on camera, AI-powered tools offer an alternative. Platforms like Synthesia and Pictory AI allow you to create videos without ever stepping in front of a camera. These tools can generate animated explainer videos, convert text into speech, and even use AI-generated avatars to present content on your behalf.

Another effective way to repurpose book content for YouTube is through short-form video clips. Platforms like TikTok, Instagram Reels, and YouTube Shorts have changed how audiences consume information, favoring concise, visually engaging snippets. If your book contains bite-sized wisdom—motivational quotes, quick tips, or thought-provoking questions—you can create short, engaging clips that tease your book's content while driving viewers to learn more.

YouTube's AI-driven analytics tools can also help refine your content strategy over time. By analyzing which videos perform well, you can adjust your approach to focus on topics that resonate most with your audience, leading to better engagement and a growing community of viewers who may eventually become readers.

While some people love reading and others prefer watching videos, a significant portion of the audience prefers listening. Podcasts have surged in popularity because they allow people to consume content passively—whether during a commute, a workout, or while doing household chores. If your book is rich in stories, insights, or thought-provoking discussions, a podcast can be the perfect way to repurpose that material into an entirely new content format.

Turning a book into a podcast doesn't have to be complicated. Some authors read excerpts from their books, adding personal commentary or reflections along the way. Others use the podcast format as a discussion platform, inviting guests—other authors, experts, or fans—to talk about the themes explored in their book.

AI-powered tools can also help streamline podcast production. Descript AI automatically transcribes and edits audio, while Play.ht and Resemble AI allow you to generate AI-powered voiceovers if you prefer a more automated approach. Hosting platforms like Anchor (by Spotify) and Podbean make distribution easy, ensuring your podcast reaches Apple Podcasts, Spotify, and other major streaming services.

Beyond engagement, podcasts open new monetization opportunities. Authors can secure sponsorship deals, offer premium content, or use the podcast as a platform to promote their book, courses, and other products. If done well, a podcast can become a self-sustaining asset, generating income while expanding your audience.

The most significant advantage of repurposing content is that it allows you to reach different audiences without constantly creating new material from scratch. Some people will find you through your blog, others through YouTube, and still others through your podcast—but at the core, they are all discovering the same insights you originally wrote in your book.

Instead of seeing your book as a one-time product, think of it as a launchpad for other content forms. AI tools can help simplify the process, from generating video scripts and podcast outlines to optimizing blog content for search engines. By diversifying your content formats, you keep your work relevant, grow your audience, and ultimately increase the long-term impact and profitability of your book, giving you a reason to be optimistic about the future.

For authors looking to build a sustainable career, repurposing content isn't just an option—it's a necessity. The key is to start small, experiment with different formats, and gradually build an ecosystem of content that keeps readers, viewers, and listeners engaged for years to come. Remember, every big success starts with a small step, so don't feel overwhelmed.

Licensing and Collaborations with Other Creators

Writing a book is just the beginning of its journey. While direct sales can generate income, licensing and collaborations open the door to long-term revenue, expanded reach, and opportunities to bring your work to new audiences. Many successful authors maximize their earnings by allowing their content to be adapted, repurposed, and co-created with others—whether through foreign translations, film and TV adaptations, partnerships with content creators, or brand collaborations.

By harnessing the power of AI-powered analytics and automation tools, authors can take control of their business, identifying lucrative licensing opportunities, negotiating partnerships, and streamlining collaborations without the manual effort that traditionally made such deals complex. In this way, licensing and collaborations not only help scale an author's business but also establish their work as a brand that extends beyond books, instilling a sense of confidence and empowerment.

One of the most powerful ways to monetize intellectual property is through licensing—allowing others to legally use your book's content in exchange for royalties or a one-time fee. Licensing agreements can cover various forms, including foreign language rights, audiobook deals, movie and TV rights, and educational use.

Selling translation rights is one of the easiest ways to expand your book's reach globally without doing additional writing. Many international readers are eager for books originally written in English, and licensing your book to foreign publishers allows them to handle the translation, distribution, and marketing while you earn royalties.

AI-powered platforms like DeepL and Google Translate AI have also made the translation process easier, allowing independent authors to explore self-publishing in multiple languages. However, for a professional touch, working with human translators and foreign publishers remains the best option.

The audiobook market has grown tremendously, and licensing your book for audio production can significantly increase sales.

Traditionally, audiobooks were expensive to produce, requiring professional narrators and sound engineers. However, AI-powered voice synthesis tools like Play.ht, Speechki, and Amazon Polly now enable cost-effective audiobook creation, making it easier for authors to produce and distribute their work in audio format.

Some authors choose to license audiobook rights to companies like Audible Studios, Findaway Voices, or Storytel, which handle production and distribution while the author receives royalties. Others may use AI-generated narration to self-publish audiobooks and retain complete control over pricing and sales.

For fiction writers, the prospect of licensing a book for film or television adaptation is one of the most thrilling opportunities. Platforms like Netflix, Amazon Prime, and HBO are constantly seeking new content, and book adaptations remain one of their most popular sources of storytelling, creating a sense of anticipation and excitement for the author.

AI-driven analytics tools like Bookstat and Wattpad Insights help authors determine whether their book has strong adaptation potential by analyzing engagement metrics, audience demand, and genre trends. Independent authors can also pitch their books directly to producers using AI-assisted proposal tools like ScriptBook, which evaluate a book's cinematic potential.

Collaboration is another keyway for authors to expand their influence, reach new audiences, and create innovative content. Partnering with other creators—whether fellow writers, YouTubers, podcasters, artists, or brands—fosters a sense of community, introducing your book to new fans while offering fresh ways to engage existing readers and sharing in the success of the collaboration.

Teaming up with another author, particularly one in a complementary genre or niche, can help both writers expand their readership and share marketing efforts. This collaboration could take the form of:

- Co-writing a new book together.

- Bundling books as a special promotion.
- Guest writing for each other's blogs or newsletters.

AI-powered writing tools like Sudowrite, ChatGPT, and Grammarly AI help co-authors streamline the process by generating drafts, editing for consistency, and ensuring stylistic harmony.

Content creators on YouTube, TikTok, and podcasts have massive, engaged audiences, making them ideal partners for book promotions. By collaborating with influencers, authors can reach a broader audience through interviews, book reviews, and guest appearances.

AI-powered matchmaking platforms like Upfluence, Heepsy, and BuzzSumo help authors find relevant influencers based on audience demographics and content style. Some authors even create branded content where their book is featured in a larger discussion—whether that's a podcast episode about the book's themes or a YouTube documentary-style video.

Books don't have to be confined to print. Licensing book-related content for merchandising, special editions, and collectors' items can create additional revenue streams. Merchandise—such as T-shirts, posters, mugs, and limited-edition hardcover versions—can appeal to dedicated fans and collectors.

AI-driven platforms like Printify, Redbubble, and Teespring allow authors to automate merchandise production and fulfillment, making it easy to offer themed products without managing inventory.

Licensing and collaborations turn an author's work into an expanding brand rather than a single product. Instead of relying solely on book sales, these strategies create multiple revenue streams that generate income long after the book's release.

Whether you're licensing foreign rights, adapting your book into an audiobook, partnering with content creators, or turning your book into an entire merchandise line, AI-powered tools make these opportunities more accessible than ever. By thinking beyond the traditional book market, authors can transform their creative work into a long-term, scalable business with unlimited growth potential.

For authors looking to scale their success, licensing and collaborations are not just optional—they're the key to building a lasting legacy in the publishing world.

AI-Powered Tools for Managing Royalties and Income Tracking

Managing book royalties, tracking income, and understanding financial performance can quickly become overwhelming for authors—especially those publishing across multiple platforms like Amazon KDP, Apple Books, Kobo, and IngramSpark. Unlike traditional publishing, where a single publisher typically handles royalty payments, self-published and hybrid authors must juggle earnings from various sources, track irregular payment schedules, and analyze sales data on their own. This fragmentation makes it difficult to maintain a clear financial picture or make timely, informed decisions.

Thankfully, AI-powered tools are now transforming how authors manage their income. These systems automate royalty tracking, consolidate reports across platforms, forecast earnings, and provide real-time financial insights. Instead of logging into multiple dashboards or manually updating spreadsheets, authors can now rely on smart platforms that collect and interpret the data for them—saving time and significantly reducing the risk of errors or missed payments.

By analyzing past sales performance, AI helps forecast future income trends, allowing authors to set realistic budgets, adjust pricing, and plan promotions more effectively. Many tools also offer seamless integration with a range of sales channels, giving authors a single, unified view of their total earnings—whether their books are sold on Amazon, downloaded via subscription services, or purchased from lesser-known international platforms.

Beyond royalties, these tools are also helpful for managing expenses. From ad spend and cover design to formatting and software subscriptions, AI-powered systems categorize costs and generate tax-ready reports. This reduces the burden of bookkeeping and ensures authors are financially prepared for quarterly or annual filings.

Tool	Best For	Key Features	Price
Book Report	Self-published authors on Amazon KDP	AI-powered Amazon KDP sales tracking, real-time earnings updates, income breakdowns by book	Free for low sales; Paid plans start at $10/month
ScribeCount	Authors publishing across multiple platforms	Tracks royalties from Amazon KDP, Apple Books, Kobo, Google Play, and more; visual earnings dashboard	$15–$20/month
TrackerBox	Authors with multiple revenue streams	AI consolidates earnings from different stores, customizable financial reports	One-time fee of $89
Publishwide	Wide-distribution authors	Automated sales reports, AI-powered sales forecasting, multi-currency support	$8–$12/month
Reedsy Royalty Calculator	Beginner authors estimating potential earnings	AI estimates royalties based on book price, format, and store commission rates	Free
KDP Champ	Amazon KDP-focused authors	AI-driven data visualization, daily earnings alerts, ad revenue tracking	$10–$25/month
QuickBooks AI	Authors needing full business financial tracking	Tracks book royalties, expenses, advertising costs, and tax deductions	Starts at $25/month
Wave Accounting AI	Indie authors managing small business finances	AI categorizes book-related income and expenses, generates tax reports	Free (with paid add-ons)

Choosing the right AI tool to manage your book royalties and financial data depends mainly on where and how you publish. For authors who are exclusively using Amazon KDP, tools like Book Report and KDP Champ are excellent options. They provide real-time tracking of sales, earnings, and page reads, giving you immediate insight into your book's performance. These platforms are simple, intuitive, and designed specifically for Kindle authors who want to stay on top of their daily revenue.

If you publish across multiple platforms—such as Apple Books, Kobo, Barnes & Noble, and IngramSpark—then more robust, multi-platform solutions are necessary. ScribeCount and Publishwide stand out in this category. They consolidate royalty data from all major vendors into one clean, user-friendly dashboard. This saves countless hours of downloading reports from separate sites and allows you to analyze your full publishing income in one place, with visualizations that make it easier to spot patterns and trends.

For authors who need deeper financial oversight, especially those running their writing as a business, accounting tools with AI integration are a wise investment. Platforms like QuickBooks AI and Wave Accounting go beyond royalty tracking. They also monitor advertising expenses, book production costs, and other business-related spending. These tools can categorize expenses automatically, help you prepare for tax season, and even generate profit-and-loss statements—all while syncing with your bank accounts and payment platforms.

If your primary concern is income forecasting—understanding how much you're likely to earn next month or next quarter—tools like TrackerBox and KDP Champ provide simple yet powerful AI-driven sales projections. They analyze historical data to give you an idea of future trends, helping you set goals, plan promotions, and decide when to release your next title.

Ultimately, the best tool for you depends on the complexity of your publishing strategy. If you sell exclusively on Amazon, you might only need a lightweight tracker, which focuses on sales and royalty tracking. But if you're operating like a small publishing company—selling across formats, regions, and platforms—then a more comprehensive financial system, which includes features like expense tracking, tax preparation, and income forecasting, can give you the oversight you need to stay profitable and organized.

AI-powered financial tools empower you with the insights needed to make smarter decisions. They automate royalty tracking, monitor sales trends, and forecast income, giving you the control and confidence to adjust your pricing, budget for marketing, or time your next launch.

By integrating AI into your workflow, you're not just making things easier—you're creating a sustainable, data-driven foundation for long-term success. Whether you're a self-published author navigating global sales or a hybrid author managing multiple revenue streams, these tools offer the clarity, accuracy, and efficiency that every writer deserves. And the best part? They give you more time to focus on what you love most—writing. It's important to note that these tools use AI in a secure and privacy-conscious manner, ensuring that your financial data is protected.

Part 8: The Future of Publishing

The publishing industry is evolving faster than ever. What was once dominated by traditional publishing houses and print media has now expanded into a tech-driven landscape, where AI, digital platforms, and new reader behaviors are reshaping how books are written, marketed, and consumed.

For authors, this shift presents both challenges and exciting opportunities. Artificial intelligence is transforming the book creation process, from AI-assisted writing and editing to predictive analytics that enable authors to anticipate reader preferences before writing. Self-publishing has become more accessible, allowing writers to bypass traditional gatekeepers and reach a global audience with tools that automate everything from formatting to distribution. Meanwhile, new monetization models—from subscription-based platforms to blockchain publishing—are redefining how authors earn from their work.

In this section, we'll explore the key trends shaping the future of publishing. From AI-powered storytelling and personalized reader experiences to emerging technologies like NFTs, Web3 publishing, and immersive storytelling formats, we'll look at how the next generation of authors can stay ahead of the curve. Whether you're an indie writer or traditionally published, understanding these trends will help you adapt, innovate, and thrive in the rapidly evolving world of publishing.

AI's Role in Shaping Tomorrow's Bestsellers

The art of storytelling has always been a journey of evolution, and now, with the advent of artificial intelligence, a new chapter of wonder and excitement is unfolding. From the invention of the printing press to the rise of e-books, every innovation has reshaped how stories are told, distributed, and consumed. AI is now ushering in a new era for authors and publishers, fundamentally transforming the way books are written, edited, marketed, and even conceptualized.

AI is not just a tool for automation—it's a powerful and inspiring partner in the creative process. AI-driven writing assistants empower authors to draft and refine manuscripts, predictive analytics inspire new themes and genres, and machine learning algorithms personalize book recommendations for readers. With AI-generated audiobooks, automated translations, and adaptive storytelling, the publishing landscape is evolving at an unprecedented pace.

But with this transformation comes important questions: Will AI-generated books become indistinguishable from human-written ones? How will authors balance creativity with algorithm-driven trends? And what does this mean for the future of originality in literature?

In this chapter, we explore how AI is shaping the creation of tomorrow's bestsellers, encompassing AI-assisted writing, data-driven storytelling insights, and AI-powered book marketing strategies. Whether you view AI as an opportunity or a disruption, one thing is sure—the future of publishing will be shaped by those who are motivated to embrace innovation while staying true to the heart of storytelling.

Emerging Trends in AI and Publishing

The rapid advancement of artificial intelligence is not just changing how books are written, but how they are marketed, distributed, and even read. What once required extensive human effort—structuring a compelling story, finding the right audience, and navigating the complexities of book promotion—can now be enhanced or entirely streamlined by AI. As technology evolves, authors, publishers, and readers are adapting to a landscape where AI is no longer just a tool but an integral part of the publishing ecosystem.

One of the most noticeable shifts is in AI-assisted writing and editing. While human creativity remains at the heart of storytelling,

AI-powered tools now help authors brainstorm ideas, refine prose, and even generate entire drafts. Writing assistants like ChatGPT and Jasper AI can suggest plot developments, enhance dialogue, and analyze readability, allowing authors to work more efficiently. Some AI systems are even capable of mimicking distinct writing styles, raising new questions about originality and authorship. While AI is unlikely to replace human writers, it is becoming an indispensable co-writer, particularly in genre fiction, self-help, and serialized content.

Another significant development is the rise of data-driven publishing. Traditional publishing has long relied on intuition and market trends, but AI is now offering a more precise, predictive approach to identifying bestsellers. By analyzing reader behavior, sales patterns, and engagement metrics, AI can determine which genres, topics, and writing styles are most likely to succeed. Platforms like Amazon and Wattpad already use machine learning to personalize book recommendations. Still, AI is now going further—helping publishers decide which manuscripts to acquire based on real-time demand and audience preferences. In the self-publishing world, independent authors are leveraging these insights to adjust their marketing strategies, optimize book titles and covers, and fine-tune their storytelling for maximum engagement.

The way books are consumed is also evolving. Audiobooks, for example, have seen a surge in popularity, and AI is playing a key role in their accessibility and affordability. AI-generated narration, powered by advanced text-to-speech models, is making it possible to produce audiobooks without the high costs of human voice actors. Companies like Google and Apple are already experimenting with AI narration that sounds remarkably human, opening new opportunities for authors who previously couldn't afford professional audio production.

Interactive and immersive storytelling is another trend gaining momentum. AI-driven narratives are enabling new forms of personalized fiction, where readers can influence the storyline based on their choices. Interactive storytelling platforms are using machine learning to adapt narratives in real time, creating customized reading experiences that blur the line between books and games. This shift is particularly evident in digital-first platforms, where AI-generated branching narratives allow readers to engage with a story in dynamic and unpredictable ways.

Beyond storytelling, AI is reshaping the business models of publishing. Subscription-based platforms like Kindle Unlimited, Scribd, and Radish are leveraging AI to analyze reader habits and tailor content delivery, optimizing what books get promoted to whom. Meanwhile, blockchain and AI-powered digital rights management (DRM) systems are exploring ways to track ownership, combat piracy, and introduce new revenue streams for authors, such as NFT-backed books and tokenized royalties.

Despite these advancements, the increasing presence of AI in publishing raises important ethical and philosophical questions. Will AI-generated content flood the market, diluting the value of human-written stories? How will copyright and intellectual property laws evolve to accommodate AI-generated works? At what point does AI transition from a tool to a competitor of human authors? These debates will shape the industry in the coming years, as regulators, publishers, and writers navigate the balance between technological efficiency and artistic integrity.

One thing is sure: AI is no longer a distant possibility—it is actively redefining every aspect of publishing, from creation to consumption. Whether this leads to more opportunities for authors and readers or a fundamental shift in what it means to write and publish a book remains to be seen. But those who embrace these emerging trends and adapt to new tools will be best positioned to thrive in the next era of storytelling.

The Ethical Debate: How Much AI Is Too Much?

The rise of artificial intelligence in publishing has sparked both excitement and concern. AI-powered tools are making it easier than ever for authors to write, edit, market, and distribute their books, but as these technologies advance, they also raise a pressing ethical question: How much AI is too much?

At what point does AI stop being a tool and start becoming the creator? If AI can generate compelling novels, assist in character development, and even mimic the style of famous authors, does it challenge the fundamental idea of authorship? And if AI-written content floods the market, will it dilute the value of human creativity or democratize storytelling by making publishing more accessible to everyone, thereby opening up new avenues for diverse voices and stories?

One of the most controversial issues is AI-generated writing. Today's AI writing assistants can draft entire book chapters, suggest dialogue, and even replicate an author's tone and style with remarkable accuracy. While many authors use AI as a creative assistant—helping with brainstorming, outlining, and editing—it's important to remember that human input is always required for a job to be considered truly original. This reassures us that AI can never replace the unique touch of human creativity.

Copyright law adds another layer of complexity to this debate. Traditionally, copyright belongs to the creator of a work, but who owns the rights to AI-generated content? If an AI model writes a book based on a dataset of existing works, is it infringing on intellectual property? Some publishing platforms have already banned AI-generated books, while others have introduced disclosure requirements, forcing authors to state whether AI was used in the writing process. Yet, as AI becomes more sophisticated, enforcing these regulations may become increasingly complex. This underscores the need for balanced regulation to ensure the rights of all creators are protected.

Another ethical concern is bias and authenticity in AI-generated content. AI models are trained on vast datasets, which means they inherently reflect the biases present in those sources. This has led to concerns about representation, diversity, and originality in AI-generated works. Can AI truly create stories that reflect the lived experiences of human authors? Or will it reinforce stereotypes and homogenize storytelling, favoring specific themes and structures based on algorithmic predictions of what sells best?

Beyond writing, AI is reshaping reader engagement and content recommendations in ways that may not always be ethical. Algorithms now dictate which books get promoted, which voices are amplified, and which works get buried in search results. While AI-driven personalization helps readers find books tailored to their interests, it also raises concerns about gatekeeping and manipulation. If AI controls what gets visibility, does this limit literary diversity and reduce exposure to unconventional or underrepresented voices?

The rise of AI in publishing also brings economic implications. As AI tools become more advanced, some fear they could replace jobs traditionally held by human editors, translators, audiobook narrators, and even cover designers. AI-generated voice narration is already challenging professional voice actors, and AI-assisted translations are competing with human linguists. While AI makes publishing more cost-effective for authors, it also disrupts traditional roles in the publishing industry. Will AI lead to a creative revolution, or will it erode opportunities for human professionals?

Despite these concerns, AI is not inherently a threat—it is a tool, and like any tool, its impact depends on how it is used. Many authors see AI as a way to enhance human creativity rather than replace it. Instead of viewing AI as a competitor, some argue that it should be seen as a co-pilot, helping authors refine their ideas, explore new storytelling possibilities, and streamline the more technical aspects of publishing. AI can also open up new opportunities for authors, such as reaching broader audiences and experimenting with new genres or styles.

Ultimately, the ethical debate surrounding AI in publishing is not about whether AI should be used—it already is. The real question is how much human involvement should remain in the creative process and where we draw the line between AI-assisted and AI-authored works. As technology continues to evolve, the industry will need to strike a balance between embracing innovation and preserving the integrity of human storytelling. Whether that means setting more straightforward guidelines for AI-generated works, redefining intellectual property laws, or ensuring AI remains a supporting tool rather than a replacement, the decisions made today will shape the future of literature for generations to come. It's crucial to start discussing and implementing these solutions now to ensure a smooth transition into the AI-driven future of publishing.

Preparing for the Future of Storytelling in a Digital-First World

Storytelling has always been in sync with technological advancements, from oral traditions to digital publishing. As we step into an era where AI, immersive experiences, and interactive storytelling redefine narrative consumption, authors and creators must gear up for a digital-first world. This is a world where AI, immersive experiences, and interactive storytelling are redefining narrative consumption and where the boundaries between books, media, and technology are becoming increasingly blurred.

The rise of e-books, audiobooks, and subscription-based reading platforms has already changed how readers engage with stories. But the next wave of innovation goes beyond simple digital formats—it introduces AI-generated narratives, interactive fiction, personalized storytelling experiences, and even blockchain-backed publishing models. Readers are no longer just passive consumers; they are becoming participants in dynamic, evolving narratives shaped by their choices and engagement.

One of the most significant shifts is the growing influence of AI-driven content creation. AI-assisted writing tools are making it easier for authors to draft, edit, and refine their work, while machine learning algorithms analyze market trends to predict what readers will want next. In this new landscape, storytelling is no longer just about creativity—it's about understanding data, audience behavior, and how technology can enhance the reading experience.

Immersive storytelling is another key trend shaping the future. Augmented reality (AR), virtual reality (VR), and AI-driven narratives are opening new doors for creative expression. Imagine a novel that allows readers to step into the world of the story through a VR headset, or an AI-powered app that adapts the storyline based on a reader's emotional responses. These innovations challenge traditional storytelling structures and offer a multi-sensory, interactive experience that appeals to a new generation of tech-savvy readers.

However, with all these digital transformations, authors must also adapt their publishing and marketing strategies to thrive in an AI-driven world. The days of simply publishing a book and relying on word-of-mouth are fading. Instead, AI-powered marketing tools, predictive analytics, and personalized recommendation engines are now essential for reaching the right audience. Social media algorithms favor short-form content, making it increasingly important for authors to leverage video marketing, podcasts, and digital storytelling techniques to engage their audience beyond the page.

Monetization models are also evolving. Traditional book sales are no longer the only path to success. Subscription platforms, crowdfunding, direct-to-reader publishing, and even NFT-backed books and blockchain-based royalties are creating new revenue streams for authors willing to embrace digital-first business models. AI-driven distribution platforms are optimizing pricing strategies, while global translation AI tools are making books more accessible to international audiences without the high costs of traditional translation services.

However, with all these advancements comes the challenge of maintaining the human essence of storytelling. As AI-generated books become more common and algorithms shape what gets published, the role of human creativity remains not just important, but central. The future of storytelling is not about AI replacing authors, but about how technology can enhance the art of storytelling, making it more engaging, accessible, and interactive than ever before. Your unique voice and creativity are irreplaceable in this landscape.

For authors, preparing for the future means not just adapting to new tools but also feeling empowered by them. It means understanding how AI can streamline creative workflows, how digital platforms can amplify reach, and how to create meaningful connections with readers in an era of algorithm-driven content. Those who adapt to these changes—leveraging AI without losing the human voice in their narratives—will be the ones who not only survive but thrive in the digital-first publishing landscape.

The Future is Yours to Write

You've now journeyed through the entire lifecycle of a modern author, from brainstorming and writing to publishing, marketing, and scaling your success. The world of publishing is no longer confined to traditional gatekeepers—technology has democratized storytelling, giving you the tools and freedom to craft, publish, and promote your book on your terms. Whether you choose to self-publish, go hybrid, or partner with a traditional publisher, you now have the knowledge and resources to navigate this ever-evolving landscape with confidence.

One thing is sure: AI is here to stay. It's revolutionizing the way books are written, edited, marketed, and consumed. But the heart of storytelling will always belong to human creativity. AI can assist, streamline, and optimize the process, but machines cannot replicate the passion, originality, and depth of human experience. Your voice matters. Your stories are unique. Technology is just the tool—how you wield it is up to you.

Now, as you step forward in your publishing journey, ask yourself:

- What's your next book idea?
- How will you apply what you've learned to reach more readers?
- What new opportunities will you explore to grow as an author?

The landscape of publishing will continue to evolve, and the most successful authors will be those who adapt, innovate, and embrace the tools available to them. You've already taken the first step by learning how to harness AI and modern publishing strategies—now, it's time to act, share your story with the world, and build the author career you've always envisioned. Your story is unique and valuable, and the world is waiting to hear it.

This is just the beginning. The future of publishing is unfolding, and you have the power to shape it. So go out there, write, publish, and make your mark—because the next bestseller could be yours.

Olena Berezovska's books

1. Мій шлях до вічного. Березовська О.А. — 90 стор. Самовидав. Івано-Франківськ, Україна, 1995.
2. Интернет: Мифы и реальность заработка. Березовская Е.П. — 110 стр. Несколько онлайн-публикаций. Украина-Россия-Беларусь, 2000. (Ebook ISBN: 978-0-9867786-5-0)
3. Тысячиии… вопросов и ответов по гинекологии. Березовская Е.П. — 360 стр. Пресс-экспресс. Львов, Україна, 2008. (Print ISBN: 966-8360-08-7)
4. Ангел. Березовская Е.П. — 94 стр. Торонто, Канада, 2008. (Print ISBN: 978-1-997797-06-7, Ebook ISBN: 978-0-9867786-2-9)
5. День серебристого дождя. Березовская Е.П. — 107 стр. Торонто, Канада, 2008. (Ebook ISBN: 978-0-9867786-3-6)
6. Настольное пособие для беременных женщин. Березовская Е.П. — 400 стр. International Academy of Healthy Life. Канада-Украина, 2010. (Print ISBN: 978-0-9867786-1-2)
7. Подготовка к беременности. Березовская Е.П. — 200 стр. International Academy of Healthy Life. Канада-Украина, 2012. (Print ISBN: 978-0-9867786-0-5)
8. Гормонотерапия в акушерстве и гинекологии: иллюзии и реальность. Березовская Е.П. — 600 стр. International Academy of Healthy Life. Канада, 2013. (Ebook ISBN: 978-0-9867786-6-7)
9. 9 месяцев счастья. Настольное пособие для беременных женщин. Березовская Е.П. — 596 стр. ЭКСМО. Москва, Россия, 2015. (Print and Ebook ISBN: 978-5-699-80102-2)
10. Настільний посібник для вагітних. Березовська О.П. — 400 стор. Электронна версія. International Academy of Healthy Life. Торонто, Канада, 2016. (Ebook ISBN: 978-0-9867786-1-2)
11. Підготовка до вагітності. Березовська О.П. — 205 стор. Электронна версія. International Academy of Healthy Life. Торонто, Канада, 2016. (Print ISBN: 978-0-9867786-0-5)

12. Посібник для вагітних. Березовська О.П. — 392 стор. Манускрипт. Львів, Україна, 2016. (Print ISBN: 978-966-2400-55-7)

13. 1000 вопросов и ответов по гинекологии. Березовская Е.П. — 432 стр. ЭКСМО. Москва, Россия, 2017. (Print and Ebook ISBN: 978-5-699-80101-5)

14. Дочки-матери: Все, о чем вам не рассказывала ваша мама и чему стоит научить свою дочь. Березовская Е.П. — 288 стр. ЭКСМО. Москва, Россия, 2018. (Print and Ebook ISBN: 978-5-04-090021-3)

15. 9 місяців щастя. Березовська О.П. — 576 стор. BookChef. Київ, Україна, 2018. (Print and Ebook ISBN: 978-617-7559-18-3)

16. 9 месяцев счастья (второе издание). Настольное пособие для беременных женщин. Березовская Е.П. — 596 стр. ЭКСМО. Москва, Россия, 2019. (Print and Ebook ISBN: 978-5-04-098981-2)

17. Это все гормоны! Березовская Е.П. — 410 стр. ЭКСМО. Москва, Россия, 2019. (Print and Ebook ISBN: 978-5-04-101870-2)

18. Малыш, ты скоро? Березовская Е.П. — 384 стр. ЭКСМО. Москва, Россия, 2019. (Print and Ebook ISBN: 978-5-04-103359-0)

19. Когда ты будешь готова. Березовская Е.П. — 348 стр. ЭКСМО. Москва, Россия, 2020. (Print and Ebook ISBN: 978-5-04-116932-9)

20. Здравствуй, малыш. Березовская Е.П. — 320 стр. ЭКСМО. Москва, Россия, 2021. (Print and Ebook ISBN 978-5-04-121120-2)

21. Педіатрія: у 3-х т. Т. 3: підручник для студ. вищих мед. навч. закладів IV рівня акред. Катілов О., Варзарь А., Валіуліс А., Дмитрієв Д., та ін. — 656 стор. Нова Книга. Вінниця, Україна, 2022. (Print ISBN: 978-966-382-931-9)

22. 9 місяців щастя. Посібник для вагітних (оновлене й доповнене видання). Березовська О.П. — 624 стор. BookChef. Київ, Україна, 2023. (Print and Ebook ISBN: 978-617-548-122-6)

23. Коли тобі 35+. Як завагітніти й народити дитину. Березовська О.П. — 256 стор. BookChef. Київ, Україна, 2023. (Print and Ebook ISBN: 978-617-548-124-0)

24. Когда тебе 35+. Как забеременеть и родить ребенка. Березовская Е.П. — 290 стр. International Academy of Healthy Life. Торонто, Канада, 2024. (Ebook ISBN: 978-0-9867786-7-4)

25. Angel. Olena Berezovska. — 256 p. International Academy of Healthy Life. Toronto, Canada, 2024. (Ebook ISBN: 978-0-9867786-8-1)

26. Ангел. Березовська О.П. — 270 стор. International Academy of Healthy Life. Торонто, Канада, 2024. (Print ISBN 978-0-9867786-9-8, Ebook ISBN 978-1-997797-00-5)

27. Grandma Lena's Bedtime Stories. Olena Berezovska. — 154 p. International Academy of Healthy Life. Toronto, Canada, 2024. (Print ISBN: 978-1-0691603-0-0)

28. Привіт, малюк! Як пройти четвертий триместр без турбот і хвилювань. Березовська О.П. — 290 стор. International Academy of Healthy Life. Торонто, Канада, 2024. (Print ISBN: 978-1-0691603-3-1)

29. Growing Up Strong: A Guide to Girls' Health and Well-Being. Olena Berezovska. — 422 p. International Academy of Healthy Life. Toronto, Canada, 2025. (Print ISBN: 978-1-0691603-4-8, Ebook ISBN: 978-1-0694544-6-1)

30. Вечірні казочки бабусі Олени. Березовська О.П. — 180 стор. International Academy of Healthy Life. Toronto, Canada, 2025 (Print ISBN: 978-1-0691603-1-7)

31. Вечерние сказки бабушки Лены. Березовская Е.П. — 172 стр. International Academy of Healthy Life. Toronto, Canada, 2025 (Ebook ISBN: 978-1-0691603-2-4).

32. The Curious Escapades of a Corpse Named Jack. Book 1. Olena Berezovska. — 190 p. International Academy of Healthy Life. Toronto, Canada, 2025 (Print ISBN: 978-1-0691603-5-5, Ebook ISBN: 978-1-997797-02-9)

33. Основи здоров'я дівчаток: Практичний путівник для батьків. Березовська О. — 570 стор. International Academy of Healthy

Life. Toronto, Canada, 2025 (Print ISBN: 978-1-0691603-6-2, Ebook ISBN: 978-1-0694544-7-8)

34. The Curious Escapades of a Corpse Named Jack. Book 2. Olena Berezovska. — 112 p. International Academy of Healthy Life. Toronto, Canada, 2025 (Print ISBN: 978-1-0691603-7-9, Ebook ISBN: 978-1-997797-03-6)

35. Hormonal Intelligence: How Hormones Shape Health and Well-being. Olena Berezovska. — 478 p. International Academy of Healthy Life. Toronto, Canada, 2025 (Print ISBN: 978-1-0691603-8-6, Ebook ISBN: 978-1-0694544-4-7)

36. Все про гормони: Таємна мова вашого тіла. Олена Березовська. — 460 с. International Academy of Healthy Life. Торонто, Канада, 2025 (Print ISBN: 978-1-0691603-9-3, Ebook ISBN: 978-1-0694544-5-4)

37. Дивовижні пригоди трупа на ім'я Джек: Книга 1. Олена Березовська. — 180 с. International Academy of Healthy Life. Торонто, Канада, 2025 (Print ISBN: 978-1-0694544-0-9, Ebook ISBN: 978-1-997797-04-3)

38. Підготовка до вагітності: Посібник з усвідомленого батьківства. Олена Березовська. — 468 с. International Academy of Healthy Life. Торонто, Канада, 25 травня 2025 (Print ISBN: 978-1-0694544-41-6, Ebook ISBN: 978-1-0694544-8-5)

39. DIY Bestseller: How to Write, Publish, and Market Your Book in the AI Era. Olena Berezovska. — 432 p. International Academy of Healthy Life. Toronto, Canada, 2025. (Print ISBN: 978-1-0694544-2-3, Ebook ISBN: 978-1-997797-01-2)

40. Mind Over Muscle: A Journal for Teen Athletes. Olena Berezovska. — 58 p. International Academy of Healthy Life. Toronto, Canada, 2025. (Print ISBN: 978-1-0694544-3-0, Ebook ISBN: 978-1-0694544-3-0)

41. Kopf schlägt Muskeln: Ein Journal für jugendliche Athleten. Olena Berezovska. — 58 p. International Academy of Healthy Life. Toronto, Canada, 2025. (Print ISBN: 978-1-997797-07-4 , Ebook ISBN: 979-8-231304-94-3)

42. After Delivery: A Doctor's Guide to Postpartum Healing and Recovery. Olena Berezovska. – 400 p. International Academy of Healthy Life. Toronto, Canada, 2025 (Print ISBN: 978-1-997797-08-1, Ebook ISBN: 978-1-997797-09-8)

43. Дивовижні пригоди трупа на ім'я Джек: Книга 2. Олена Березовська. — 123 с. International Academy of Healthy Life. Торонто, Канада, 2025 (Print ISBN: 978-1-997797-12-8, Ebook ISBN: 978-1-997797-14-2)

44. DIY Bestseller: Как написать, издать и продвинуть свою книгу в эпоху искусственного интеллекта. Olena Berezovska. — 432 p. International Academy of Healthy Life. Toronto, Canada, 2025. (Print ISBN: 978-1-997797-13-5, Ebook ISBN: 979-8-232129-42-2)

About the author

Olena Berezovska

Doctor-researcher, obstetrician-gynecologist, author of books, writer, speaker, lecturer, founder and CEO of the International Academy of Healthy Life, Inc, (Canada)
Email: intacadenyhl@gmail.com

- 20 years of experience at Mount Sinai Hospital (Toronto, Canada) at Clinical Research Unit of the Department of Obstetrics and Gynecology.
- Additional certification in gynecological oncology, female sexology, reproductive medicine, evidence-based medicine, psychology, nutrition, and alternative medicine.
- Visiting lecturer for medical students, doctors, midwives, and nurses in medical schools and hospitals of Ukraine: Medical State University of Ivano-Frankivsk, Odessa, Vinnitsa, Kharkiv, Ivano-Frankivsk Medical college, Ivano-Frankivsk Regional maternity hospital and regional children's hospital, Lviv Regional Reproductive Center, Dr. Artemchuk's clinic (Kharkiv), Evidence Clinic Vinnitsa), Dr. Valikhnovsky's hospital, Amosov National Institute of Cardiovascular Pathology (Kyiv), Clinic "Miy likar" (Poltava), Lyudmila Lototska's Family Health Center (Lviv), Dr. Komarovsky's Klinikom, etc.
- Lecturer at School of sexual education for teenagers and parents (UNICEF UKRAINE, UNICEF GERMANY)
- Author of over 20 books on women's health and pregnancy, 8 of which are bestsellers ("9 Months of Happiness", "1000 questions and answers in gynecology", "When you'll be ready", "It's all hormones", "Baby, are you coming soon?", "Hello, baby", "When you are 35+ years old"). Books are successfully published and reprinted in Ukraine, Russia, Belorussia, Kazakhstan, and other countries.

- In 2008–2011 founder of health magazine Sanatate (Republic of Moldova), Chief and Medical editor.
- In 2004–2012 - Lead Consultant in Obstetrics and gynecology in the medical network Likar.Info (Ukraine)
- In 2009–2012 official expert of the project Health@Mail.ru (Russia).
- More than 200 conferences, seminars, and others educational activities for people without medical education in many countries, as well as meetings with subscribers and readers (Ukraine, Russia, Spain, Poland, Canada, USA, etc).
- Articles in the American Journal of Obstetrics and Gynecology, Journal of Obstetrics and Gynaecology of Canada, "A Word on Health!", "Health of Ukraine", "Preschool Nurse", Proceedings of Russian Academy of DNA-genealogy, etc.
- Over 500 articles and interviews in famous popular magazines such as Cosmopolitan, Vogue, CHIPS Journal,"Ukrainska Pravda", "Observer", "Focus", "Lvivska newspaper", "People's Correspondent", "My child", "Interlocutor", "Komsomolskaya Pravda", "Women's health", "Peasant life", "Beauty and health", "Doctor Peter", Letidor, Zdrave.to, WOMO, Sanatate, NEN, Nur KZ and many other magazines of Ukraine, Russia, Kazakhstan, Poland, Bulgaria, Moldova, Belarus.
- Since 2015, a frequent guest on television (Snidanok 1+1, Vezha, Za Zhive, TRK Karpaty, Paradise Breakfast, IRT Poltava, Obzrevatel TV, TV channel "VINTERA", Direct channel, Territoriya Pozitiva, Short.Media, Telekanal Kyiv, Important stories) and radio (The Highest Gift, Radio Era.fm, Vezha, Gorod S, Radio Russkaya Reklama New York).

OFFICIAL AND SOCIAL PAGES

In English:
Author's pages:
Instagram https://www.instagram.com/olenaberezovska_author
Facebook: https://www.facebook.com/profile.php?id=61583299100580

YouTube https://www.youtube.com/@DrOOlenaBerezovska/
Facebook https://www.facebook.com/DrOlenaB
Instagram https://instagram.com/dr_olena_b
LinkedIn https://www.linkedin.com/in/olena-berezovska-3a56389/

Art:
Etsy Art from Olena's Heart https://www.etsy.com/ca/shop/OberezovArt
Art on Instagram https://instagram.com/oberezob_art
YouTube Art from Olena's Heart -
https://m.youtube.com/@artfromolenasheart9506

Personal:
Instagram - https://instagram.com/oberezov
Facebook - https://www.facebook.com/olena.berezovska

In Ukrainian and Russian:
Official page www.doctorberezovska.com
YouTube - https://m.youtube.com/@DrOlenaB (Silver YouTube Creator Award)
Facebook - https://www.facebook.com/dr.olena.berezovska
Instagram - https://instagram.com/dr_olena_berezovska
Instagram Ukrainian https://www.instagram.com/dr_olena_obgyn/
Telegram - https://t.me/doctor_berezovska
Festina Cookbook https://www.instagram.com/festina_cookbook

www.ingramcontent.com/pod-product-compliance
Lightning Source LLC
LaVergne TN
LVHW090308210926
848480LV00001B/172